2007
A BRAND-NEW YEAR—
A PROMISING NEW START

With expert readings and forecasts, you can chart a course to romance, adventure, good health, or career opportunities while gaining valuable insight into yourself and others. Offering a daily outlook for 18 full months, this fascinating guide shows you:

- The important dates in your life
- What to expect from an astrological reading
- How the stars can help you stay healthy and fit And more!

Let this sound advice guide you through a year of heavenly possibilities—for today and for every day of 2007!

SYDNEY OMARR'S® DAY-BY-DAY ASTROLOGICAL GUIDE FOR

ARIES—March 21–April 19
TAURUS—April 20–May 20
GEMINI—May 21–June 20
CANCER—June 21–July 22
LEO—July 23–August 22
VIRGO—August 23–September 22
LIBRA—September 23–October 22
SCORPIO—October 23–November 21
SAGITTARIUS—November 22–December 21
CAPRICORN—December 22–January 19
AQUARIUS—January 20–February 18
PISCES—February 19–March 20

IN 2007

Sydney Omarr's®

DAY-BY-DAY ASTROLOGICAL GUIDE FOR

SAGITTARIUS

NOVEMBER 22–DECEMBER 21

2007

By Trish MacGregor
with Carol Tonsing

A SIGNET BOOK

SIGNET
Published by New American Library, a division of
Penguin Group (USA) Inc., 375 Hudson Street,
New York, New York 10014, USA
Penguin Group (Canada), 90 Eglinton Avenue East, Suite 700, Toronto,
Ontario M4P 2Y3, Canada (a division of Pearson Penguin Canada Inc.)
Penguin Books Ltd., 80 Strand, London WC2R 0RL, England
Penguin Ireland, 25 St. Stephen's Green, Dublin 2,
Ireland (a division of Penguin Books Ltd.)
Penguin Group (Australia), 250 Camberwell Road, Camberwell, Victoria 3124,
Australia (a division of Pearson Australia Group Pty. Ltd.)
Penguin Books India Pvt. Ltd., 11 Community Centre, Panchsheel Park,
New Delhi - 110 017, India
Penguin Group (NZ), cnr Airborne and Rosedale Roads, Albany,
Auckland 1310, New Zealand (a division of Pearson New Zealand Ltd.)
Penguin Books (South Africa) (Pty.) Ltd., 24 Sturdee Avenue,
Rosebank, Johannesburg 2196, South Africa

Penguin Books Ltd., Registered Offices:
80 Strand, London WC2R 0RL, England

First published by Signet, an imprint of New American Library,
a division of Penguin Group (USA) Inc.

First Printing, June 2006
10 9 8 7 6 5 4 3 2 1

CONTENTS

INTRODUCTION

Astrology to Use Every Day

Are you living your life to the fullest? Whether you want a more rewarding career, financial freedom, better relationships, or a romantic love life, astrology can help you make it happen. No matter what your goal, astrology's age-old techniques work just as well today as they did thousands of years ago. You can apply them to so many areas of your life to make the best decisions concerning your career, love, money, health, and even clothing and vacations.

In relationships, astrology can help you understand every sun-sign combination, which is very handy when you meet someone special. You'll be amazed at how knowing only the person's sun sign can help resolve a conflict or improve communication. What's more, astrology gives you a way to troubleshoot potential problems in advance and, if they crop up, find a way to turn them around.

On a deeper level, astrology can be a tool for personal growth and insight into your own special place in the cosmos. Like your genetic imprint, your astrology chart is unique. It is a map of your moment in time, which has its own code, based on the sun, moon, and planets at the time and place you were born. What is especially intriguing is that this system can offer specific, practical guidance, even when using only one of the elements of the code, your sun sign.

For those who would like to know more about astrology, this book provides user-friendly information to start you on your astrological journey. Then you can put your whole astrological portrait together by looking up the other planets in your horoscope. If you want to delve deeper, we'll show you the best astrology Web sites, where you can find sophisticated software and free education. If you're interested in connecting with other astrologers, we provide an extensive resource list of contacts and organizations, as well as computer program recommendations for fun or serious study.

As the saying goes, "Timing is everything." We'll deal in many ways with the question of timing: the difficult times (which also present positive challenges), times with potential for delays and misunderstandings, and the best times to take risks and to kick back and relax. You will learn when to use the downtime when Mercury is retrograde to reconnect with old friends, troubleshoot, and reevaluate where you're going and with whom.

This guide provides the tools you need to plan the best year ever, to enhance every aspect of your life, plus astonishingly accurate day-by-day forecasts to follow along in your own activities. Let it empower you to make 2007 a year of growth and prosperity!

CHAPTER 1

The Big Trends of 2007

Prepare for Changes Ahead

Astrologers judge the trends of a year by following the slow-moving planets, from Jupiter through Pluto. A change in sign indicates a new cycle, with new emphasis. The farthest planets (Uranus, Neptune, and Pluto), which stay in a sign for at least seven years, cause a very significant change in the atmosphere when they change signs. Shifts in Jupiter, which changes every year, and Saturn, every two years, are more obvious in current events and daily lives. Jupiter generally brings a fortunate, expansive emphasis to its new sign, while Saturn's two-year cycle is a reality check, bringing tests of maturity, discipline, and responsibility.

Sagittarius Is the Sign to Watch

In the final year of Pluto's transit of Sagittarius, it will be accompanied and intensified by Jupiter, the planet of expansion. This duo is superpowerful because Sagittarius is the sign Jupiter rules, making 2007 the grand finale for many of the key trends that began in 1995, when Pluto first entered Sagittarius.

Until January 2008, slow-moving Pluto will be emphasizing everything associated with Sagittarius to prepare us philosophically and spiritually for things to come. Perhaps the most pervasive sign of Pluto in Sagittarius over the past few years has been globalization in all its forms. We are re-forming boundaries, creating new forms of travel, interacting with exotic cultures and religions as never before.

In truth-telling Sagittarius, Pluto has shifted our emphasis away from acquiring wealth to a quest for the meaning of it all, as upward strivers discover that money and power are not enough and religious extremists assert themselves. We search the cosmos for something to believe in when many lies and scandals are brought to public view, exposing leaders in the corporate, political and religious domains. When ideals and idols are shattered, we reevaluate our goals and ask ourselves what is really important.

Sagittarius is the sign of linking everything together; therefore, the trend has been to find ways to connect on spiritual, philosophical, and intellectual levels. The spiritual emphasis of Pluto in Sagittarius has filtered down to our home lives, as religion and religious controversy have entered local communities. Vast church complexes that combine religious activities with sports centers, health clubs, malls, and theme parks are being built. Religious education and book publishing have expanded as well.

Sagittarius is known for love of animals, especially horses. It's no surprise that horse racing has become popular again and that America has never been more pet happy. Look for extremes related to animal welfare, such as vegetarianism as a lifestyle. As habitats are destroyed, the care, feeding, and control of wild animals will become a larger issue, especially when deer, bears, and coyotes invade our backyards.

The Sagittarius love of the outdoors combined with Pluto's power has already promoted extreme sports, especially those that require strong legs, like rock climbing, trekking, or snowboarding. Expect the trend toward more adventurous travel to continue, as well as fitness- or sports-oriented vacations. Exotic hiking trips to unexplored territories, mountain-climbing expeditions, spa vacations, and sports-associated resorts are part of this trend.

Publishing, which is associated with Sagittarius, has been transformed by global conglomerates and the Internet. Look for more inspirational books aimed at those who are interested in spirituality outside of traditional religions.

What's Next? Capricorn Brings Us Down to Earth

Next year, Pluto will join Jupiter in Capricorn, which marks a major shift in emphasis to Capricorn-related themes. Capricorn is a practical, building, healing earth sign. It is an active, cardinal sign that symbolizes rising from the waters of the emotions to the top of the mountain, surmounting obstacles all the way, demanding maturity and down-to-earth common sense. Capricorn relates to structures, institutions, order, mountains and mountain countries, mineral rights, issues involving the elderly and growing older—all of which will be emphasized in the coming years.

This shift begins in December 2007, which starts activating all the cardinal signs (Aries, Cancer, Libra, Capricorn). At the end of 2007, you should feel the rumblings of change in the Capricorn area of your horoscope and in the world at large. The last time Pluto was in Capricorn was the period of the Revolutionary War. Therefore this may be an important time in U.S. politics, as well as a reflection of the aging and maturing of American society in general.

Saturn Moves from Leo to Virgo: The Maturing of the Baby Boomers, Reforms in Care and Maintenance

Saturn, the planet of limitation, testing, and restriction, has been transiting Leo since mid-July 2005, forcing us to grow up and get serious in the Leo areas of our lives. Many of the fun things in life fall under the banner of Leo: entertainment, show business, children, play, recreation, love affairs, hobbies, performing, talent, the creative arts, and recognition by others. Since Saturn tends to put a damper on Leo's fun, expect some restrictions on the entertainment business, shows with more serious themes and actors. Leo is associated with children, and with Saturn come the burdens and responsibilities of bringing them up.

The subject of aging in general belongs to Saturn, and

the Leo archetype in this area is the aging film star determined to hold on to youth. Love affairs and flirtations, part of Leo's sunny side, may this year involve older people. Maturing baby boomers will demand more awareness from the media. Therefore we will see more older people on television and in films, more entertainment tailored to an aging population, a harbinger of the even stronger Saturnian trends coming up in 2008. Since Leo is also associated with speculation and gambling, in fact all games, expect more stringent regulation and controversy around big-time casinos and sports.

Saturn in Leo demands hard work in creative ventures, responsibility when interacting with others. Leo types can't get away with casual love. affairs, or with being high-handed, arrogant, or divalike in any way. Leo divas will have to earn their applause. This could tone down the blatant celebrity-worshipping culture that has arisen over the past few years. No longer will it be enough to be famous for being famous. The emphasis will be on true values rather than the trappings of success. Flashy lifestyles, bling bling jewelry, and showing off will be out.

Saturn moves into Virgo on September 2, 2007, which is followed soon after by a solar eclipse in Virgo on September 11. This is a time when Virgo issues—health care and maintenance and moral standards and controls—will come to the fore. We will adjust the structures of our lives, making changes so that we can function at an efficient level. We'll be challenged with a reality check in areas where we have been too optimistic or expansive.

Jupiter in Sagittarius

During the year that Jupiter remains in a sign, the fields associated with that sign—comedy, fun, travel, laughter—will be the ones that arouse excitement and enthusiasm, usually providing excellent opportunities for expansion, fame, and fortune. Jupiter remains in fun-loving Sagittarius, the sign it rules, until December 18.

One place we will notice the Jupiter influence is in fashion, which should have a cheerful, colorful look. Sagittarius has great fashion flair, which should show up in ethnic influences and exciting new sportswear.

Those born under Sagittarius should have many opportunities during the year. However, keep your feet on the ground. The flip side of Jupiter is that there are no limits. You can expand off the planet under a Jupiter transit, which is why the planet is often called the Gateway to Heaven. If something is going to burst (such as an artery) or overextend or go over the top in some way, it could happen under a supposedly lucky Jupiter transit. So be aware.

Those born under Gemini may find their best opportunities working with partners this year, as Jupiter will be transiting their seventh house of relationships.

Continuing Trends

Uranus and Neptune continue to do a kind of astrological dance called a mutual reception. This is a supportive relationship where Uranus is in Pisces, the sign ruled by Neptune, while Neptune is in Aquarius, the sign ruled by Uranus. When this dance is over in 2011, it is likely that we will be living under very different political and social circumstances.

Uranus in Pisces

Uranus, known as the Great Awakener, tends to cause both upheaval and innovation in the sign it transits. During previous episodes of Uranus in Pisces, great religions and spiritual movements have come into being, most recently Mormonism and Christian Fundamentalism. In its most positive mode, Pisces promotes imagination and creativity, the art of illusion in theater and film, the inspiration of great artists. A water sign, Pisces is naturally associated with all things liquid—oceans, oil, alcohol—and with those creatures that live in the water—fish, the fishing industry, fish habitats, and fish farming. Currently there is a great debate going on about overfishing, contamination of fish, and fish farming. The underdog, the enslaved, and the disenfranchised should also benefit from Uranus in Pisces.

Since Uranus is a disruptive influence that aims to challenge the status quo, the forces of nature that manifest will most likely be in the Pisces area: oceans, seas, and rivers. We have seen unprecedented rainy seasons, floods, mud slides, and disastrous hurricanes. Note that 2005's devastating Hurricane Katrina hit an area known for both the oil and fishing industries.

Pisces is associated with the prenatal phase of life, which is related to regenerative medicine. The controversy over embryonic stem cell research should continue to be debated. Petroleum issues, both in the oil-producing countries and offshore oil drilling, will come to a head. Uranus in Pisces suggests that development of new hydroelectric sources may provide the power we need to continue our current power-thirsty lifestyle.

As in previous eras, there should continue to be a flourishing of the arts. We are seeing many new artistic forms developing now, such as computer-created actors and special effects. The sky's the limit on this influence.

Those who have problems with Uranus are those who resist change, so the key is to embrace the future.

Neptune in Aquarius

Neptune is a planet of imagination and creativity, but also of deception and illusion. Neptune is associated with hospitals, which have been the subject of much controversy. On the positive side, hospitals are acquiring cutting-edge technology. The atmosphere of many hospitals is already changing from the intimidating and sterile environment of the past to that of a health-promoting spa. Alternative therapies, such as massage, diet counseling, and aromatherapy, are becoming commonplace, which expresses this Neptune trend. New procedures in plastic surgery, also a Neptune glamour field, and anti-aging therapies are restoring the illusion of youth.

However, issues involving the expense and quality of

health care and the evolving relationship between doctors, drug companies, and HMOs reflect a darker side of this trend.

What About the New Planets?

Our solar system is becoming more complex; astronomers continue to discover new objects circling the sun. In addition to the familiar planets, there are comets, cometoids, asteroids, and strange icy bodies in the Kuiper Belt beyond Neptune. The newest object at this writing is a planetlike orb that has a tiny moon. It is tentatively nicknamed Xena, after the TV heroine. Once Xena's orbit is established, astrologers will observe what effect this planet has on our horoscopes. Astrologers have long hypothesized about distant planets on the outer reaches of the solar system, but most astrologers stop with Pluto, which itself is quite controversial. Some scientists insist that tiny Pluto, only one-fifth the size of Earth, is not a full-fledged planet. However, anyone experiencing a zap to the horoscope from this little object knows that it is a force to be reckoned with! Time will tell about Xena and her yet to be discovered siblings!

CHAPTER 2

Your Best Times This Year

Have you ever felt that success is a matter of timing, that you could set your schedule on a successful course if you coordinated your activities with times when the planets give you the green light? On the other hand, it's useful to know when not to act, when it would be better to kick back and review where you're going.

For instance, when mischievous Mercury creates havoc with communications and you can't seem to make progress with projects, you'll use the time to best advantage by backing up your vital computer files, clearing out your files and closets and reading between the lines of contracts. That's the time to be extra patient with coworkers and double-check all messages. Mark your social calendar when Venus passes through your sign—that's when you're the flavor of the month. You've got extra sex appeal, so it's time to get a knockout new outfit or hairstyle. Then ask someone you'd like to know better to dinner. Venus timing can also help you charm clients with a stunning sales pitch or make an offer they won't refuse.

In this chapter, you will learn how to find your best times as well as which times to avoid. You will also learn how to read the moods of the moon and make them work for you. Use the information and tables in this chapter and the planet tables in this book, and also use the moon sign listings in your daily forecasts.

Here are the happenings to note on your agenda:

- Dates of your sun sign (high-energy period)
- The month previous to your sun sign (low-energy period)
- Dates of planets in your sign this year

- Full and new moons (pay special attention when these fall in your sun sign!)
- Eclipses
- Moon in your sun sign every month, as well as moon in the opposite sign (listed in daily forecast)
- Mercury retrogrades
- Other retrograde periods

Your High-Power Time

Every birthday starts off a new cycle of solar energy for you. You should feel a new surge of vitality as the powerful sun enters your sign. This is the time when predominant energies are most favorable to you. So go for it! Start new projects, make your big moves (especially when the new moon is in your sign, doubling your charisma). You'll get the recognition you deserve now, when everyone is attuned to your sun sign. Look in the tables in this book to see if other planets will also be passing through your sun sign at this time. Venus (love, beauty), Mars (energy, drive), and Mercury (communication, mental sharpness) reinforce the sun and give an extra boost to your life in the areas they affect. Venus will rev up your social and love life, making you seem especially attractive. Mars amplifies your energy and drive. Mercury fuels your brainpower and helps you communicate. Jupiter signals an especially lucky period of expansion.

There are two downtimes related to the sun. During the month before your birthday period, when you are winding up your annual cycle, you could be feeling especially vulnerable and depleted. So at that time get extra rest, watch your diet, and take it easy. Don't overstress yourself. Use this time to gear up for a big "push" when the sun enters your sign.

Another downtime is when the sun is in a sign opposite your sun sign (six months from your birthday). That's when the prevailing energies are very different from yours. You may feel at odds with the world. You'll have to work harder for recognition because people are not on your wavelength.

11

However, this could be a good time to work on a team, in cooperation with others, or behind the scenes.

Plan Your Day with the Moon

The moon is a powerful tool to divine the mood of the moment. You can work with the moon in two ways. Plan by the *sign* the moon is in; plan by the *phase* of the moon. The sign will tell you the kind of activities that suit the moon's mood. The phase will tell you the best time to start or finish a certain activity.

Working with the phases of the moon is as easy as looking up at the night sky. During the new moon, when both the sun and moon are in the same sign, begin new ventures—especially activities that are favored by that sign. Then you'll utilize the powerful energies pulling you in the same direction. You'll be focused outward, toward action, and in a doing mode. Postpone breaking off, terminating, deliberating, or reflecting—activities that require introspection and passive work. These are better suited to a later moon phase.

Get your project under way during the first quarter. Then go public at the full moon, a time of high intensity, when feelings come out into the open. This is your time to shine—to express yourself. Be aware, however, that because pressures are being released, other people will also be letting off steam. Since confrontations are possible, take advantage of this time either to air grievances or to avoid arguments. Traditionally, astrologers often advise against surgery at this time, which could produce heavier bleeding.

About three days after the full moon comes the disseminating phase, a time when the energy of the cycle begins to wind down. From the last quarter of the moon to the next new moon, it's a time to cut off unproductive relationships, do serious thinking, and focus on inward-directed activities.

You'll feel some new and full moons more strongly than others, especially those new moons that fall in your sun sign and full moons in your opposite sign. Because that full moon happens at your low-energy time of year, it is likely to be an especially stressful time in a relationship, when any hidden problems or unexpressed emotions could surface.

Full and New Moons in 2007

All dates are calculated for eastern standard time and eastern daylight time.

Full Moon—January 3 in Cancer
New Moon—January 18 in Capricorn

Full Moon—February 2 in Leo
New Moon—February 17 in Aquarius

Full Moon—March 3 in Virgo (lunar eclipse)
New Moon—March 18 in Pisces (total solar eclipse)

Full Moon—April 2 in Libra
New Moon—April 17 in Aries

Full Moon—May 2 in Scorpio
New Moon—May 16 in Taurus

Full Moon—May 31 in Sagittarius
New Moon—June 14 in Gemini

Full Moon—June 30 in Capricorn
New Moon—July 14 in Cancer

Full Moon—July 29 in Aquarius
New Moon—August 12 in Leo

Full Moon—August 28 in Pisces (lunar eclipse)
New Moon—September 11 in Virgo (solar eclipse)

Full Moon—September 26 in Aries
New Moon—October 11 in Libra

Full Moon—October 26 in Taurus
New Moon—November 9 in Scorpio

Full Moon—November 24 in Gemini
New Moon—December 9 in Sagittarius
Full Moon—December 23 in Cancer

How to Time by the Moon Sign

To forecast the daily emotional "weather," to determine your monthly high and low days, or to synchronize your activities with the cycles of the moon, take note of the moon sign under your daily forecast at the end of the book. Here are some of the activities favored and the moods you are likely to encounter under each moon sign.

Moon in Aries: Get Moving!

The new moon in Aries is an ideal time to start new projects. Everyone is pushy, raring to go, rather impatient, and short-tempered. Leave details and follow-up for later. Competitive sports or martial arts are great ways to let off steam. Quiet types could use some assertiveness, but it's a great day for dynamos. Be careful not to step on too many toes.

Moon in Taurus: Lay the Foundations for Success

Do solid, methodical tasks like follow-through or backup work. Make investments, buy real estate, do appraisals, do some hard bargaining. Attend to your property. Get out in the country or spend some time in your garden. Enjoy creature comforts, music, a good dinner, sensual lovemaking. Forget starting a diet—this is a day when you'll feel self-indulgent.

Moon in Gemini: Communicate

Talk means action today. Telephone, write letters, fax! Make new contacts, stay in touch with steady customers.

You can juggle lots of tasks today. It's a great time for mental activity of any kind. Don't try to pin people down—they, too, are feeling restless. Keep it light. Flirtations and socializing are good. Watch gossip—and don't give away secrets.

Moon in Cancer: Pay Attention to Loved Ones

This is a moody, sensitive, emotional time. People respond to personal attention, to mothering. Stay at home, have a family dinner, call your mother. Nostalgia, memories, and psychic powers are heightened. You'll want to hang on to people and things (don't clean out your closets now). You could have shrewd insights into what others really need and want. Pay attention to dreams, intuition, and gut reactions.

Moon in Leo: Be Confident

Everybody is in a much more confident, warm, generous mood. It's a good day to ask for a raise, show what you can do, dress like a star. People will respond to flattery, enjoy a bit of drama and theater. You may be extravagant, treat yourself royally, and show off a bit—but don't break the bank! Be careful you don't promise more than you can deliver.

Moon in Virgo: Be Practical

Do practical down-to-earth chores. Review your budget, make repairs, be an efficiency expert. Not a day to ask for a raise. Tend to personal care and maintenance. Have a health checkup, go on a diet, buy vitamins or health food. Make your home spotless. Take care of details and piled-up chores. Reorganize your work and life so they run more smoothly and efficiently. Save money. Be prepared for others to be in a critical, faultfinding mood.

Moon in Libra: Be Diplomatic

Attend to legal matters. Negotiate contracts. Arbitrate. Do things with your favorite partner. Socialize. Be romantic. Buy a special gift, a beautiful object. Decorate yourself or your surroundings. Buy new clothes. Throw a party. Have an elegant, romantic evening. Smooth over any ruffled feathers. Avoid confrontations. Stick to civilized discussions.

Moon in Scorpio: Solve Problems

This is a day to do things with passion. You'll have excellent concentration and focus. Try not to get too intense emotionally. Avoid sharp exchanges with loved ones. Others may tend to go to extremes, get jealous, overreact. Great for troubleshooting, problem solving, research, scientific work—and making love. Pay attention to those psychic vibes.

Moon in Sagittarius: Sell and Motivate

A great time for travel, philosophical discussions, setting long-range career goals. Work out, do sports, buy athletic equipment. Others will be feeling upbeat, exuberant, and adventurous. Risk taking is favored. You may feel like taking a gamble, betting on the horses, visiting a local casino, buying a lottery ticket. Teaching, writing, and spiritual activities also get the green light. Relax outdoors. Take care of animals.

Moon in Capricorn: Get Organized

You can accomplish a lot now, so get on the ball! Attend to business. Issues concerning your basic responsibilities, duties, family, and elderly parents could crop up. You'll be expected to deliver on promises. Weed out the deadwood from your life. Get a dental checkup. Not a good day for gambling or taking risks.

Moon in Aquarius: Join the Group

A great day for doing things with groups—clubs, meetings, outings, politics, parties. Campaign for your candidate. Work for a worthy cause. Deal with larger issues that affect humanity—the environment and metaphysical questions. Buy a computer or electronic gadget. Watch TV. Wear something outrageous. Try something you've never done before. Present an original idea. Don't stick to a rigid schedule—go with the flow. Take a class in meditation, mind control, yoga.

Moon in Pisces: Be Creative

This can be a very creative day, so let your imagination work overtime. Film, theater, music, ballet could inspire you. Spend some time alone, resting and reflecting, reading or writing poetry. Daydreams can also be profitable. Help those less fortunate. Lend a listening ear to someone who may be feeling blue. Don't overindulge in self-pity or escapism, however. People are especially vulnerable to substance abuse now. Turn your thoughts to romance and someone special.

Retrogrades: When the Planets Seem to Backstep

All the planets, except for the sun and moon, have times when they appear to move backward—or retrograde—as it seems from our point of view on earth. At these times, planets do not work as they normally do. So it's best to "take a break" from that planet's energies in our life and to do some work on an inner level.

Mercury Retrograde: The Key Is in "Re"

Mercury goes retrograde most often, and its effects can be especially irritating. When it reaches a short distance ahead of the sun several times a year, it seems to move backward from our point of view. Astrologers often compare retrograde motion to the optical illusion that occurs when we ride on a train that passes another train traveling at a different speed—the second train appears to be moving in reverse.

What this means to you is that the Mercury-ruled areas of your life—analytical thought processes, communications, scheduling—are subject to all kinds of confusion. Be prepared. Communications equipment can break down. Schedules may be changed on short notice. People are late for appointments or don't show up at all. Traffic is terrible. Major purchases malfunction, don't work out, or get delivered in the wrong color. Letters don't arrive or are delivered to the wrong address. Employees will make errors that have to be corrected later. Contracts don't work out or must be renegotiated.

Since most of us can't put our lives on "hold" during Mercury retrogrades, we should learn to tame the trickster and make it work for us. The key is in the prefix *re-*. This is the time to go back over things in your life, *re*flect on what you've done during the previous months. Now you can get deeper insights, spot errors you've missed. So take time to *re*view and *re*evaluate what has happened. *Re*st and *re*ward yourself—it's a good time to take a vacation, especially if you *re*visit a favorite place. *Re*organize your work and finish up projects that are backed up. Clean out your desk and closets. Throw away what you can't *re*cycle. If you must sign contracts or agreements, do so with a contingency clause that lets you *re*evaluate the terms later.

Postpone major purchases or commitments for the time being. Don't get married (unless you're *re*marrying the same person). Try not to *re*ly on other people keeping appointments, contracts, or agreements to the letter; have several alternatives. Double-check and *re*ad between the lines. Don't buy anything connected with communications or transportation (if you must, be sure to cover yourself).

Mercury retrograding through your sun sign will intensify its effect on your life.

If Mercury was retrograde when you were born, you may be one of the lucky people who don't suffer the frustrations of this period. If so, your mind probably works in a very intuitive, insightful way.

The sign in which Mercury is retrograding can give you an idea of what's in store—as well as the sun signs that will be especially challenged.

Mercury Retrogrades in 2007

Mercury has three retrograde periods this year.
  February 14 to March 8 from Pisces back to Aquarius
  June 15 to July 9 in Cancer
  October 11 to November 1 from Scorpio back to Libra

Venus Retrograde: Relationships Move Backward

Retrograding Venus can cause your relationships to take a backward step, or it can make you extravagant and impractical. Shopping till you drop and buying what you cannot afford are problems at this time. It's *not* a good time to redecorate—you'll hate the color of the walls later. Postpone getting a new hairstyle. Try not to fall in love either. But if you wish to make amends in an already troubled relationship, make peaceful overtures at this time.

Venus Retrogrades in 2007

Venus turns retrograde in Virgo from July 27 until September 8, when it turns direct in Leo.

Use the Go Power of Mars

Mars shows how and when to get where you want to go. Timing your moves with Mars on your side can give you a big push. On the other hand, pushing Mars the wrong way can guarantee that you'll run into frustrations in every corner. Your best times to forge ahead are during the weeks when Mars is traveling through your sun sign or your Mars sign (look these up in the tables in this book). Also consider times when Mars is in a compatible sign (fire with air signs, or earth with water signs). You'll be sure to have planetary power on your side.

Mars Retrogrades in 2007

Mars turns retrograde on November 15 until January 30, 2008, from Cancer to Gemini.

When Other Planets Retrograde

The slower-moving planets stay retrograde for months at a time (Jupiter, Saturn, Neptune, Uranus, and Pluto).

When Saturn is retrograde, it's an uphill battle with self-discipline. You may not be in the mood for work. You may feel more like hanging out at the beach than getting things done.

Neptune retrograde promotes a dreamy escapism from reality, when you may feel you're in a fog (Pisces will feel this, especially).

Uranus retrograde may mean setbacks in areas where there have been sudden changes, when you may be forced to regroup or reevaluate the situation.

Pluto retrograde is a time to work on establishing proportion and balance in areas where there have been recent dramatic transformations.

When the planets move forward again, there's a shift in the atmosphere. Activities connected with each planet start moving ahead, plans that were stalled get rolling. Make a special note of those days on your calendar and proceed accordingly.

Other Retrogrades in 2007

The five slower-moving planets all go retrograde in 2007.

Jupiter retrogrades four months from April 5 to August 6 in Sagittarius.

Saturn turned retrograde on December 5, 2006, until

April 19, 2007. It turns retrograde again on December 19 for the duration of the year.

Uranus retrogrades from June 23 to November 24 in Pisces.

Neptune retrogrades from May 24 to October 31 in Aquarius.

Pluto retrogrades from March 31 to September 7 in Sagittarius.

CHAPTER 3

What Planets Could Rock Your World This Year

It's been said that knowledge is power, so why not use astrology's wisdom to ride with the tide this year and make the planets work for you?

Eclipses Clear the Air

Eclipses can bring on milestones in your life, if they aspect a key point in your horoscope. In general, they shake up the status quo, bringing hidden areas out into the open. During this time, problems you've been avoiding or have brushed aside can surface to demand your attention. A good coping strategy is to accept whatever comes up as a challenge that could make a positive difference in your life. And don't forget the power of your sense of humor. If you can laugh at something, you'll never be afraid of it.

What Is the Best Thing to Do During an Eclipse?

When the natural rhythms of the sun and moon are disturbed, it's best to postpone important activities. Be sure to mark eclipse days on your calendar, especially if the eclipse falls in your birth sign. This year, those born under Aries, Pisces, and Virgo should take special note of the feelings that arise. With lunar eclipses, some possibilities could be a break from attachments or the healing of an illness or substance abuse, which had been triggered by the subconscious. The temporary event could be a healing time, when you gain perspective. During solar eclipses, when you might be in a highly subjective state, pay attention to the hidden subconscious patterns that surface, the emotional truth that is revealed at this time.

The effect of the eclipse can reverberate for some time, often months after the event. But it is especially important to stay cool and make no major moves during the period known as the shadow of the eclipse, which begins about a week before and lasts until at least three days after the eclipse. After three days, the daily rhythms should return to normal, and you can proceed with business as usual.

This Year's Eclipse Dates

March 3: Lunar eclipse in Virgo
March 18: Solar eclipse in Pisces
August 28: Lunar eclipse in Pisces
September 11: Solar eclipse in Virgo

Saturn Gives You a Reality Check

When Saturn hits a critical point in your horoscope, you can count on an experience that will make you slow up, pull back, and reexamine your life. It is a call to eliminate what is not working, to shape up, to set priorities, to examine the boundaries and structures in your life (or lack of them) and set new ones. During this process, you may feel restricted, frustrated, or inhibited—not a fun time, but one that will serve you well in the long run. You may need to take on more responsibilities that will test your limits.

By the end of its twenty-eight-year trip around the zodiac, Saturn will have tested you in all areas of your life. The major tests happen in seven-year cycles, when Saturn passes over the angles of your chart, which means your rising sign, the top of your chart or midheaven, your descendant, and the nadir or bottom of your chart. This is when the real life-changing experiences happen. But you are also in for a testing period whenever Saturn passes a planet in your chart or stresses that planet from a distance. It is useful to check your planetary positions with the timetable of Saturn or prepare in advance, or at least to brace yourself.

When Saturn returns to its location at the time of your birth, at approximately age twenty-eight, you'll have your first Saturn return. At this time, a person usually takes stock or settles down to find his mission in life and assume full adult duties and responsibilities.

Another way Saturn helps us is to reveal the karmic lessons from previous lives and give us the chance to overcome them. So look at Saturn's challenges as much-needed opportunities for self-improvement.

Outwitting the Planets

Second-guessing Saturn and the eclipses this year is easy if you have a copy of your horoscope calculated by a computer. This enables you to pinpoint the area of your life that will be affected. However, you can make an educated guess, by setting up a rough diagram on your own. If you'd like to find out which area of your life this year's Saturn change is most likely to affect, follow these easy steps.

First, you must know the time of day you were born and look up your rising sign listed on the tables in this book (see chapter 7). Set up an estimated horoscope by drawing a circle, then dividing it into four parts by making a cross directly through the center. Continue to divide each of the parts into thirds, as if you were dividing a cake, until you have twelve slices. Write your rising sign on the middle left-hand slice, which would be the nine o'clock point, if you were looking at your watch. Then write the following signs on the dividing line of each slice, working counterclockwise, until you have listed all twelve signs of the zodiac.

You should now have a basic diagram of your horoscope chart (minus the planets, of course). Starting with your rising-sign slice, number each portion consecutively, again working counterclockwise.

Since this year's eclipses will fall in Pisces and Virgo, find the number of these slices, or houses, on the chart and read the following descriptions for the kinds of issues that are likely to be emphasized. On September 2, Saturn will move from Leo to Virgo, so check those houses in your chart for Saturn-related events.

If an eclipse or Saturn falls in your FIRST HOUSE:

Events cause you to examine the ways you are acting independently and push you to become more visible, to assert yourself. This is a time when you feel compelled to make your own decisions. You may want to change your physical appearance, body image, or style of dress in some way. Under affliction, there might be illness or physical harm.

If an eclipse or Saturn falls in your SECOND HOUSE:

This is the place where you consider all matters of security. You consolidate your resources, earn money, acquire property, and decide what you value and what you want to own. On a deeper level, this house reveals your sense of self-worth.

If an eclipse or Saturn falls in your THIRD HOUSE:

Here you reach out to others, express your ideas, and explore different courses of action. You may feel especially restless or have confrontations with neighbors or siblings. In your search for more knowledge, you may decide to improve your skills, get more education, or sign up for a course that interests you. Local transportation, especially your car, might be affected by an eclipse here.

If an eclipse or Saturn falls in your FOURTH HOUSE:

Here is where you put down roots and establish a base. You'll consider what home really means to you. Issues involving parents, the physical setup or location of your home, and your immediate family demand your attention. You may be especially concerned with parenting or relationships with your own mother. You may consider moving your home to a new location or leaving home.

If an eclipse or Saturn falls in your FIFTH HOUSE:
Here is where you express yourself, either through your personal talents or through procreating children. You are interested in making your special talents visible. This is also the house of love affairs and the romantic aspect of life, where you flirt, have fun, and enjoy the excitement of love. Hobbies and crafts fall in this area.

If an eclipse or Saturn falls in your SIXTH HOUSE:
How well are you doing your job? This is your maintenance department, where you take care of your health, organize your life, and set up a daily routine. It is also the place where you perfect your skills and add polish to your life. The chores you do every day, the skills you learn, and the techniques you use fall here. If something doesn't work in your life, an eclipse is sure to bring this to light. If you've been neglecting your health, diet, and fitness, you'll probably pay the consequences during an eclipse. Or you may be faced with work that requires much routine organization and steady effort, rather than creative ability. Or you may be required to perform services for others.

If an eclipse or Saturn falls in your SEVENTH HOUSE:
This is the area of committed relationships, of those which involve legal agreements, of working in a close relationship with another. Here you'll be dealing with how you relate, what you'll be willing to give up for the sake of a marriage or partnership. Eclipses here can put extra pressure on a relationship and, if it's not working, precipitate a breakup. Lawsuits and open enemies also reside here.

If an eclipse or Saturn falls in your EIGHTH HOUSE:
This area is concerned with power and control. Consider what you are willing to give up in order that something might happen. Power struggles, intense relationships, and desires to penetrate deeper mysteries belong here. Debts, loans, financial matters that involve another party, and wheeling and dealing also come into focus. So does sex, where you surrender your individual power to create a new life together. Matters involving birth and death are also involved here.

If an eclipse or Saturn falls in your NINTH HOUSE:

Here is where you look at the big picture. You'll seek information that helps you find meaning in life: higher education, religion, travel, global issues. Eclipses here can push you to get out of your rut, to explore something you've never done before, and to expand your horizons.

If an eclipse or Saturn falls in your TENTH HOUSE:

This is the high-profile point in your chart. Here is where you consider how society looks at you and your position in the outside world. You'll be concerned about whether you receive proper credit for your work and if you're recognized by higher-ups. Promotions, raises, and other forms of recognition can be given or denied. If you have worked hard, Saturn can give you well-deserved rewards here. Either your standing in your career or in your community can be challenged, or you'll be publicly acknowledged for achieving a goal. An eclipse here can make you famous or burst your balloon if you've been too ambitious or neglecting other areas of your life.

If an eclipse or Saturn falls in your ELEVENTH HOUSE:

Your relationship with groups of people comes under scrutiny during an eclipse: whom you are identified with, whom you socialize with, and how well you are accepted by other members of your team. Activities of clubs and political parties, networking, and other social interactions become important. You'll be concerned about what other people think.

If an eclipse or Saturn falls in your TWELFTH HOUSE:

This is the time when the focus turns to your inner life. An especially favorable eclipse here might bring you great insight and inspiration. On the other hand, events may happen that cause you to retreat from public life. Here is where we go to be alone or to work in retreats, hospitals, or religious institutions, or to explore psychotherapy. Here is where you deliver selfless service, through charitable acts. Good aspects from an eclipse could promote an ability to go with the flow or to rise above the competition to find an inner, almost mystical strength that enables you to connect with the deepest needs of others.

CHAPTER 4

The Moon and Your Emotions

How do you react to life's problems? What do you care about? What makes you feel comfortable, secure, or romantic? The answers are a few secrets revealed by the moon sign in your horoscope, where the moon represents your receptive, reflective, female, nurturing self. It also reflects who you were nurtured by—the mother or mother figure in your chart. In a man's chart, the moon position describes his receptive, emotional, yin side, as well as the woman in his life who will have the deepest effect, usually his mother. (Venus reveals the kind of woman who will attract him physically.)

It's well worth having an accurate chart cast to determine your moon sign or that of someone you'd like to know better, since this reveals much about your inner life. You can learn what appeals to a person subconsciously by knowing the person's moon sign, which reflects the instinctive emotional nature.

The moon is more at home in some signs than others. It rules maternal Cancer and is exalted in Taurus—both comforting, home-loving signs where the natural emotional energies of the moon are easily and productively expressed. But when the moon is in the opposite signs—Capricorn and Scorpio—it leaves the comfortable nest and deals with emotional issues of power and achievement in the outside world. Those of you with the moon in these signs are likely to find your emotional role more challenging in life.

Since detailed moon tables are too extensive for this book, check through the following listing to find the moon sign that feels most familiar.

Moon in Aries

This placement makes you both independent and ardent. An idealist, you tend to fall in and out of love easily. You love a challenge but could cool once your quarry is captured. Your emotional reactions are fast and fiery, quickly expressed and quickly forgotten. You may not think before expressing your feelings. It's not easy to hide how you feel. Channeling all your emotional energy could be one of your big challenges.

Moon in Taurus

A sentimental soul, you are very fond of the good life, and you gravitate toward solid, secure relationships. You like displays of affection and creature comforts—all the tangible trappings of a cozy, safe, calm atmosphere. You are sensual and steady emotionally, but very stubborn, possessive, and determined. You can't be pushed, and you tend to dislike changes. You should make an effort to broaden your horizons and to take a risk sometimes. You may become very attached to your home turf. You may also be a collector of objects that are meaningful to you.

Moon in Gemini

You crave mental stimulation and variety in life, which you usually get through either an ever-varied social life, the excitement of flirtation and/or multiple professional involvements. You may marry more than once and have a rather chaotic emotional life due to your difficulty with commitment and settling down, as well as your need to be constantly on the go. (Be sure to find a partner who is as outgoing as you are.) You will have to learn at some point to focus your energies because you tend to be somewhat fragmented—to do two things at once, to have two homes or even two lovers. If you can find a creative way to express your many-faceted nature, you'll be ahead of the game.

Moon in Cancer

This is the most powerful lunar position, which is sure to make a deep imprint on your character. Your needs are very much associated with your reaction to the needs of others. You are very sensitive, caring, and self-protective, though some of you may mask this with a hard shell, like the moon-sensitive crab. This placement also gives an excellent memory, keen intuition, and an uncanny ability to perceive the needs of others. All of the lunar phases will affect you, especially full moons and eclipses, so you would do well to mark them on your calendar. Because you're happiest at home, you may work at home or turn your office into a second home, where you can nurture and comfort people. (You may tend to mother the world.) With natural psychic, intuitive ability, you might be drawn to occult work in some way. Or you may get professionally involved with providing food and shelter to others.

Moon in Leo

This warm, passionate moon takes everything to heart. You are attracted to all that is noble, generous, and aristocratic in life (and may be a bit of a snob). You have an innate ability to take command emotionally, but you do need strong support, loyalty, and loud applause from those you love. You are possessive of your loved ones and your turf and will roar if anyone threatens to take over your territory.

Moon in Virgo

You are rather cool until you decide if others measure up. But once someone or something meets your ideal standards, you hold up your end of the arrangement perfectly. You may, in fact, drive yourself too hard to attain some notion of perfection. Try to be a bit easier on yourself and others. Don't always act the censor! You love to be the teacher and are drawn to situations where you can change others for the better, but sometimes you must learn to accept others for what they are—enjoy what you have!

Moon in Libra

Like other air-sign moons, you think before you feel. Therefore, you may not immediately recognize the emotional needs of others. However, you are relationship oriented and may find it difficult to be alone or to do things alone. After you have learned emotional balance by leaning on yourself first, you can have excellent partnerships. It is best for you to avoid extremes, which set your scales swinging and can make your love life precarious. You thrive in a rather conservative, traditional, romantic relationship, where you receive attention and flattery—but not possessiveness—from your partner. You'll be your most charming in an elegant, harmonious atmosphere.

Moon in Scorpio

This is a moon that enjoys and responds to intense, passionate feelings. You may go to extremes and have a very dramatic emotional life, full of ardor, suspicion, jealousy, and obsession. It would be much healthier to channel your need for power and control into meaningful work. This is a good position for anyone in the fields of medicine, police work, research, the occult, psychoanalysis, or intuitive work, because life-and-death situations don't faze you. However, you do take personal disappointments very hard.

Moon in Sagittarius

You take life's ups and downs with good humor and the proverbial grain of salt. You'll love 'em and leave 'em—take off on a great adventure at a moment's notice. Born free could be your slogan. Attracted by the exotic, you have wanderlust mentally and physically. You may be too much in search of new mental and spiritual stimulation to ever settle down.

Moon in Capricorn

Are you ever accused of being too cool and calculating? You have an earthy side, but you take prestige and position very seriously. Your strong drive to succeed extends to your romantic life, where you will be devoted to improving your lifestyle, rising to the top. A structured situation where you can advance methodically makes you feel wonderfully secure. You may be attracted to someone older or very much younger or from a different social world. It may be difficult to look at the lighter side of emotional relationships. Though this moon is placed in the sign of its detriment, the good news is that you tend to be very dutiful and responsible to those you care for.

Moon in Aquarius

You are a people collector with many friends of all backgrounds. You are happiest surrounded by people and may feel uneasy when left alone. Though you usually stay friends with lovers, intense emotions and demanding one-on-one relationships turn you off. You don't like anything to be too rigid or scheduled. Though tolerant and understanding, you can be emotionally unpredictable and may opt for an unconventional love life. With plenty of space, you will be able to sustain relationships with liberal, freedom-loving types.

Moon in Pisces

You are very responsive and empathetic to others, especially if they have problems or are the underdog. (Be on guard against attracting too many people with sob stories.) You'll be happiest if you can express your creative imagination in the arts or in the spiritual or healing professions. Because you may tend to escape in fantasies or overreact to the moods of others, you need an emotional anchor to help you keep a firm foothold in reality. Steer clear of too much escapism (especially in alcohol) or reclusiveness. Places near water soothe your moods. Working in a field that gives you emotional variety will also help you be productive.

CHAPTER 5

Basic Astrology: Your Owner's Manual

You probably know your zodiac sign and those of your friends. But do you know the difference between a sign and a constellation? And what is a house? Is yours an earth sign or a water sign? If you'd like to venture around the zodiac into the deeper areas of astrology, this chapter can get you up and running. It's a quick owner's manual, your fast track to understanding the basic principles of this fascinating but often confusing subject.

Signs and Constellations: What's the Difference?

First, let's get our sign language straight, because for most readers, that's the starting point of astrology.

Signs are actually a type of celestial real estate, located on the zodiac, an imaginary 360-degree belt circling the earth. This belt is divided into twelve equal thirty-degree portions, which are the signs. There's a lot of confusion about the difference between the signs and the constellations of the zodiac. The latter are patterns of stars that originally marked the twelve divisions, like signposts. Though a sign is named after the constellation that once marked the same area, the constellations are no longer in the same place relative to the earth that they were many centuries ago. Over hundreds of years, the earth's orbit has shifted, so that from our point of view here on earth, the constellations seem to have moved. However, the signs remain in place. (Most Western astrology uses the twelve-equal-part division of the zodiac, though there are some other methods of astrology that still use the constellations instead of the signs.)

Most people think of themselves in terms of their sun sign. A sun sign refers to the sign the sun is orbiting through at a given moment (from our point of view here on earth). For instance, "I'm an Aries" means that the sun was passing through Aries when that person was born. However, there are nine other planets (plus asteroids, fixed stars, and sensitive points) that also form our total astrological personality, and some or many of these will be located in other signs. No one is completely Aries, with all astrological components in one sign! (Please note that, in astrology, the sun and moon are usually referred to as planets, though of course they're not.)

As we mentioned before, the sun signs are places on the zodiac. They do not do anything (the planets are the doers). However, they are associated with many things, depending on their location.

How We Define the Signs

The definitions of the signs evolved systematically from four components that interrelate. These four different criteria are a sign's element: its quality, its polarity or sex, and its order in the progression of the zodiac. All these factors work together to tell us what the sign is like.

The system is magically mathematical. The number 12—as in the twelve signs of the zodiac—is divisible by 4, by 3, and by 2. There are four elements, three qualities, and two polarities, which follow each other in sequence around the zodiac.

The four elements (earth, air, fire, and water) are the building blocks of astrology. The use of an element to describe a sign probably dates from man's first attempts to categorize what he saw. Ancient sages believed that all things were composed of combinations of these basic elements—earth, air, fire, and water. This included the human character, which was fiery/choleric, earthy/melancholy, airy/sanguine, or watery/phlegmatic. The elements also correspond to our emotional (water), physical (earth), mental (air) and spiritual (fire) natures. The energies of each of the elements were then observed to be related to the time of year when the sun was passing through a certain segment of the zodiac.

Those born with the sun in fire signs—Aries, Leo, Sagittarius—embody the characteristic of that element. Optimism, warmth, hot tempers, enthusiasm, and spirit are typical of these signs. Taurus, Virgo, and Capricorn are earthy—more grounded, physical, materialistic, organized and deliberate than fire-sign people. Air-sign people—Gemini, Libra, and Aquarius—are mentally oriented communicators. Water signs—Cancer, Scorpio, and Pisces—are emotional, sensitive, and creative.

Think of what each element does to the others. Water puts out fire or evaporates under heat. Air fans the flames or blows them out. Earth smothers fire, drifts and erodes with too much wind, becomes mud or fertile soil with water. Those are often perfect analogies for the relationships between people of different sun-sign elements. This astro-chemistry was one of the first ways man described his relationships. Fortunately, no one is entirely air or fire. We all have a bit, or a lot, of each element in our horoscopes. It is this unique mix that defines each astrological personality.

Within each element, there are three qualities that describe types of behavior associated with the sign. Those of cardinal signs are activists, go-getters. These four signs—Aries, Cancer, Libra, and Capricorn—begin each season. Fixed signs, which happen in the middle of the season, are associated with builders, stabilizers. You'll find that sun signs Taurus, Leo, Scorpio, and Aquarius are usually gifted with concentration, stamina, and focus. Mutable signs—Gemini, Virgo, Sagittarius, and Pisces—fall at the end of each season and thus are considered catalysts for change. People born under mutable signs are flexible, adaptable.

The polarity of a sign is either its positive or negative charge. It can be masculine, active, positive, and yang like air or fire signs. Or feminine, reactive, negative, and yin like the water and earth signs.

Finally, we consider the sign's place in the order of the

35

zodiac. This is vital to the balance of all the forces and the transmission of energy moving through the signs. You may have noticed that your sign is quite different from your neighboring sign on either side. Yet each seems to grow out of its predecessor like links in a chain and transmits a synthesis of energy gathered along the chain to the following sign, beginning with the fire-powered, active, positive charge of Aries.

How the Signs Add Up

SIGN	ELEMENT	QUALITY	POLARITY	PLACE
Aries	fire	cardinal	masculine	first
Taurus	earth	fixed	feminine	second
Gemini	air	mutable	masculine	third
Cancer	water	cardinal	feminine	fourth
Leo	fire	fixed	masculine	fifth
Virgo	earth	mutable	feminine	sixth
Libra	air	cardinal	masculine	seventh
Scorpio	water	fixed	feminine	eighth
Sagittarius	fire	mutable	masculine	ninth
Capricorn	earth	cardinal	feminine	tenth
Aquarius	air	fixed	masculine	eleventh
Pisces	water	mutable	feminine	twelfth

Your Sign's Special Planet

Each sign has a ruling planet that is most compatible with its energies. Mars adds its fiery assertive characteristics to

Aries. The sensual beauty and comfort-loving side of Venus rules Taurus, whereas the idealistic side of Venus rules Libra. Quick-moving Mercury rules two mutable signs, Gemini and Virgo. Its mental agility belongs to Gemini while its analytical, critical side is best expressed in Virgo. The changeable emotional moon is associated with Cancer, while the outgoing Leo personality is ruled by the sun. Scorpio originally shared Mars, but when Pluto was discovered in this century, its powerful magnetic energies were deemed more suitable to the intense vibrations of the fixed water sign Scorpio. Disciplined Capricorn is ruled by Saturn, and expansive Sagittarius by Jupiter. Unpredictable Aquarius is ruled by Uranus and creative, imaginative Pisces by Neptune. In a horoscope, if a planet is placed in the sign it rules, it is sure to be especially powerful.

The Layout of a Horoscope Chart

A horoscope chart is a map of the heavens at a given moment in time. It looks like a wheel divided with twelve spokes. In between each of the spokes is a section called a house.

Each house deals with a different area of life and is influenced by a special sign and a planet. Astrologers look at the house to tell in what area of life an event is happening or about to happen.

The house is governed by the sign passing over the spoke (or cusp of the house) at that particular moment. Though the first house is naturally associated with Aries and Mars, it would also have an additional Capricorn influence if that sign was passing over the house cusp at the time the chart was cast. The sequence of the houses starts with the first house located at the left center spoke (or the number 9 position, if you were reading a clock). The houses are then read counterclockwise around the chart, with the fourth house at the bottom of the chart, the tenth house at the top or twelve o'clock position.

Where do the planets belong? Around the horoscope, planets are placed within the houses according to their location at the time of the chart. That is why it is so important to have an accurate time; with no specific time, the planets have no specific location in the houses and one cannot determine which area of life they will apply to. Since the signs move across the houses as the earth turns, planets in a house will naturally intensify the importance of that house. The house that contains the sun is naturally one of the most prominent.

The First House: Home of Aries and Mars

The sign passing over the first house at the time of your birth is known as your *ascendant*, or *rising sign*. The first house is the house of "firsts"—the first impression you make, how you initiate matters, the image you choose to project. This is where you advertise yourself, where you project your personality. Planets that fall here will intensify the way you come across to others.

The Second House: Home of Taurus and Venus

This house is where you experience the material world— what you value. Here are your attitudes about money, possessions, finances, whatever belongs to you, and what you own, as well as your earning and spending capacity. On a deeper level, this house reveals your sense of self-worth, the inner values that draw wealth in various forms.

The Third House: Home of Gemini and Mercury

This house describes how you communicate with others, how you reach out to others nearby, and how you interact with the immediate environment. It shows how your thinking process works and the way you express your thoughts. Are you articulate or tongue-tied? Can you think on your feet? This house also shows your first relationships, your experiences with brothers and sisters, and how you deal with people close to you such as your neighbors or pals. It's where you take short trips, write letters, or use the telephone. It shows how your mind works in terms of left-brain logical and analytical functions.

The Fourth House: Home of Cancer and the Moon

The fourth house shows the foundation of life, the psychological underpinnings. At the bottom of the chart, this house shows how you are nurtured and made to feel secure—your roots! It shows your early home environment and the circumstances at the end of your life (your final "home") as well as the place you call home now. Astrologers look here for information about the parental nurturers in your life.

The Fifth House: Home of Leo and the Sun

The fifth house is where the creative potential develops. Here you express yourself and procreate in the sense that children are outgrowths of your creative ability. But this house most represents your inner childlike self who delights in play. If your inner security has been established by the time you reach this house, you are now free to have fun, romance, and love affairs and to give of yourself. This is also the place astrologers look for playful love affairs, flirtations, and brief romantic encounters (rather than long-term commitments).

The Sixth House: Home of Virgo and Mercury

The sixth house has been called the "care and maintenance" department. This house shows how you take care of your body and organize yourself to perform efficiently in the world. Here is where you get things done, where you look after others, and fulfill service duties such as taking care of pets. Here is what you do to survive on a day-to-day basis. The sixth house demands order in your life; otherwise there would be chaos. This house is your "job" (as opposed to your career, which is the domain of the tenth house), your diet, and your health and fitness regimens.

The Seventh House: Home of Libra and Venus

This house shows your attitude toward partners and those with whom you enter into commitments, contracts, or agreements. Here is the way you relate to others, as well as your close, intimate, one-on-one relationships (including open enemies—those you "face off" with). Open hostilities, lawsuits, divorces, and marriages happen here. If the first house represents the "I," the seventh or opposite house is the "not-I"—the complementary partner you attract by the way you come across. If you are having trouble with partnerships, consider what you are attracting by the energies of your first and seventh houses.

The Eighth House: Home of Scorpio and Pluto (also Mars)

The eighth house refers to how you merge with something or someone, and how you handle power and control. This is one of the most mysterious and powerful houses, where your energy transforms itself from "I" to "we." As you give up power and control by uniting with something or someone, two kinds of energies merge and become something greater, leading to a regeneration of the self on a higher level. Here are your attitudes toward sex, shared resources, taxes (what you share with the government). Because this house involves what belongs to others, you face issues of control and power struggles, or undergo a deep psychological transformation as you bond with another. Here you transcend yourself with dreams, drugs, and occult or psychic experiences that reflect the collective unconscious.

The Ninth House: Home of Sagittarius and Jupiter

The ninth house shows your search for wisdom and higher knowledge—your belief system. As the third house represents the "lower mind," its opposite on the wheel, the ninth house, is the "higher mind"—the abstract, intuitive, spiritual mind that asks "big" questions like "Why are we here?" After the third house has explored what was close at hand, the ninth stretches out to broaden you mentally with higher education and travel. Here you stretch spiritually with religious activity. Since you are concerned with how everything is related, you tend to push boundaries, take risks. Here is where you express your ideas in a book or thesis, where you pontificate, philosophize, or preach.

The Tenth House: Home of Capricorn and Saturn

The tenth house is associated with your public life and high-profile activities. Located directly overhead at the "high noon" position on the horoscope wheel, this is the most "visible" house in the chart, the one where the world sees you. It deals with your career (but not your routine "job") and your reputation. Here is where you go public, take on responsibilities, (as opposed to the fourth house, where you stay home). This will affect the career you choose and your "public relations." This house is also associated with your father figure or the main authority figure in your life.

The Eleventh House: Home of Aquarius and Uranus

The eleventh house is where you extend yourself to a group, a goal, or a belief system. This house is where you define what you really want, the kinds of friends you have, your political affiliations, and the kind of groups you identify with as an equal. Here is where you become concerned with "what other people think" or where you rebel against social conventions. Here is where you could become a socially conscious humanitarian or a partygoing social butterfly. It's where you look to others to stimulate you and discover your kinship to the rest of humanity. The sign on this house can help you understand what you gain and lose from friendships.

The Twelfth House: Home of Pisces and Neptune

Old-fashioned astrologers used to put a rather negative spin on this house, calling it the house of self-undoing. When we undo ourselves, we surrender control, boundaries, limits, and rules. The twelfth house is where the boundaries between yourself and others become blurred and you become selfless. But instead of being self-undoing, the twelfth house can be a place of great creativity and talent. It is the place where you can tap into the collective unconscious, where your imagination is limitless.

In your trip around the zodiac, you've gone from the I of self-assertion in the first house to the final house, which symbolizes the dissolution that happens before rebirth. The twelfth house is where accumulated experiences are processed in the unconscious. Spiritually oriented astrologers look to this house for evidence of past lives and karma. Places where we go for solitude or to do spiritual or reparatory work belong here, such as retreats, religious institutions, or hospitals. Here is also where we withdraw from society voluntarily or involuntarily or are put in prison because of antisocial activity. Selfless giving through charitable acts is part of this house, as is dependence on charity.

In your daily life, the twelfth house reveals your deepest intimacies, your best-kept secrets, especially those you hide from yourself and keep repressed deep in the unconscious. It is where we surrender a sense of a separate self to a deep feeling of wholeness, such as selfless service in religion or any activity that involves merging with the greater whole. Many sports stars have important planets in the twelfth house that enable them to play in the zone, finding an inner, almost mystical, strength that transcends their limits.

Who's Home in Your Houses?

Houses are stronger or weaker depending on how many planets are inhabiting them. If there are many planets in a given house, it follows that the activities of that house will be especially important in your life. If the planet that rules the house is also located there, this too adds power to the house.

CHAPTER 6

Your Planetary Recipe

Besides the sun and moon, there are eight planets in your horoscope. Each is an ingredient representing a basic force in life that interacts with the other planets to make up a recipe that is uniquely yours. The location of a planet in your horoscope can determine how strongly that planet will affect you. A planet that's close to your rising sign will be emphasized in your chart. If two or more planets are grouped together in one sign, they usually operate together, playing off each other, rather than expressing their energy singularly. A lone planet that stands far away from the others is usually outstanding and often calls the shots in a horoscope.

The sign of each planet also has a powerful influence. In some signs, the planetary energies are very much at home and can easily express themselves. In others, the planet has to work harder and is slightly out of sorts. The sign that most corresponds to the energies of a planet is said to be ruled by that planet and obviously is the best place for it to be. The next best place is in a sign where it is exalted, or especially harmonious. On the other hand, there are places in the horoscope where a planet has to work harder to play its role, such as the sign opposite a planet's rulership, which embodies the opposite area of life, and the sign opposite its exaltation. However, a planet that must work harder can actually be more complete, because it must stretch itself to meet the challenges of living in a more difficult sign. Like world leaders who've had to struggle for greatness, this planet may actually develop great strength and character.

Here's a list of the best places for each planet to be. Note that, as new planets were discovered, they replaced

44

the traditional rulers of signs which best complemented their energies.

ARIES—Mars
TAURUS—Venus, in its most sensual form
GEMINI—Mercury, in its communicative role
CANCER—the moon
LEO—the sun
VIRGO—also Mercury, this time in its more critical capacity
LIBRA—also Venus, in its more aesthetic, judgmental form
SCORPIO—Pluto, replacing Mars, the sign's original ruler
SAGITTARIUS—Jupiter
CAPRICORN—Saturn
AQUARIUS—Uranus, replacing Saturn, its original ruler
PISCES—Neptune, replacing Jupiter, its original ruler

A person who has many planets in exalted signs is lucky indeed, for here is where the planet can accomplish the most and be its most influential and creative.

SUN—exalted in Aries, where its energy creates action
MOON—exalted in Taurus, where instincts and reactions operate on a highly creative level
MERCURY—exalted in Aquarius, where it can reach analytical heights
VENUS—exalted in Pisces, a sign whose sensitivity encourages love and creativity
MARS—exalted in Capricorn, a sign that puts energy to work productively
JUPITER—exalted in Cancer, where it encourages nurturing and growth
SATURN—at home in Libra, where it steadies the scales of justice and promotes balanced, responsible judgment
URANUS—powerful in Scorpio, where it promotes transformation
NEPTUNE—especially favored in Cancer, where it gains the security to transcend to a higher state
PLUTO—exalted in Pisces, where it dissolves the old cycle to make way for transition to the new

The Personal Planets: Mercury, Venus, and Mars

These planets work in your immediate personal life.

Mercury affects how you communicate and how your mental processes work. Are you a quick study who grasps information rapidly? Or do you learn more slowly and thoroughly? How is your concentration? Can you express yourself easily? Are you a good writer? All these questions can be answered by your Mercury placement.

Venus shows what you react to. What turns you on? What appeals to you aesthetically? Are you charming to others? Are you attractive to look at? Your taste, your refinement, your sense of balance and proportion are all Venus-ruled.

Mars is your outgoing energy, your drive and ambition. Do you reach out for new adventures? Are you assertive? Are you motivated? Self-confident? Hot-tempered? How you channel your energy and drive is revealed by your Mars placement.

Mercury Shows How Your Mind Works

In our cookbook analogy, Mercury would be the recipe instructions. Mercury shows how you think and speak, how logical you are. Since it stays close to the sun, read the description for Mercury in your sun sign, then the sign preceding and following it. Then decide which reflects the way you think.

Mercury in Aries

Your mind is very active and assertive. It approaches a plan aggressively. You never hesitate to say what you think, never shy away from a battle. In fact, you may relish a verbal confrontation. Tact is not your strong point, so you may have to learn not to trip over your tongue.

Mercury in Taurus

This is a cautious Mercury. Though you may be a slow learner, you have good concentration and mental stamina. You want to make your ideas really happen. You'll attack a problem methodically and consider every angle thoroughly, never jumping to conclusions. You'll stick with a subject until you master it.

Mercury in Gemini

You are a wonderful communicator with great facility for expressing yourself both verbally and in writing. You love gathering all kinds of information. You probably finish other people's sentences, and express yourself with eloquent hand gestures. You can talk to anybody anytime . . . and probably have phone and e-mail bills to prove it. You read anything from sci-fi to Shakespeare, and might need an extra room just for your book collection. Though you learn fast, you may lack focus and discipline. Watch a tendency to jump from subject to subject.

Mercury in Cancer

You rely on intuition more than logic. Your mental processes are usually colored by your emotions, so you may seem shy or hesitant to voice your opinions. However, this placement gives you the advantage of great imagination and empathy in the way you communicate with others.

Mercury in Leo

You are enthusiastic and very dramatic in the way you express yourself. You like to hold the attention of groups, and could be a great public speaker. Your mind thinks big, so you prefer to deal with the overall picture rather than with the details.

Mercury in Virgo

This is one of the best places for Mercury. It should give you critical ability, attention to details, and thorough analysis. Your mind focuses on the practical side of things. This type of thinking is very well suited to being a teacher or editor.

Mercury in Libra

You're either a born diplomat who smoothes over ruffled feathers or a talented debater. Many lawyers have this placement. However, since you're forever weighing the pros and cons of a situation, you may vacillate when making decisions.

Mercury in Scorpio

This is an investigative mind that stops at nothing to get the answers. You may have a sarcastic, stinging wit or a gift for the cutting remark. There's always a grain of truth to your verbal sallies, thanks to your penetrating insight.

Mercury in Sagittarius

You are a supersalesman with a tendency to expound. Though you are very broad-minded, you can be dogmatic when it comes to telling others what's good for them. You won't hesitate to tell the truth as you see it, so watch a tendency toward tactlessness. On the plus side, you have a great sense of humor. This position of Mercury is often considered by astrologers to be at a disadvantage because Sagittarius opposes Gemini, the sign Mercury rules, and squares off with Virgo, another Mercury-ruled sign. What often happens is that Mercury in Sagittarius oversteps its bounds and loses sight of the facts in a situation. Do a reality check before making promises you may not be able to deliver.

Mercury in Capricorn

This placement endows good mental discipline. You have a love of learning and a very orderly approach to your subjects. You will patiently plod through the facts and figures until you have mastered the tasks. You grasp structured situations easily, but may be short on creativity.

Mercury in Aquarius

An independent, original thinker, you'll have more cutting-edge ideas than the average person. You will be quick to check out any unusual opportunities. Your opinions are so well-researched and grounded that once your mind is made up, it is difficult to change.

Mercury in Pisces

You have the psychic and intuitive mind of a natural poet. Learn to make use of your creative imagination. You may think in terms of helping others, but check a tendency to be vague and forgetful of details.

Venus: The Sweet Things

In our recipe analogy, Venus would be dessert. Venus shows where you receive pleasure, what you love to do. Find your Venus placement from the charts at the end of this chapter by looking for the year of your birth in the left-hand column. Then follow the line of that year across the page until you reach the time period of your birthday. The sign heading that column will be your Venus. If you were born on a day when Venus was changing signs, check the signs preceding or following that day to determine if that sign feels more like your Venus nature.

Venus in Aries

You can't stand to be bored, confined, or ordered around. But a good challenge, maybe even a rousing row, turns you on. Confess—don't you pick a fight now and then just to get someone stirred up? You're attracted by the chase, not the catch, which could cause some problems in your love life if the object of your affection becomes too attainable. You like to wear red, and you can spot a trend before anyone else.

Venus in Taurus

All your senses work in high gear. You love to be surrounded by glorious tastes, smells, textures, sounds, and visuals. Austerity is not for you! Neither is being rushed. You like time to enjoy your pleasures. Soothing surroundings with plenty of creature comforts are your cup of tea. You like to feel secure in your nest, with no sudden jolts or surprises. You like familiar objects—in fact, you may hate to let anything or anyone go.

Venus in Gemini

You are a lively, sparkling personality who thrives in a situation that affords a constant variety and a frequent change of scenery. A varied social life is important to you, with plenty of stimulation and a chance to engage in some light flirtation. Commitment may be difficult, because playing the field is so much fun.

Venus in Cancer

An atmosphere where you feel protected, coddled, and mothered is best for you. You love to be surrounded by children in a cozy, homelike situation. You are attracted to those who are tender and nurturing, who make you feel secure and well provided for. You may be quite secretive about your emotional life, or attracted to clandestine relationships.

Venus in Leo

First-class attention in large doses turns you on, and so does the glitter of real gold and the flash of mirrors. You like to feel like a star at all times, surrounded by your admiring audience. The side effect is that you may be attracted to flatterers and tinsel, while the real gold requires some digging.

Venus in Virgo

Everything neatly in its place? On the surface, you are attracted to an atmosphere where everything is in perfect order, but underneath are some basic, earthy urges. You are attracted to those who appeal to your need to teach, to be of service, or to play out a Pygmalion fantasy. You are at your best when you are busy doing something useful.

Venus in Libra

Elegance and harmony are your key words. You can't abide an atmosphere of contention. Your taste tends toward the classic, with light harmonies of color—nothing clashing, trendy, or outrageous. You love doing things with a partner, and should be careful to pick one who is decisive but patient enough to let you weigh the pros and cons. And steer clear of argumentative types!

Venus in Scorpio

Hidden mysteries intrigue you. In fact, anything that is too open and aboveboard is a bit of a bore. You surely have a stack of whodunits by the bed, along with an erotic magazine or two. You like to solve puzzles, and may also be fascinated with the occult, crime, or scientific research. Intense, all-or-nothing situations add spice to your life, and you love to ferret out the secrets of others. But you could get burned by your flair for living dangerously. The color black, spicy food, dark wood furniture, and heady perfume all get you in the right mood.

Venus in Sagittarius

If you are not actually a world traveler, your surroundings are sure to reflect your love of faraway places. You like a casual outdoor atmosphere and a dog or two to pet. There should be plenty of room for athletic equipment and suitcases. You're attracted to kindred souls who love to travel and who share your freedom-loving philosophy of life. Athletics and spiritual or New Age pursuits could be other interests.

Venus in Capricorn

No fly-by-night relationships for you! You want substance in life, and you are attracted to whatever will help you get where you are going. Status objects turn you on. And so do those who have a serious, responsible, businesslike approach as well as those who remind you of a beloved parent. It is characteristic of this placement to be attracted to someone of a different generation. Antiques, traditional clothing, and dignified behavior are becoming to you.

Venus in Aquarius

This Venus wants to make friends, to be "cool." You like to be in a group, particularly one pushing a worthy cause. You feel quite at home surrounded by people, and could even court fame. Yet all the while you remain detached from any intense commitment. Original ideas and unpredictable people fascinate you. You don't like everything to be planned out in advance, preferring spontaneity and delightful surprises.

Venus in Pisces

This Venus loves to give of yourself, and you find plenty of takers. Stray animals and people appeal to your heart and your pocketbook, but be careful to look at their motives realistically once in a while. You are extremely vulnerable to sob stories of all kinds. Fantasy, the arts (especially film, dance, and theater), and psychic or spiritual activities also speak to you.

Mars: Hot and Spicy

In your cosmic recipe, Mars provides the heat and spice. It is the mover and shaker in your life. It shows how you pursue your goals, whether you have energy to burn or proceed at a slow, steady pace. It will also show how you get angry. Do you explode or do a slow burn or hold everything inside, then get revenge later?

To find your Mars, turn to the charts on pages 86–94. Then find your birth year in the left-hand column and trace the line across horizontally until you come to the column headed by the month of your birth. There you will find an abbreviation of your Mars sign. If the description of your Mars sign doesn't ring true, read the description of the sign preceding and following it. You may have been born on a day when Mars was changing signs, in which case your Mars might be in the adjacent sign.

Mars in Aries

In the sign it rules, Mars shows its brilliant fiery nature. You have an explosive temper and can be quite impatient. On the other hand, you have tremendous courage, energy, and drive. You'll let nothing stand in your way as you race to be first! Obstacles are met head-on and broken through by force. However, those that require patience and persistence can have you exploding in rage. You're a great starter, but not necessarily around for the finish.

Mars in Taurus

Slow, steady, concentrated energy gives you staying power to last until the finish line. You have great stamina, and you never give up. Your tactic is to wear away obstacles with your persistence. Often you come out a winner because you've had the patience to hang in there. When angered, you do a slow burn.

Mars in Gemini

You can't sit still for long. This Mars craves variety. You often have two or more things going on at once—it's all an amusing game to you. Your life can get very complicated, but that only adds spice and stimulation. What drives you into a nervous, hyper state? Boredom, sameness, routine, and confinement. You can do wonderful things with your hands, and you have a way with words.

Mars in Cancer

You rarely attack head-on. Instead, you'll keep things to yourself, make plans in secret, and always cover your actions. This might be interpreted by some as manipulative, but you are only being self-protective. You get furious when anyone knows too much about you. But you do like to know all about others. Your mothering and feeding instincts can be put to good use if you work in the food, hotel, or child-care business. You may have to overcome your fragile sense of security, which prompts you not to take risks and to get physically upset when criticized. Don't take things so personally!

Mars in Leo

You have a very dominant personality that takes center stage. Modesty is not one of your traits, nor is taking a backseat. You prefer giving the orders, and have been known to make a dramatic scene if they are not obeyed. Properly used, this Mars confers leadership ability, endurance, and courage.

Mars in Virgo

You are the faultfinder of the zodiac. You notice every detail. Mistakes of any kind make you very nervous. You may worry, even if everything is going smoothly. You may not express your anger directly, but you sure can nag. You have definite likes and dislikes, and you are sure you can do the job better than anyone else. You are certainly more industrious and detail-oriented than other signs. Your Mars energy is often most positively expressed in some kind of teaching role.

Mars in Libra

This Mars will have a passion for beauty, justice, and art. Generally, you will avoid confrontations at all costs. You prefer to spend your energy finding diplomatic solutions or weighing pros and cons. Your other techniques are passive aggression or exercising your well-known charm to get people to do what you want.

Mars in Scorpio

This is a powerful placement, so intense that it demands careful channeling into worthwhile activities. Otherwise, you could become obsessed with your sexuality or might use your need for power and control to manipulate others. You are strong-willed, shrewd, and very private about your affairs, and you'll usually have a secret agenda behind your actions. Your great stamina, focus, and discipline would be excellent assets for careers in the military or medical fields, especially research or surgery. When angry, you don't get mad—you get even!

Mars in Sagittarius

This expansive Mars often propels people into sales, travel, athletics, or philosophy. Your energies function well when you are on the move. You have a hot temper, and are inclined to say what you think before you consider the consequences. You shoot for high goals—and talk endlessly about them—but you may be weak on groundwork. This Mars needs a solid foundation. Watch a tendency to take unnecessary risks.

Mars in Capricorn

This is an ambitious Mars with an excellent sense of timing. You have an eye for those who can be of use to you, and you may dismiss people ruthlessly when you're angry, but you drive yourself hard and deliver full value. This is a good placement for an executive. You'll aim for status and a high material position in life, and you'll keep climbing despite the odds. A great Mars to have!

Mars in Aquarius

This is the most rebellious Mars. You seem to have a drive to assert yourself against the status quo. You may enjoy provoking people, shocking them out of traditional views. Or this placement could express itself in an offbeat sex life. Somehow you often find yourself in unconventional situations. You enjoy being a leader of an active group, which pursues forward-looking studies, politics, or goals.

Mars in Pisces

This Mars is a good actor who knows just how to appeal to the sympathies of others. You create and project wonderful fantasies, or you use your sensitive antennae to crusade for those less fortunate. You get what you want through creating a veil of illusion and glamour. This is a good Mars for someone in the creative and imaginative fields—a dancer, performer, photographer, actor. Many famous film stars have this placement. Watch a tendency to manipulate by making others feel sorry for you.

Jupiter Piles the Plate High

In our recipe analogy, Jupiter would be the high-carb dish that can add on pounds. This big, bright, swirling mass of gases is associated with abundance, prosperity, and the kind of windfall you get without too much hard work. You're optimistic under Jupiter's influence, when anything seems possible. You'll travel, expand your mind with higher education, and publish to share your knowledge widely. On the other hand, Jupiter's influence is neither discriminating nor disciplined. It represents the principle of growth without judgment, and therefore could result in extravagance, weight gain, laziness, and carelessness, if not kept in check.

Be sure to look up your Jupiter in the tables in this book. When the current position of Jupiter is favorable, you may get that lucky break. This is a great time to try new things, take risks, travel, or get more education. Opportunities seem to open up easily, so take advantage of them.

Once a year, Jupiter changes signs. That means you are due for an expansive time every twelve years, when Jupiter travels through your sun sign. You'll also have up periods every four years, when Jupiter is in the same element as your sun sign.

Jupiter in Aries

You are the soul of enthusiasm and optimism. Your luckiest times are when you are getting started on an exciting project or selling an idea that you really believe in. You may have to watch a tendency to be arrogant with those who do not share your enthusiasm. You follow your impulses, often ignoring budget or other commonsense limitations. To produce real, solid benefits, you'll need patience and follow-through wherever this Jupiter falls in your horoscope.

Jupiter in Taurus

You'll spend on beautiful material things, especially those that come from nature—items made of rare woods, natural fabrics, or precious gems, for instance. You can't have too much comfort or too many sensual pleasures. Watch a tendency to overindulge in good food, or to overpamper yourself with nothing but the best. Spartan living is not for you! You may be especially lucky in matters of real estate.

Jupiter in Gemini

You are the great talker of the zodiac, and you may be a great writer, too. But restlessness could be your weak point. You jump around, talk too much, and could be a jack-of-all-trades. Keeping a secret is especially difficult, so you'll have to watch a tendency to spill the beans. Since you love to be at the center of a beehive of activity, you'll have a vibrant social life. Your best opportunities will come through your talent for language—speaking, writing, communicating, and selling.

Jupiter in Cancer

You are luckiest in situations where you can find emotional closeness or deal with basic security needs such as food, nurturing, or shelter. You may be a great collector. Or you may simply love to accumulate things—you are the one who stashes things away for a rainy day. You probably have a very good memory and love children. In fact, you may have many children to care for. The food, hotel, child-care, and shipping businesses hold good opportunities for you.

Jupiter in Leo

You are a natural showman who loves to live in a larger-than-life way. Yours is a personality full of color that always finds its way into the limelight. You can't have too much attention or applause. Showbiz is a natural place for you, and so is any area where you can play to a crowd. Exercising your flair for drama, your natural playfulness, and your romantic nature brings you good fortune. But watch a tendency to be overly extravagant or to monopolize center stage.

Jupiter in Virgo

You actually love those minute details others find boring. To you, they make all the difference between the perfect and the ordinary. You are the fine craftsman who spots every flaw. You expand your awareness by finding the most efficient methods and by being of service to others. Many of you will be drawn to medical or teaching fields. You'll also have luck in publishing, crafts, nutrition, and service professions. Watch out for a tendency to overwork.

Jupiter in Libra

This is an other-directed Jupiter that develops best with a partner. The stimulation of others helps you grow. You are also most comfortable in harmonious, beautiful situations and you work well with artistic people. You have a great sense of fair play and an ability to evaluate the pros and cons of a situation. You usually prefer to play the role of diplomat rather than adversary.

Jupiter in Scorpio

You love the feeling of power and control, of taking things to their limit. You can't resist a mystery. Your shrewd, penetrating mind sees right through to the heart of most situations and people. You have luck in work that provides for solutions to matters of life and death. You may be drawn to undercover work, behind-the-scenes intrigue, psychotherapy, the occult, and sex-related ventures. Your challenge will be to develop a sense of moderation and tolerance for other beliefs. This Jupiter can be fanatical. You may have luck in handling other people's money— insurance, taxes, and inheritance can bring you a windfall.

Jupiter in Sagittarius

Independent, outgoing, and idealistic, you'll shoot for the stars. This Jupiter compels you to travel far and wide, both physically and mentally, via higher education. You may have luck while traveling in an exotic place. You also have luck with outdoor ventures, exercise, and animals, particularly horses. Since you tend to be very open about your opinions, watch a tendency to be tactless and to exaggerate. Instead, use your wonderful sense of humor to make your point.

Jupiter in Capricorn

Jupiter is much more restrained in Capricorn, the sign of rules and authority. Here, Jupiter can make you overwork and heighten any ambition or sense of duty you may have.

You'll expand in areas that advance your position, putting you farther up the social or corporate ladder. You are lucky working within the establishment in a very structured situation where you can show off your ability to organize and reap rewards for your hard work.

Jupiter in Aquarius

This is another freedom-loving Jupiter, with great tolerance and originality. You are at your best when you are working for a humanitarian cause and in the company of many supporters. This is a good Jupiter for a political career. You'll relate to all kinds of people on all social levels. You have an abundance of original ideas, but you are best off away from routine and any situation that imposes rigid rules. You need mental stimulation!

Jupiter in Pisces

You are a giver whose feelings and pocketbook are easily touched by others, so choose your companions with care. You could be the original sucker for a hard-luck story. Better find a worthy hospital or a charity that will appreciate your selfless support. You have a great creative imagination. You may attract good fortune in fields related to oil, perfume, pharmaceuticals, petroleum, dance, footwear, and alcohol. But beware of overindulgence in alcohol—focus on a creative outlet instead.

Saturn Is a Disciplined Diet

Jupiter speeds you up with *lucky breaks* and quick energy. Then along comes Saturn to slow you down with the *disciplinary brakes* and slow-burning energy. It is the part of your planetary diet that helps you achieve lasting goals. Saturn has unfairly been called a malefic planet, one of the bad guys of the zodiac. On the contrary, Saturn is one of our best friends, the kind who tells you what you need to hear even if it's not good news. Under a Saturn transit, we grow up, take responsibility for our lives, and emerge from whatever test this planet has in store as far wiser, more capable and mature human beings. It is when we are under pressure that we grow stronger.

Look up your natal Saturn in the tables in this book for clues on where you need work.

Saturn in Aries

Saturn here puts the brakes on Aries' natural drive and enthusiasm. There is often an angry side to this placement. You don't let anyone push you around, and you know what's best for yourself. Following orders is not your strong point, and neither is diplomacy. You tend to be quick to go on the offensive in relationships, attacking first, before anyone attacks you. Because no one quite lives up to your standards, you often wind up doing everything yourself. You'll have to learn to cooperate and tone down self-centeredness. Both Pat Buchanan and Saddam Hussein have this Saturn.

Saturn in Taurus

A big issue is getting control of the cash flow. There will be lean periods that can be frightening, but you have the patience and endurance to stick them out and the methodical drive to prosper in the end. Learn to take a philosophical attitude, like Ben Franklin, who also had this placement and who said, "A penny saved is a penny earned."

Saturn in Gemini

You are a serious student of life, but you may have difficulty communicating or sharing your knowledge. You may be shy, speak slowly, or have fears about communicating, like Eleanor Roosevelt. You dwell in the realms of science, theory, or abstract analysis—even when you are dealing with the emotions, like Sigmund Freud, who also had this placement.

Saturn in Cancer

Your tests come with establishing a secure emotional base. In doing so, you may have to deal with some very basic fears centering on your early home environment. Most of your Saturn tests will have emotional roots in those early childhood experiences. You may have difficulty remaining objective in terms of what you try to achieve. So it will be especially important for you to deal with negative feelings such as guilt, paranoia, jealousy, resentment, and suspicion. Galileo and Michelangelo also navigated these murky waters.

Saturn in Leo

This is an authoritarian Saturn—a strict, demanding parent who may deny the pleasure principle in your zeal to see that rules are followed. Though you may feel guilty about taking the spotlight, you are very ambitious and loyal. You have to watch a tendency toward rigidity, also toward overwork and holding back affection. Joseph Kennedy and Billy Graham share this placement.

Saturn in Virgo

This is a cautious, exacting Saturn. You are intensely hard on yourself. Most of all, you give yourself the roughest time with your constant worries about every little detail, often making yourself sick. You may have difficulties setting priorities and getting the job done. Your tests will come in learning tolerance and understanding of others. Charles de Gaulle, Mae West, and Nathaniel Hawthorne had this meticulous Saturn.

Saturn in Libra

Saturn is exalted here, which makes this planet an ally. You may choose very serious, older partners in life, perhaps stemming from a fear of dependency. You need to learn to stand solidly on your own before you commit to another. You are extremely cautious as you deliberate every involvement—with good reason. It is best that you find an occupation that makes good use of your sense of duty and honor. Steer clear of fly-by-night situations. Both Khruschev and Mao Tse-tung had this placement.

Saturn in Scorpio

You have great staying power. This Saturn tests you in situations involving the control of others. You may feel drawn to some kind of intrigue or undercover work, like J. Edgar Hoover. Or there may be an air of mystery surrounding your life and death, like Marilyn Monroe and Robert Kennedy, who both had this placement. There are lessons to be learned from your sexual involvements. Often sex is used for manipulation or is somehow out of the ordinary. The Roman emperor Caligula and the transsexual Christine Jorgensen are extreme cases.

Saturn in Sagittarius

Your challenges and lessons will come from tests of your spiritual and philosophical values, as happened to Martin Luther King and Gandhi. You are high-minded and sincere with this reflective, moral placement. Uncompromising in your ethical standards, you could become a benevolent despot.

Saturn in Capricorn

With the help of Saturn at maximum strength, your judgment will improve with age. And like Spencer Tracy's screen image, you'll be the gray-haired hero with a strong sense of responsibility. You advance in life slowly but steadily, always with a strong hand at the helm and an eye for the advantageous situation. Like Pat Robertson, you're likely to stand for conservative values. Negatively, you may be a loner, prone to periods of melancholy.

Saturn in Aquarius

Your tests come from relationships with groups. Do you care too much about what others think? Do you feel like an outsider, like Greta Garbo? You may fear being different from others and therefore slight your own unique, forward-looking gifts. Or like Lord Byron and Howard Hughes, you may take the opposite tack and rebel in the extreme. You can apply discipline to accomplish great humanitarian goals, as Albert Schweitzer did.

Saturn in Pisces

Your fear of the unknown and the irrational may lead you to the safety and protection of an institution. You may go on the run like Jesse James, who had this placement, to avoid looking too deeply inside. Or you might go in the opposite, more positive direction and develop a disciplined psychoanalytic approach, which puts you more in control of your feelings. Some of you will take refuge in work with hospitals, charities, or religious institutions. Queen Victoria, who had this placement, symbolized an era when institutions of all kinds were sustained. Discipline applied to artistic work, especially poetry and dance, or to spiritual work, such as yoga or meditation, might be helpful.

How Uranus, Neptune, and Pluto Influence a Whole Generation

These three planets remain in signs such a long time that a whole generation bears the imprint of the sign. Mass movements, great sweeping changes, fads that characterize a generation, even the issues of the conflicts and wars of the time are influenced by these "outer three" planets. When one of those distant planets changes signs, there is a definite shift in the atmosphere, the feeling of the end of an era.

Since these planets are so far away from the sun—too distant to be seen by the naked eye—they pick up signals from the universe at large. These planetary receivers literally link the sun with distant energies, and then perform a similar function in your horoscope by linking your central character with intuitive, spiritual, transformative forces from the cosmos. Each planet has a special domain, and will reflect this in the area of your chart where it falls.

Uranus Is the Surprise Ingredient

In your cosmic recipe, Uranus is the unexpected ingredient that sets you and your generation apart. There is nothing ordinary about this quirky green planet that seems to be traveling on its side, surrounded by a swarm of moons. Is it any wonder that astrologers assigned it to Aquarius, the most eccentric and gregarious sign? Uranus seems to wend its way around the sun, marching to its own tune.

Significantly, Uranus follows Saturn, the planet of limitations and structures. Often we get caught up in the structures we have created to give ourselves a sense of security. However, if we lose contact with our spiritual roots, then Uranus is likely to jolt us out of our comfortable rut and wake us up.

Uranus energy is electrical, happening in sudden flashes. It is not influenced by karma or past events, nor does it regard tradition, sex, or sentiment. The Uranus key words are surprise and awakening. Suddenly, there's that flash of inspiration, that bright idea, that totally new approach to revolutionize whatever scheme you were undertaking. A Uranus event takes you by surprise; it happens from out of the blue, for better or for worse. The Uranus place in your life is where you awaken and become your own person, leaving the structures of Saturn behind. And it is probably the most unconventional place in your chart.

Look up the sign of Uranus at the time of your birth and see where you follow your own tune.

Uranus in Aries

Birth Dates:
    March 31, 1927–November 4, 1927

January 13, 1928–June 6, 1934
October 10, 1934–March 28, 1935
Your generation is original, creative, pioneering. It developed the computer, the airplane, and the cyclotron. You let nothing hold you back from exploring the unknown, and you have a powerful mixture of fire and electricity behind you. Women of your generation were among the first to be liberated. You were the unforgettable style setters. You have a surprise in store for everyone. Like Yoko Ono, Grace Kelly, and Jacqueline Onassis, your life may be jolted by sudden and violent changes.

Uranus in Taurus

Birth Dates:
June 6, 1934–October 10, 1934
March 28, 1935–August 7, 1941
October 5, 1941–May 15, 1942
The great territorial shake-ups of World War II began during your generation. You are independent, probably self-employed or would like to be. You have original ideas about making money, and you brace yourself for sudden changes of fortune. This Uranus can cause shake-ups, particularly in finances, but it can also make you a born entrepreneur.

Uranus in Gemini

Birth Dates:
August 7, 1941–October 5, 1941
May 15, 1942–August 30, 1948
November 12, 1948–June 10, 1949
You were the first children to be influenced by television. Now, in your adult years, your generation stocks up on answering machines, cell phones, computers, and fax machines—any new way you can communicate. You have an inquiring mind, but your interests may be rather short-lived. This Uranus can be easily fragmented if there is no structure and focus.

Uranus in Cancer

Birth Dates:
  August 30, 1948–November 12, 1948
  June 10, 1949–August 24, 1955
  January 28, 1956–June 10, 1956

This generation came at a time when divorce was becoming commonplace, so your home image is unconventional. You may have an unusual relationship with your parents; you may have come from a broken home or an unconventional one. You'll have unorthodox ideas about parenting, intimacy, food, and shelter. You may also be interested in dreams, psychic phenomena, and memory work.

Uranus in Leo

Birth Dates:
  August 24, 1955–January 28, 1956
  June 10, 1956–November 1, 1961
  January 10, 1962–August 10, 1962

This generation understood how to use electronic media. Many of your group are now leaders in the high-tech industries, and you also understand how to use the new media to promote yourself. Like Isadora Duncan, you may have a very eccentric kind of charisma and a life that is sparked by unusual love affairs. Your children, too, may have traits that are out of the ordinary. Where this planet falls in your chart, you'll have a love of freedom, be a bit of an egomaniac, and show the full force of your personality in a unique way, like tennis great Martina Navratilova.

Uranus in Virgo

Birth Dates:
  November 1, 1961–January 10, 1962
  August 10, 1962–September 28, 1968
  May 20, 1969–June 24, 1969

You'll have highly individual work methods. Many of you will be finding newer, more practical ways to use computers. Like Einstein, who had this placement, you'll break the rules brilliantly. Your generation came at a time of student rebellions, the civil rights movement, and the general acceptance of health foods. Chances are, you're concerned about pollution and cleaning up the environment. You may also be involved with nontraditional healing methods.

Uranus in Libra

Birth Dates:
  September 28, 1968–May 20, 1969
  June 24, 1969–November 21, 1974
  May 1, 1975–September 8, 1975
Your generation will be always changing partners. Born during the era of women's liberation, you may have come from a broken home and have no clear image of what a marriage entails. There will be many sudden splits and experiments before you settle down. Your generation will be much involved in legal and political reforms and in changing artistic and fashion looks.

Uranus in Scorpio

Birth Dates:
  November 21, 1974–May 1, 1975
  September 8, 1975–February 17, 1981
  March 20, 1981–November 16, 1981
Interest in transformation, meditation, and life after death signaled the beginning of New Age consciousness. Your generation recognizes no boundaries, no limits, and no external controls. You'll have new attitudes toward death and dying, psychic phenomena, and the occult. Like Mae West and Casanova, you'll shock 'em sexually, too.

Uranus in Sagittarius

Birth Dates:
  February 17, 1981–March 20, 1981
  November 16, 1981–February 15, 1988
  May 27, 1988–December 2, 1988
Could this generation be the first to travel in outer space? An earlier generation with this placement included Charles Lindbergh and a time when the first zeppelins and

the Wright Brothers were conquering the skies. Uranus here forecasts great discoveries, mind expansion, and long-distance travel. Like Galileo and Martin Luther, those born in these years will generate new theories about the cosmos and mankind's relation to it.

Uranus in Capricorn

Birth Dates:
    December 20, 1904–January 30, 1912
    September 4, 1912–November 12, 1912
    February 15, 1988–May 27, 1988
    December 2, 1988–April 1, 1995
    June 9, 1995–January 12, 1996
This generation, now growing up, will challenge traditions with the help of electronic gadgets. In these years, we got organized with the help of technology put to practical use. The Internet was born following the great economic boom of the 1990s. Great leaders who were movers and shakers of history, like Julius Caesar and Henry VIII, were born under this placement.

Uranus in Aquarius

Birth Dates:
    January 30, 1912–September 4, 1912
    November 12, 1912–April 1, 1919
    August 16, 1919–January 22, 1920
    April 1, 1995–June 9, 1995
    January 12, 1996–March 10, 2003
    September 15, 2003–December 30, 2003
Uranus in Aquarius is the strongest placement for this planet. Recently we've had the opportunity to witness the full force of its power of innovation, as well as its sudden wake-up calls and insistence on humanitarian values. This was a time of high-tech development, when home computers became as ubiquitous as television. It was a time of globalization, of surprise attacks (9/11), and underdeveloped countries demanding attention. The last generation with this placement produced great innovative minds such as Leonard Bernstein and Orson Welles. The next will be-

come another radical breakthrough generation, much concerned with global issues that involve all humanity.

Uranus in Pisces

Birth Dates:
  April 1, 1919–August 16, 1919
  January 22, 1920–March 31, 1927
  November 4, 1927–January 12, 1928
  March 10, 2003–September 15, 2003
  December 20, 2003–May 28, 2010

Uranus is now in Pisces, ushering in a new generation. In the past century, Uranus in Pisces focused attention on the rise of electronic entertainment—radio and the cinema—and the secretiveness of Prohibition. This produced a generation of idealists exemplified by Judy Garland's theme "Somewhere over the Rainbow." Uranus in Pisces also hints at stealth activities, at hospital and prison reform, at high-tech drugs and medical experiments, at shake-ups and reforms in the Pisces-ruled petroleum industry. Issues regarding the water and oil supply, water-related storm damage, sudden hurricanes, and floods demand our attention.

Neptune Is the Magic Solvent

Neptune is the liquid in your horoscope recipe that dissolves other ingredients and creates a magical, inspired result. It is often maligned as the planet of illusions that dissolves reality, enabling you to escape the material world. Under Neptune's influence, you see what you want to see. But Neptune also encourages you to create. It embodies glamour, subtlety, mystery, and mysticism, and it governs anything that takes you beyond the mundane world, including out-of-body experiences.

Neptune acts to transcend your ordinary perceptions to take you to another level, where you experience either confusion or ecstasy. Its force can pull you off course only if you allow this to happen. Those who use Neptune wisely can translate their daydreams into poetry, theater, design, or inspired moves in the business world, avoiding the tricky "con artist" side of this planet.

Find your Neptune listed below.

Neptune in Cancer

Birth Dates:

July 19, 1901–December 25, 1901
May 21, 1902–September 23, 1914
December 14, 1914–July 19, 1915
March 19, 1916–May 2, 1916

Dreams of the homeland, idealistic patriotism, and glamorization of the nurturing assets of women characterized this time. You who were born here have unusual psychic ability and deep insights into basic needs of others.

Neptune in Leo

Birth Dates:

September 23, 1914–December 14, 1914
July 19, 1915–March 19, 1916
May 2, 1916–September 21, 1928
February 19, 1929–July 24, 1929

Neptune in Leo brought us the glamour and high living of the 1920s and the big spenders of that time. The Neptune temptations of gambling, seduction, theater, and lavish entertaining distracted from the realities of the age. Those born in that generation also made great advances in the arts.

Neptune in Virgo

Birth Dates:

September 21, 1928–February 19, 1929
July 24, 1929–October 3, 1942
April 17, 1943–August 2, 1943

Neptune in Virgo encompassed the 1930s, the Great Depression, and the beginning of World War II, when a new order was born. There was a time of facing "what doesn't work." Many were unemployed and found solace at the movies, watching the great Virgo star Greta Garbo or the escapist dance films of Busby Berkeley. New public services were born. Those with Neptune in Virgo later spread the gospel of health and fitness. This generation's devotion to spending hours at the office inspired the term *workaholic*.

Neptune in Libra

Birth Dates:
    October 3, 1942–April 17, 1943
    August 2, 1943–December 24, 1955
    March 12, 1956–October 19, 1956
    June 15, 1957–August 6, 1957
This was the time of World War II and the postwar period, when the world regained balance and returned to relative stability. Neptune in Libra was the romantic generation who would later be concerned with relating. As this generation matured, there was a new trend toward marriage and commitment. Racial and sexual equality became important issues, as they redesigned traditional roles to suit modern times.

Neptune in Scorpio

Birth Dates:
    December 24, 1955–March 12, 1956
    October 19, 1956–June 15, 1957
    August 6, 1957–January 4, 1970
    May 3, 1970–November 6, 1970
Neptune in Scorpio brought in a generation that would become interested in transformative power. Born in an era that glamorized sex, drugs, rock and roll, and Eastern religion, they matured in a more sobering time of AIDS, cocaine abuse, and New Age spirituality. As they evolve, they will become active in healing the planet from the results of the abuse of power.

Neptune in Sagittarius

Birth Dates:
    January 4, 1970–May 3, 1970
    November 6, 1970–January 19, 1984

June 23, 1984–November 21, 1984

Neptune in Sagittarius was the time when space and astronaut travel became a reality. The Neptune influence glamorized new approaches to mysticism, religion, and mind expansion. This generation will take a new approach to spiritual life, with emphasis on visions, mysticism, and clairvoyance.

Neptune in Capricorn

Birth Dates:
  January 19, 1984–June 23, 1984
  November 21, 1984–January 29, 1998

Neptune in Capricorn brought a time when delusions about material power were glamorized in the mid–1980s and 1990s. There was a boom in the stock market, and the Internet era spawned young tycoons who later lost it all. It was also a time when the psychic and occult worlds spawned a new category of business enterprise, and sold services on television.

Neptune in Aquarius

Birth Dates:
  January 29, 1998–April 4, 2011

This should continue to be a time of breakthroughs. Here the creative influence of Neptune reaches a universal audience. This is a time of dissolving barriers, of globalization—when we truly become one world. During this transit of high-tech Aquarius, new kinds of entertainment media reach across cultural differences. However, the transit of Neptune has also raised boundary issues between cultures, especially in Middle Eastern countries with Neptune-ruled oil fields. As Neptune raises issues of social and political structures not being as solid as they seem, this could continue to produce rebellion and chaos in the environment. However, by using imagination (Neptune) in partnership with a global view (Aquarius) we could reach creative solutions.

Those born with this placement should be true citizens of the world with a remarkable creative ability to transcend social and cultural barriers.

Pluto Can Transform You

Add a small touch of Pluto to your recipe and it will change the dish completely! Though it is a tiny planet, its influence is great. When Pluto zaps a strategic point in your horoscope, your life changes dramatically.

This little planet is the power behind the scenes; it affects you at deep levels of consciousness, causing events to come to the surface that will transform you and your generation. Nothing escapes, or is sacred, with this probing planet. Its purpose is to wipe out the past so something new can happen.

The Pluto place in your horoscope is where you have invisible power (Mars governs the visible power), where you can transform, heal, and affect the unconscious needs of the masses. Pluto tells lots about how your generation projects power, what makes it seem cool to others. And when Pluto changes signs, there is a whole new concept of what's cool. Pluto's strange elliptical orbit occasionally runs inside the orbit of neighboring Neptune. Because of its eccentric path, the length of time Pluto stays in any given sign can vary from thirteen to thirty-two years. It covered only seven signs in the last century.

Pluto in Gemini

Birth Dates:
   Late 1800s–May 26, 1914
   This was a time of mass suggestion and breakthroughs in communications, a time when many brilliant writers such as Ernest Hemingway and F. Scott Fitzgerald were born. Henry Miller, D. H. Lawrence, and James Joyce scandalized society by using explicit sexual images and language in their literature. "Muckraking" journalists exposed corruption. Pluto-ruled Scorpio President Theodore Roosevelt said, "Speak softly, but carry a big stick." This generation had an intense need to communicate and made major breakthroughs in knowledge. A compulsive restlessness and a thirst for a variety of experiences characterized many of this generation.

Pluto in Cancer

Birth Dates:
    May 26, 1914–June 14, 1939
    Dictators and mass media arose to wield emotional power over the masses. Women's rights was a popular issue. Deep sentimental feelings, acquisitiveness, and possessiveness characterized these times and people. Most of the great stars of the Hollywood era that embodied the American image were born during this period: Grace Kelly, Esther Williams, Frank Sinatra, Lana Turner, to name a few.

Pluto in Leo

Birth Dates:
    June 14, 1939–August, 19, 1957
    The performing arts played on the emotions of the masses. Mick Jagger, John Lennon, and rock and roll were born at this time. So were "baby boomers" like Bill and Hillary Clinton. Those born here tend to be self-centered, powerful, and boisterous. This generation does its own thing, for better or for worse.

Pluto in Virgo

Birth Dates:
    August 19, 1957–October 5, 1971
    April 17, 1972–July 30, 1972
    This is the "yuppie" generation that sparked a mass movement toward fitness, health, and career. It is a much more sober, serious, driven generation than the fun-loving Pluto in Leo. During this time, machines were invented to process detail work efficiently. Inventions took a practical turn with answering machines, fax machines, car phones, and home office equipment—all making the workplace far more efficient.

Pluto in Libra

Birth Dates:
    October 5, 1971–April 17, 1972

July 30, 1972–November 5, 1983
May 18, 1984–August 27, 1984

A mellower generation, people born at this time are concerned with partnerships, working together, and finding diplomatic solutions to problems. Marriage is important to this generation, and they will define it by combining traditional values with equal partnership. This was a time of women's liberation, gay rights, ERA, and legal battles over abortion, all of which transformed our ideas about relationships.

Pluto in Scorpio

Birth Dates:

November 5, 1983–May 18, 1984
August 27, 1984–January 17, 1995

Pluto was in the sign it rules for a comparatively short period of time. However, this was a time of record achievements, destructive sexually transmitted diseases, nuclear power controversies, and explosive political issues. Pluto destroys in order to create new understanding—the phoenix rising from the ashes—which should be some consolation for those of you who felt Pluto's force before 1995. Sexual shockers were par for the course during these intense years when black clothing, transvestites, body piercing, tattoos, and sexually explicit advertising pushed the boundaries of good taste.

Pluto in Sagittarius

Birth Dates:

January 17, 1995–April 20, 1995
November 10, 1995–January 26, 2008

During our current Pluto transit, we are being pushed to expand our horizons, to find deeper spiritual meaning in life. Pluto's opposition with Saturn in 2001 brought an enormous conflict between traditional societies and the forces of change. It signals a time when religious convictions will exert more power in our political life as well.

Since Sagittarius is the sign that rules travel, there's a good possibility that Pluto, the planet of extremes, will make space travel a reality for some of us. Already, we are seeing wealthy adventurers paying for the privilege of travel on space shuttles. Discovery of life-forms on other planets could transform our ideas about where we came from.

New dimensions in electronic publishing, concern with animal rights and the environment, and an increasing emphasis on extreme forms of religion are other signs of these times. Look for charismatic religious leaders to arise now. We'll also be developing far-reaching philosophies designed to elevate our lives with a new sense of purpose.

VENUS SIGNS 1901–2007

	Aries	Taurus	Gemini	Cancer	Leo	Virgo
1901	3/29–4/22	4/22–5/17	5/17–6/10	6/10–7/5	7/5–7/29	7/29–8/23
1902	5/7–6/3	6/3–6/30	6/30–7/25	7/25–8/19	8/19–9/13	9/13–10/7
1903	2/28–3/24	3/24–4/18	4/18–5/13	5/13–6/9	6/9–7/7	7/7–8/17
						9/6–11/8
1904	3/13–5/7	5/7–6/1	6/1–6/25	6/25–7/19	7/19–8/13	8/13–9/6
1905	2/3–3/6	3/6–4/9	7/8–8/6	8/6–9/1	9/1–9/27	9/27–10/21
	4/9–5/28	5/28–7/8				
1906	3/1–4/7	4/7–5/2	5/2–5/26	5/26–6/20	6/20–7/16	7/16–8/11
1907	4/27–5/22	5/22–6/16	6/16–7/11	7/11–8/4	8/4–8/29	8/29–9/22
1908	2/14–3/10	3/10–4/5	4/5–5/5	5/5–9/8	9/8–10/8	10/8–11/3
1909	3/29–4/22	4/22–5/16	5/16–6/10	6/10–7/4	7/4–7/29	7/29–8/23
1910	5/7–6/3	6/4–6/29	6/30–7/24	7/25–8/18	8/19–9/12	9/13–10/6
1911	2/28–3/23	3/24–4/17	4/18–5/12	5/13–6/8	6/9–7/7	7/8–11/18
1912	4/13–5/6	5/7–5/31	6/1–6/24	6/24–7/18	7/19–8/12	8/13–9/5
1913	2/3–3/6	3/7–5/1	7/8–8/5	8/6–8/31	9/1–9/26	9/27–10/20
	5/2–5/30	5/31–7/7				
1914	3/14–4/6	4/7–5/1	5/2–5/25	5/26–6/19	6/20–7/15	7/16–8/10
1915	4/27–5/21	5/22–6/15	6/16–7/10	7/11–8/3	8/4–8/28	8/29–9/21
1916	2/14–3/9	3/10–4/5	4/6–5/5	5/6–9/8	9/9–10/7	10/8–11/2
1917	3/29–4/21	4/22–5/15	5/16–6/9	6/10–7/3	7/4–7/28	7/29–8/21
1918	5/7–6/2	6/3–6/28	6/29–7/24	7/25–8/18	8/19–9/11	9/12–10/5
1919	2/27–3/22	3/23–4/16	4/17–5/12	5/13–6/7	6/8–7/7	7/8–11/8
1920	4/12–5/6	5/7–5/30	5/31–6/23	6/24–7/18	7/19–8/11	8/12–9/4
1921	2/3–3/6	3/7–4/25	7/8–8/5	8/6–8/31	9/1–9/25	9/26–10/20
	4/26–6/1	6/2–7/7				
1922	3/13–4/6	4/7–4/30	5/1–5/25	5/26–6/19	6/20–7/14	7/15–8/9
1923	4/27–5/21	5/22–6/14	6/15–7/9	7/10–8/3	8/4–8/27	8/28–9/20
1924	2/13–3/8	3/9–4/4	4/5–5/5	5/6–9/8	9/9–10/7	10/8–11/12
1925	3/28–4/20	4/21–5/15	5/16–6/8	6/9–7/3	7/4–7/27	7/28–8/21

Libra	Scorpio	Sagittarius	Capricorn	Aquarius	Pisces
8/23–9/17	9/17–10/12	10/12–1/16	1/16–2/9	2/9–3/5	3/5–3/29
			11/7–12/5	12/5–1/11	
10/7–10/31	10/31–11/24	11/24–12/18	12/18–1/11	2/6–4/4	1/11–2/6
					4/4–5/7
8/17–9/6	12/9–1/5			1/11–2/4	2/4–2/28
11/8–12/9					
9/6–9/30	9/30–10/25	1/5–1/30	1/30–2/24	2/24–3/19	3/19–4/13
		10/25–11/18	11/18–12/13	12/13–1/7	
10/21–11/14	11/14–12/8	12/8–1/1/06			1/7–2/3
8/11–9/7	9/7–10/9	10/9–12/15	1/1–1/25	1/25–2/18	2/18–3/14
	12/15–12/25	12/25–2/6			
9/22–10/16	10/16–11/9	11/9–12/3	2/6–3/6	3/6–4/2	4/2–4/27
			12/3–12/27	12/27–1/20	
11/3–11/28	11/28–12/22	12/22–1/15			1/20–2/4
8/23–9/17	9/17–10/12	10/12–11/17	1/15–2/9	2/9–3/5	3/5–3/29
			11/17–12/5	12/5–1/15	
10/7–10/30	10/31–11/23	11/24–12/17	12/18–12/31	1/1–1/15	1/16–1/28
				1/29–4/4	4/5–5/6
11/19–12/8	12/9–12/31		1/1–1/10	1/11–2/2	2/3–2/27
9/6–9/30	1/1–1/4	1/5–1/29	1/30–2/23	2/24–3/18	3/19–4/12
	10/1–10/24	10/25–11/17	11/18–12/12	12/13–12/31	
10/21–11/13	11/14–12/7	12/8–12/31		1/1–1/6	1/7–2/2
8/11–9/6	9/7–10/9	10/10–12/5	1/1–1/24	1/25–2/17	2/18–3/13
	12/6–12/30	12/31			
9/22–10/15	10/16–11/8	1/1–2/6	2/7–3/6	3/7–4/1	4/2–4/26
		11/9–12/2	12/3–12/26	12/27–12/31	
11/3–11/27	11/28–12/21	12/22–12/31		1/1–1/19	1/20–2/13
8/22–9/16	9/17–10/11	1/1–1/14	1/15–2/7	2/8–3/4	3/5–3/28
		10/12–11/6	11/7–12/5	12/6–12/31	
10/6–10/29	10/30–11/22	11/23–12/16	12/17–12/31	1/1–4/5	4/6–5/6
11/9–12/8	12/9–12/31		1/1–1/9	1/10–2/2	2/3–2/26
9/5–9/30	1/1–1/3	1/4–1/28	1/29–2/22	2/23–3/18	3/19–4/11
	9/31–10/23	10/24–11/17	11/18–12/11	12/12–12/31	
10/21–11/13	11/14–12/7	12/8–12/31		1/1–1/6	1/7–2/2
8/10–9/6	9/7–10/10	10/11–11/28	1/1–1/24	1/25–2/16	2/17–3/12
	11/29–12/31				
9/21–10/14	1/1	1/2–2/6	2/7–3/5	3/6–3/31	4/1–4/26
	10/15–11/7	11/8–12/1	12/2–12/25	12/26–12/31	
11/13–11/26	11/27–12/21	12/22–12/31		1/1–1/19	1/20–2/12
8/22–9/15	9/16–10/11	1/1–1/14	1/15–2/7	2/8–3/3	3/4–3/27
		10/12–11/6	11/7–12/5	12/6–12/31	

VENUS SIGNS 1901–2007

	Aries	Taurus	Gemini	Cancer	Leo	Virgo
1926	5/7–6/2	6/3–6/28	6/29–7/23	7/24–8/17	8/18–9/11	9/12–10/5
1927	2/27–3/22	3/23–4/16	4/17–5/11	5/12–6/7	6/8–7/7	7/8–11/9
1928	4/12–5/5	5/6–5/29	5/30–6/23	6/24–7/17	7/18–8/11	8/12–9/4
1929	2/3–3/7	3/8–4/19	7/8–8/4	8/5–8/30	8/31–9/25	9/26–10/19
	4/20–6/2	6/3–7/7				
1930	3/13–4/5	4/6–4/30	5/1–5/24	5/25–6/18	6/19–7/14	7/15–8/9
1931	4/26–5/20	5/21–6/13	6/14–7/8	7/9–8/2	8/3–8/26	8/27–9/19
1932	2/12–3/8	3/9–4/3	4/4–5/5	5/6–7/12	9/9–10/6	10/7–11/1
			7/13–7/27	7/28–9/8		
1933	3/27–4/19	4/20–5/28	5/29–6/8	6/9–7/2	7/3–7/26	7/27–8/20
1934	5/6–6/1	6/2–6/27	6/28–7/22	7/23–8/16	8/17–9/10	9/11–10/4
1935	2/26–3/21	3/22–4/15	4/16–5/10	5/11–6/6	6/7–7/6	7/7–11/8
1936	4/11–5/4	5/5–5/28	5/29–6/22	6/23–7/16	7/17–8/10	8/11–9/4
1937	2/2–3/8	3/9–4/13	7/7–8/3	8/4–8/29	8/30–9/24	9/25–10/18
	4/14–6/3	6/4–7/6				
1938	3/12–4/4	4/5–4/28	4/29–5/23	5/24–6/18	6/19–7/13	7/14–8/8
1939	4/25–5/19	5/20–6/13	6/14–7/8	7/9–8/1	8/2–8/25	8/26–9/19
1940	2/12–3/7	3/8–4/3	4/4–5/5	5/6–7/4	9/9–10/5	10/6–10/31
			7/5–7/31	8/1–9/8		
1941	3/27–4/19	4/20–5/13	5/14–6/6	6/7–7/1	7/2–7/26	7/27–8/20
1942	5/6–6/1	6/2–6/26	6/27–7/22	7/23–8/16	8/17–9/9	9/10–10/3
1943	2/25–3/20	3/21–4/14	4/15–5/10	5/11–6/6	6/7–7/6	7/7–11/8
1944	4/10–5/3	5/4–5/28	5/29–6/21	6/22–7/16	7/17–8/9	8/10–9/2
1945	2/2–3/10	3/11–4/6	7/7–8/3	8/4–8/29	8/30–9/23	9/24–10/18
	4/7–6/3	6/4–7/6				
1946	3/11–4/4	4/5–4/28	4/29–5/23	5/24–6/17	6/18–7/12	7/13–8/8
1947	4/25–5/19	5/20–6/12	6/13–7/7	7/8–8/1	8/2–8/25	8/26–9/18
1948	2/11–3/7	3/8–4/3	4/4–5/6	5/7–6/28	9/8–10/5	10/6–10/31
			6/29–8/2	8/3–9/7		
1949	3/26–4/19	4/20–5/13	5/14–6/6	6/7–6/30	7/1–7/25	7/26–8/19
1950	5/5–5/31	6/1–6/26	6/27–7/21	7/22–8/15	8/16–9/9	9/10–10/3
1951	2/25–3/21	3/22–4/15	4/16–5/10	5/11–6/6	6/7–7/7	7/8–11/9

Libra	Scorpio	Sagittarius	Capricorn	Aquarius	Pisces
10/6–10/29	10/30–11/22	11/23–12/16	12/17–12/31	1/1–4/5	4/6–5/6
11/10–12/8	12/9–12/31	1/1–1/7	1/8	1/9–2/1	2/2–2/26
9/5–9/28	1/1–1/3	1/4–1/28	1/29–2/22	2/23–3/17	3/18–4/11
	9/29–10/23	10/24–11/16	11/17–12/11	12/12–12/31	
10/20–11/12	11/13–12/6	12/7–12/30	12/31	1/1–1/5	1/6–2/2
8/10–9/6	9/7–10/11	10/12–11/21	1/1–1/23	1/24–2/16	2/17–3/12
	11/22–12/31				
9/20–10/13	1/1–1/3	1/4–2/6	2/7–3/4	3/5–3/31	4/1–4/25
	10/14–11/6	11/7–11/30	12/1–12/24	12/25–12/31	
11/2–11/25	11/26–12/20	12/21–12/31		1/1–1/18	1/19–2/11
8/21–9/14	9/15–10/10	1/1–1/13	1/14–2/6	2/7–3/2	3/3–3/26
		10/11–11/5	11/6–12/4	12/5–12/31	
10/5–10/28	10/29–11/21	11/22–12/15	12/16–12/31	1/1–4/5	4/6–5/5
11/9–12/7	12/8–12/31		1/1–1/7	1/8–1/31	2/1–2/25
9/5–9/27	1/1–1/2	1/3–1/27	1/28–2/21	2/22–3/16	3/17–4/10
	9/28–10/22	10/23–11/15	11/16–12/10	12/11–12/31	
10/19–11/11	11/12–12/5	12/6–12/29	12/30–12/31	1/1–1/5	1/6–2/1
8/9–9/6	9/7–10/13	10/14–11/14	1/1–1/22	1/23–2/15	2/16–3/11
	11/15–12/31				
9/20–10/13	1/1–1/3	1/4–2/5	2/6–3/4	3/5–3/30	3/31–4/24
	10/14–11/6	11/7–11/30	12/1–12/24	12/25–12/31	
11/1–11/25	11/26–12/19	12/20–12/31		1/1–1/18	1/19–2/11
8/21–9/14	9/15–10/9	1/1–1/12	1/13–2/5	2/6–3/1	3/2–3/26
		10/10–11/5	11/6–12/4	12/5–12/31	
10/4–10/27	10/28–11/20	11/21–12/14	12/15–12/31	1/1–4/5	4/6–5/5
11/9–12/7	12/8–12/31		1/1–1/7	1/8–1/31	2/1–2/24
9/3–9/27	1/1–1/2	1/3–1/27	1/28–2/20	2/21–3/16	3/17–4/9
	9/28–10/21	10/22–11/15	11/16–12/10	12/11–12/31	
10/19–11/11	11/12–12/5	12/6–12/29	12/30–12/31	1/1–1/4	1/5–2/1
8/9–9/6	9/7–10/15	10/16–11/7	1/1–1/21	1/22–2/14	2/15–3/10
	11/8–12/31				
9/19–10/12	1/1–1/4	1/5–2/5	2/6–3/4	3/5–3/29	3/30–4/24
	10/13–11/5	11/6–11/29	11/30–12/23	12/24–12/31	
11/1–11/25	11/26–12/19	12/20–12/31		1/1–1/17	1/18–2/10
8/20–9/14	9/15–10/9	1/1–1/12	1/13–2/5	2/6–3/1	3/2–3/25
		10/10–11/5	11/6–12/5	12/6–12/31	
10/4–10/27	10/28–11/20	11/21–12/13	12/14–12/31	1/1–4/5	4/6–5/4
11/10–12/7	12/8–12/31		1/1–1/7	1/8–1/31	2/1–2/24

VENUS SIGNS 1901–2007

	Aries	Taurus	Gemini	Cancer	Leo	Virgo
1952	4/10–5/4	5/5–5/28	5/29–6/21	6/22–7/16	7/17–8/9	8/10–9/3
1953	2/2–3/3	3/4–3/31	7/8–8/3	8/4–8/29	8/30–9/24	9/25–10/18
	4/1–6/5	6/6–7/7				
1954	3/12–4/4	4/5–4/28	4/29–5/23	5/24–6/17	6/18–7/13	7/14–8/8
1955	4/25–5/19	5/20–6/13	6/14–7/7	7/8–8/1	8/2–8/25	8/26–9/18
1956	2/12–3/7	3/8–4/4	4/5–5/7	5/8–6/23	9/9–10/5	10/6–10/31
			6/24–8/4	8/5–9/8		
1957	3/26–4/19	4/20–5/13	5/14–6/6	6/7–7/1	7/2–7/26	7/27–8/19
1958	5/6–5/31	6/1–6/26	6/27–7/22	7/23–8/15	8/16–9/9	9/10–10/3
1959	2/25–3/20	3/21–4/14	4/15–5/10	5/11–6/6	6/7–7/8	7/9–9/20
					9/21–9/24	9/25–11/9
1960	4/10–5/3	5/4–5/28	5/29–6/21	6/22–7/15	7/16–8/9	8/10–9/2
1961	2/3–6/5	6/6–7/7	7/8–8/3	8/4–8/29	8/30–9/23	9/24–10/17
1962	3/11–4/3	4/4–4/28	4/29–5/22	5/23–6/17	6/18–7/12	7/13–8/8
1963	4/24–5/18	5/19–6/12	6/13–7/7	7/8–7/31	8/1–8/25	8/26–9/18
1964	2/11–3/7	3/8–4/4	4/5–5/9	5/10–6/17	9/9–10/5	10/6–10/31
			6/18–8/5	8/6–9/8		
1965	3/26–4/18	4/19–5/12	5/13–6/6	6/7–6/30	7/1–7/25	7/26–8/19
1966	5/6–6/31	6/1–6/26	6/27–7/21	7/22–8/15	8/16–9/8	9/9–10/2
1967	2/24–3/20	3/21–4/14	4/15–5/10	5/11–6/6	6/7–7/8	7/9–9/9
					9/10–10/1	10/2–11/9
1968	4/9–5/3	5/4–5/27	5/28–6/20	6/21–7/15	7/16–8/8	8/9–9/2
1969	2/3–6/6	6/7–7/6	7/7–8/3	8/4–8/28	8/29–9/22	9/23–10/17
1970	3/11–4/3	4/4–4/27	4/28–5/22	5/23–6/16	6/17–7/12	7/13–8/8
1971	4/24–5/18	5/19–6/12	6/13–7/6	7/7–7/31	8/1–8/24	8/25–9/17
1972	2/11–3/7	3/8–4/3	4/4–5/10	5/11–6/11		
			6/12–8/6	8/7–9/8	9/9–10/5	10/6–10/30
1973	3/25–4/18	4/18–5/12	5/13–6/5	6/6–6/29	7/1–7/25	7/26–8/19
1974	5/5–5/31	6/1–6/25	6/26–7/21	7/22–8/14	8/15–9/8	9/9–10/2
1975	2/24–3/20	3/21–4/13	4/14–5/9	5/10–6/6	6/7–7/9	7/10–9/2
					9/3–10/4	10/5–11/9

82

Libra	Scorpio	Sagittarius	Capricorn	Aquarius	Pisces
9/4–9/27	1/1–1/2	1/3–1/27	1/28–2/20	2/21–3/16	3/17–4/9
	9/28–10/21	10/22–11/15	11/16–12/10	12/11–12/31	
10/19–11/11	11/12–12/5	12/6–12/29	12/30–12/31	1/1–1/5	1/6–2/1
8/9–9/6	9/7–10/22	10/23–10/27	1/1–1/22	1/23–2/15	2/16–3/11
	10/28–12/31				
9/19–10/13	1/1–1/6	1/7–2/5	2/6–3/4	3/5–3/30	3/31–4/24
	10/14–11/5	11/6–11/30	12/1–12/24	12/25–12/31	
11/1–11/25	11/26–12/19	12/20–12/31		1/1–1/17	1/18–2/11
8/20–9/14	9/15–10/9	1/1–1/12	1/13–2/5	2/6–3/1	3/2–3/25
		10/10–11/5	11/6–12/6	12/7–12/31	
10/4–10/27	10/28–11/20	11/21–12/14	12/15–12/31	1/1–4/6	4/7–5/5
11/10–12/7	12/8–12/31		1/1–1/7	1/8–1/31	2/1–2/24
9/3–9/26	1/1–1/2	1/3–1/27	1/28–2/20	2/21–3/15	3/16–4/9
	9/27–10/21	10/22–11/15	11/16–12/10	12/11–12/31	
10/18–11/11	11/12–12/4	12/5–12/28	12/29–12/31	1/1–1/5	1/6–2/2
8/9–9/6	9/7–12/31		1/1–1/21	1/22–2/14	2/15–3/10
9/19–10/12	1/1–1/6	1/7–2/5	2/6–3/4	3/5–3/29	3/30–4/23
	10/13–11/5	11/6–11/29	11/30–12/23	12/24–12/31	
11/1–11/24	11/25–12/19	12/20–12/31		1/1–1/16	1/17–2/10
8/20–9/13	9/14–10/9	1/1–1/12	1/13–2/5	2/6–3/1	3/2–3/25
		10/10–11/5	11/6–12/7	12/8–12/31	
10/3–10/26	10/27–11/19	11/20–12/13	2/7–2/25	1/1–2/6	4/7–5/5
			12/14–12/31	2/26–4/6	
11/10–12/7	12/8–12/31		1/1–1/6	1/7–1/30	1/31–2/23
9/3–9/26	1/1	1/2–1/26	1/27–2/20	2/21–3/15	3/16–4/8
	9/27–10/21	10/22–11/14	11/15–12/9	12/10–12/31	
10/18–11/10	11/11–12/4	12/5–12/28	12/29–12/31	1/1–1/4	1/5–2/2
8/9–9/7	9/8–12/31		1/1–1/21	1/22–2/14	2/15–3/10
9/18–10/11	1/1–1/7	1/8–2/5	2/6–3/4	3/5–3/29	3/30–4/23
	10/12–11/5	11/6–11/29	11/30–12/23	12/24–12/31	
	11/25–12/18	12/19–12/31		1/1–1/16	1/17–2/10
10/31–11/24					
8/20–9/13	9/14–10/8	1/1–1/12	1/13–2/4	2/5–2/28	3/1–3/24
		10/9–11/5	11/6–12/7	12/8–12/31	
			1/30–2/28	1/1–1/29	
10/3–10/26	10/27–11/19	11/20–12/13	12/14–12/31	3/1–4/6	4/7–5/4
11/10–12/7	12/8–12/31		1/1–1/6	1/7–1/30	1/31–2/23

VENUS SIGNS 1901–2007

	Aries	Taurus	Gemini	Cancer	Leo	Virgo
1976	4/8–5/2	5/2–5/27	5/27—6/20	6/20–7/14	7/14–8/8	8/8–9/1
1977	2/2–6/6	6/6–7/6	7/6–8/2	8/2–8/28	8/28–9/22	9/22–10/17
1978	3/9–4/2	4/2–4/27	4/27–5/22	5/22–6/16	6/16–7/12	7/12–8/6
1979	4/23–5/18	5/18–6/11	6/11–7/6	7/6–7/30	7/30–8/24	8/24–9/17
1980	2/9–3/6	3/6–4/3	4/3–5/12	5/12–6/5	9/7–10/4	10/4–10/30
			6/5–8/6	8/6–9/7		
1981	3/24–4/17	4/17–5/11	5/11–6/5	6/5–6/29	6/29–7/24	7/24–8/18
1982	5/4–5/30	5/30–6/25	6/25–7/20	7/20–8/14	8/14–9/7	9/7–10/2
1983	2/22–3/19	3/19–4/13	4/13–5/9	5/9–6/6	6/6–7/10	7/10–8/27
					8/27–10/5	10/5–11/9
1984	4/7–5/2	5/2–5/26	5/26–6/20	6/20–7/14	7/14–8/7	8/7–9/1
1985	2/2–6/6	6/7–7/6	7/6–8/2	8/2–8/28	8/28–9/22	9/22–10/16
1986	3/9–4/2	4/2–4/26	4/26–5/21	5/21–6/15	6/15–7/11	7/11–8/7
1987	4/22–5/17	5/17–6/11	6/11–7/5	7/5–7/30	7/30–8/23	8/23–9/16
1988	2/9–3/6	3/6–4/3	4/3–5/17	5/17–5/27	9/7–10/4	10/4–10/29
			5/27–8/6	8/28–9/22	9/22–10/16	
1989	3/23–4/16	4/16–5/11	5/11–6/4	6/4–6/29	6/29–7/24	7/24–8/18
1990	5/4–5/30	5/30–6/25	6/25–7/20	7/20–8/13	8/13–9/7	9/7–10/1
1991	2/22–3/18	3/18–4/13	4/13–5/9	5/9–6/6	6/6–7/11	7/11–8/21
					8/21–10/6	10/6–11/9
1992	4/7–5/1	5/1–5/26	5/26–6/19	6/19–7/13	7/13–8/7	8/7–8/31
1993	2/2–6/6	6/6–7/6	7/6–8/1	8/1–8/27	8/27–9/21	9/21–10/16
1994	3/8–4/1	4/1–4/26	4/26–5/21	5/21–6/15	6/15–7/11	7/11–8/7
1995	4/22–5/16	5/16–6/10	6/10–7/5	7/5–7/29	7/29–8/23	8/23–9/16
1996	2/9–3/6	3/6–4/3	4/3–8/7	8/7–9/7	9/7–10/4	10/4–10/29
1997	3/23–4/16	4/16–5/10	5/10–6/4	6/4–6/28	6/28–7/23	7/23–8/17
1998	5/3–5/29	5/29–6/24	6/24–7/19	7/19–8/13	8/13–9/6	9/6–9/30
1999	2/21–3/18	3/18–4/12	4/12–5/8	5/8–6/5	6/5–7/12	7/12–8/15
					8/15–10/7	10/7–11/9
2000	4/6–5/1	5/1–5/25	5/25–6/13	6/13–7/13	7/13–8/6	8/6–8/31
2001	2/2–6/6	6/6–7/5	7/5–8/1	8/1–8/26	8/26–9/20	9/20–10/15
2002	3/7–4/1	4/1–4/25	4/25–5/20	5/20–6/14	6/14–7/10	7/10–8/7
2003	4/21–5/16	5/16–6/9	6/9–7/4	7/4–7/29	7/29–8/22	8/22–9/15
2004	2/8–3/5	3/5–4/3	4/3–8/7	8/7–9/6	9/6–10/3	10/3–10/28
2005	3/22–4/15	4/15–5/10	5/10–6/3	6/3–6/28	6/28–7/23	7/23–8/17
2006	5/3–5/29	5/29–6/24	6/24–7/19	7/19–8/12	8/12–9/6	9/6–9/30
2007	2/21–3/16	3/17–4/10	4/11–5/7	5/8–6/4	6/5–7/13	7/14–8/7
					8/8–10/6	10/7–11/7

Libra	Scorpio	Sagittarius	Capricorn	Aquarius	Pisces
9/1–9/26	9/26–10/20	1/1–1/26	1/26–2/19	2/19–3/15	3/15–4/8
10/17–11/10	11/10–12/4	12/4–12/27	12/27–1/20/78		1/4–2/2
8/6–9/7	9/7–1/7			1/20–2/13	2/13–3/9
9/17–10/11	10/11–11/4	1/7–2/5	2/5–3/3	3/3–3/29	3/29–4/23
		11/4–11/28	11/28–12/22	12/22–1/16/80	
10/30–11/24	11/24–12/18	12/18–1/11/81			1/16–2/9
8/18–9/12	9/12–10/9	10/9–11/5	1/11–2/4	2/4–2/28	2/28–3/24
			11/5–12/8	12/8–1/23/82	
10/2–10/26	10/26–11/18	11/18–12/12	1/23–3/2	3/2–4/6	4/6–5/4
			12/12–1/5/83		
11/9–12/6	12/6–1/1/84			1/5–1/29	1/29–2/22
9/1–9/25	9/25–10/20	1/1–1/25	1/25–2/19	2/19–3/14	3/14–4/7
		10/20–11/13	11/13–12/9	12/10–1/4	
10/16–11/9	11/9–12/3	12/3–12/27	12/28–1/19		1/4–2/2
8/7–9/7	9/7–1/7			1/20–2/13	2/13–3/9
9/16–10/10	10/10–11/3	1/7–2/5	2/5–3/3	3/3–3/28	3/28–4/22
		11/3–11/28	11/28–12/22	12/22–1/15	
10/29–11/23	11/23–12/17	12/17–1/10			1/15–2/9
8/18–9/12	9/12–10/8	10/8–11/5	1/10–2/3	2/3–2/27	2/27–3/23
			11/5–12/10	12/10–1/16/90	
10/1–10/25	10/25–11/18	11/18–12/12	1/16–3/3	3/3–4/6	4/6–5/4
			12/12–1/5		
11/9–12/6	12/6–12/31	12/31–1/25/92		1/5–1/29	1/29–2/22
8/31–9/25	9/25–10/19	10/19–11/13	1/25–2/18	2/18–3/13	3/13–4/7
			11/13–12/8	12/8–1/3/93	
10/16–11/9	11/9–12/2	12/2–12/26	12/26–1/19		1/3–2/2
8/7–9/7	9/7–1/7			1/19–2/12	2/12–3/8
9/16–10/10	10/10–11/13	1/7–2/4	2/4–3/2	3/2–3/28	3/28–4/22
		11/3–11/27	11/27–12/21	12/21–1/15	
10/29–11/23	11/23–12/17	12/17–1/10/97			1/15–2/9
8/17–9/12	9/12–10/8	10/8–11/5	1/10–2/3	2/3–2/27	2/27–3/23
			11/5–12/12	12/12–1/9	
9/30–10/24	10/24–11/17	11/17–12/11	1/9–3/4	3/4–4/6	4/6–5/3
11/9–12/5	12/5–12/31	12/31–1/24		1/4–1/28	1/28–2/21
8/31–9/24	9/24–10/19	10/19–11/13	1/24–2/18	2/18–3/12	3/13–4/6
			11/13–12/8	12/8	
10/15–11/8	11/8–12/2	12/2–12/26	12/26/01–1/18/02	12/8/00–1/3/01	1/3–2/2
8/7–9/7	9/7–1/7/03			1/18–2/11	2/11–3/7
9/15–10/9	10/9–11/2	1/7–2/4	2/4–3/2	3/2–3/27	3/27–4/21
		11/2–11/26	11/26–12/21	12/21–1/14/04	
10/28–11/22	11/22–12/16	12/16–1/9/05		1/1–1/14	1/14–2/8
8/17–9/11	9/11–10/8	10/8–11/15	1/9–2/2	2/2–2/26	2/26–3/22
			11/5–12/15	12/15–1/1/06	
9/30–10/24	10/24–11/17	11/17–12/11	1/1–3/5	3/5–4/6	4/6–5/3
11/8–12/4	12/5–12/29	12/30–1/24/08		1/3–1/26	1/27–2/20

How to Use the Mars, Jupiter, and Saturn Tables

Find the year of your birth on the left side of each column. The dates when the planet entered each sign are listed on the right side of each column. (Signs are abbreviated to three letters.) Your birthday should fall on or between each date listed, and your planetary placement should correspond to the earlier sign of that period.

All planet changes are calculated for the Greenwich Mean Time zone.

MARS SIGNS 1901–2007

1901	MAR	1	Leo		OCT	1	Vir
	MAY	11	Vir		NOV	20	Lib
	JUL	13	Lib	1905	JAN	13	Scp
	AUG	31	Scp		AUG	21	Sag
	OCT	14	Sag		OCT	8	Cap
	NOV	24	Cap		NOV	18	Aqu
1902	JAN	1	Aqu		DEC	27	Pic
	FEB	8	Pic	1906	FEB	4	Ari
	MAR	19	Ari		MAR	17	Tau
	APR	27	Tau		APR	28	Gem
	JUN	7	Gem		JUN	11	Can
	JUL	20	Can		JUL	27	Leo
	SEP	4	Leo		SEP	12	Vir
	OCT	23	Vir		OCT	30	Lib
	DEC	20	Lib		DEC	17	Scp
1903	APR	19	Vir	1907	FEB	5	Sag
	MAY	30	Lib		APR	1	Cap
	AUG	6	Scp		OCT	13	Aqu
	SEP	22	Sag		NOV	29	Pic
	NOV	3	Cap	1908	JAN	11	Ari
	DEC	12	Aqu		FEB	23	Tau
1904	JAN	19	Pic		APR	7	Gem
	FEB	27	Ari		MAY	22	Can
	APR	6	Tau		JUL	8	Leo
	MAY	18	Gem		AUG	24	Vir
	JUN	30	Can		OCT	10	Lib
	AUG	15	Leo		NOV	25	Scp

1909	JAN	10	Sag		MAR	9	Pic
	FEB	24	Cap		APR	16	Ari
	APR	9	Aqu		MAY	26	Tau
	MAY	25	Pic		JUL	6	Gem
	JUL	21	Ari		AUG	19	Can
	SEP	26	Pic		OCT	7	Leo
	NOV	20	Ari	1916	MAY	28	Vir
1910	JAN	23	Tau		JUL	23	Lib
	MAR	14	Gem		SEP	8	Scp
	MAY	1	Can		OCT	22	Sag
	JUN	19	Leo		DEC	1	Cap
	AUG	6	Vir	1917	JAN	9	Aqu
	SEP	22	Lib		FEB	16	Pic
	NOV	6	Scp		MAR	26	Ari
	DEC	20	Sag		MAY	4	Tau
1911	JAN	31	Cap		JUN	14	Gem
	MAR	14	Aqu		JUL	28	Can
	APR	23	Pic		SEP	12	Leo
	JUN	2	Ari		NOV	2	Vir
	JUL	15	Tau	1918	JAN	11	Lib
	SEP	5	Gem		FEB	25	Vir
	NOV	30	Tau		JUN	23	Lib
1912	JAN	30	Gem		AUG	17	Scp
	APR	5	Can		OCT	1	Sag
	MAY	28	Leo		NOV	11	Cap
	JUL	17	Vir		DEC	20	Aqu
	SEP	2	Lib	1919	JAN	27	Pic
	OCT	18	Scp		MAR	6	Ari
	NOV	30	Sag		APR	15	Tau
1913	JAN	10	Cap		MAY	26	Gem
	FEB	19	Aqu		JUL	8	Can
	MAR	30	Pic		AUG	23	Leo
	MAY	8	Ari		OCT	10	Vir
	JUN	17	Tau		NOV	30	Lib
	JUL	29	Gem	1920	JAN	31	Scp
	SEP	15	Can		APR	23	Lib
1914	MAY	1	Leo		JUL	10	Scp
	JUN	26	Vir		SEP	4	Sag
	AUG	14	Lib		OCT	18	Cap
	SEP	29	Scp		NOV	27	Aqu
	NOV	11	Sag	1921	JAN	5	Pic
	DEC	22	Cap		FEB	13	Ari
1915	JAN	30	Aqu		MAR	25	Tau

	MAY	6	Gem		OCT	26	Scp
	JUN	18	Can		DEC	8	Sag
	AUG	3	Leo	1928	JAN	19	Cap
	SEP	19	Vir		FEB	28	Aqu
	NOV	6	Lib		APR	7	Pic
	DEC	26	Scp		MAY	16	Ari
1922	FEB	18	Sag		JUN	26	Tau
	SEP	13	Cap		AUG	9	Gem
	OCT	30	Aqu		OCT	3	Can
	DEC	11	Pic		DEC	20	Gem
1923	JAN	21	Ari	1929	MAR	10	Can
	MAR	4	Tau		MAY	13	Leo
	APR	16	Gem		JUL	4	Vir
	MAY	30	Can		AUG	21	Lib
	JUL	16	Leo		OCT	6	Scp
	SEP	1	Vir		NOV	18	Sag
	OCT	18	Lib		DEC	29	Cap
	DEC	4	Scp	1930	FEB	6	Aqu
1924	JAN	19	Sag		MAR	17	Pic
	MAR	6	Cap		APR	24	Ari
	APR	24	Aqu		JUN	3	Tau
	JUN	24	Pic		JUL	14	Gem
	AUG	24	Aqu		AUG	28	Can
	OCT	19	Pic		OCT	20	Leo
	DEC	19	Ari	1931	FEB	16	Can
1925	FEB	5	Tau		MAR	30	Leo
	MAR	24	Gem		JUN	10	Vir
	MAY	9	Can		AUG	1	Lib
	JUN	26	Leo		SEP	17	Scp
	AUG	12	Vir		OCT	30	Sag
	SEP	28	Lib		DEC	10	Cap
	NOV	13	Scp	1932	JAN	18	Aqu
	DEC	28	Sag		FEB	25	Pic
1926	FEB	9	Cap		APR	3	Ari
	MAR	23	Aqu		MAY	12	Tau
	MAY	3	Pic		JUN	22	Gem
	JUN	15	Ari		AUG	4	Can
	AUG	1	Tau		SEP	20	Leo
1927	FEB	22	Gem		NOV	13	Vir
	APR	17	Can	1933	JUL	6	Lib
	JUN	6	Leo		AUG	26	Scp
	JUL	25	Vir		OCT	9	Sag
	SEP	10	Lib		NOV	19	Cap

	DEC	28	Aqu		FEB	17	Tau
1934	FEB	4	Pic		APR	1	Gem
	MAR	14	Ari		MAY	17	Can
	APR	22	Tau		JUL	3	Leo
	JUN	2	Gem		AUG	19	Vir
	JUL	15	Can		OCT	5	Lib
	AUG	30	Leo		NOV	20	Scp
	OCT	18	Vir	1941	JAN	4	Sag
	DEC	11	Lib		FEB	17	Cap
1935	JUL	29	Scp		APR	2	Aqu
	SEP	16	Sag		MAY	16	Pic
	OCT	28	Cap		JUL	2	Ari
	DEC	7	Aqu	1942	JAN	11	Tau
1936	JAN	14	Pic		MAR	7	Gem
	FEB	22	Ari		APR	26	Can
	APR	1	Tau		JUN	14	Leo
	MAY	13	Gem		AUG	1	Vir
	JUN	25	Can		SEP	17	Lib
	AUG	10	Leo		NOV	1	Scp
	SEP	26	Vir		DEC	15	Sag
	NOV	14	Lib	1943	JAN	26	Cap
1937	JAN	5	Scp		MAR	8	Aqu
	MAR	13	Sag		APR	17	Pic
	MAY	14	Scp		MAY	27	Ari
	AUG	8	Sag		JUL	7	Tau
	SEP	30	Cap		AUG	23	Gem
	NOV	11	Aqu	1944	MAR	28	Can
	DEC	21	Pic		MAY	22	Leo
1938	JAN	30	Ari		JUL	12	Vir
	MAR	12	Tau		AUG	29	Lib
	APR	23	Gem		OCT	13	Scp
	JUN	7	Can		NOV	25	Sag
	JUL	22	Leo	1945	JAN	5	Cap
	SEP	7	Vir		FEB	14	Aqu
	OCT	25	Lib		MAR	25	Pic
	DEC	11	Scp		MAY	2	Ari
1939	JAN	29	Sag		JUN	11	Tau
	MAR	21	Cap		JUL	23	Gem
	MAY	25	Aqu		SEP	7	Can
	JUL	21	Cap		NOV	11	Leo
	SEP	24	Aqu		DEC	26	Can
	NOV	19	Pic	1946	APR	22	Leo
1940	JAN	4	Ari		JUN	20	Vir

	AUG	9	Lib		OCT	12	Cap
	SEP	24	Scp		NOV	21	Aqu
	NOV	6	Sag		DEC	30	Pic
	DEC	17	Cap	1953	FEB	8	Ari
1947	JAN	25	Aqu		MAR	20	Tau
	MAR	4	Pic		MAY	1	Gem
	APR	11	Ari		JUN	14	Can
	MAY	21	Tau		JUL	29	Leo
	JUL	1	Gem		SEP	14	Vir
	AUG	13	Can		NOV	1	Lib
	OCT	1	Leo		DEC	20	Scp
	DEC	1	Vir	1954	FEB	9	Sag
1948	FEB	12	Leo		APR	12	Cap
	MAY	18	Vir		JUL	3	Sag
	JUL	17	Lib		AUG	24	Cap
	SEP	3	Scp		OCT	21	Aqu
	OCT	17	Sag		DEC	4	Pic
	NOV	26	Cap	1955	JAN	15	Ari
1949	JAN	4	Aqu		FEB	26	Tau
	FEB	11	Pic		APR	10	Gem
	MAR	21	Ari		MAY	26	Can
	APR	30	Tau		JUL	11	Leo
	JUN	10	Gem		AUG	27	Vir
	JUL	23	Can		OCT	13	Lib
	SEP	7	Leo		NOV	29	Scp
	OCT	27	Vir	1956	JAN	14	Sag
	DEC	26	Lib		FEB	28	Cap
1950	MAR	28	Vir		APR	14	Aqu
	JUN	11	Lib		JUN	3	Pic
	AUG	10	Scp		DEC	6	Ari
	SEP	25	Sag	1957	JAN	28	Tau
	NOV	6	Cap		MAR	17	Gem
	DEC	15	Aqu		MAY	4	Can
1951	JAN	22	Pic		JUN	21	Leo
	MAR	1	Ari		AUG	8	Vir
	APR	10	Tau		SEP	24	Lib
	MAY	21	Gem		NOV	8	Scp
	JUL	3	Can		DEC	23	Sag
	AUG	18	Leo	1958	FEB	3	Cap
	OCT	5	Vir		MAR	17	Aqu
	NOV	24	Lib		APR	27	Pic
1952	JAN	20	Scp		JUN	7	Ari
	AUG	27	Sag		JUL	21	Tau

	SEP	21	Gem		NOV	6	Vir
	OCT	29	Tau	1965	JUN	29	Lib
1959	FEB	10	Gem		AUG	20	Scp
	APR	10	Can		OCT	4	Sag
	JUN	1	Leo		NOV	14	Cap
	JUL	20	Vir		DEC	23	Aqu
	SEP	5	Lib	1966	JAN	30	Pic
	OCT	21	Scp		MAR	9	Ari
	DEC	3	Sag		APR	17	Tau
1960	JAN	14	Cap		MAY	28	Gem
	FEB	23	Aqu		JUL	11	Can
	APR	2	Pic		AUG	25	Leo
	MAY	11	Ari		OCT	12	Vir
	JUN	20	Tau		DEC	4	Lib
	AUG	2	Gem	1967	FEB	12	Scp
	SEP	21	Can		MAR	31	Lib
1961	FEB	5	Gem		JUL	19	Scp
	FEB	7	Can		SEP	10	Sag
	MAY	6	Leo		OCT	23	Cap
	JUN	28	Vir		DEC	1	Aqu
	AUG	17	Lib	1968	JAN	9	Pic
	OCT	1	Scp		FEB	17	Ari
	NOV	13	Sag		MAR	27	Tau
	DEC	24	Cap		MAY	8	Gem
1962	FEB	1	Aqu		JUN	21	Can
	MAR	12	Pic		AUG	5	Leo
	APR	19	Ari		SEP	21	Vir
	MAY	28	Tau		NOV	9	Lib
	JUL	9	Gem		DEC	29	Scp
	AUG	22	Can	1969	FEB	25	Sag
	OCT	11	Leo		SEP	21	Cap
1963	JUN	3	Vir		NOV	4	Aqu
	JUL	27	Lib		DEC	15	Pic
	SEP	12	Scp	1970	JAN	24	Ari
	OCT	25	Sag		MAR	7	Tau
	DEC	5	Cap		APR	18	Gem
1964	JAN	13	Aqu		JUN	2	Can
	FEB	20	Pic		JUL	18	Leo
	MAR	29	Ari		SEP	3	Vir
	MAY	7	Tau		OCT	20	Lib
	JUN	17	Gem		DEC	6	Scp
	JUL	30	Can	1971	JAN	23	Sag
	SEP	15	Leo		MAR	12	Cap

	MAY	3	Aqu		JUN	6	Tau
	NOV	6	Pic		JUL	17	Gem
	DEC	26	Ari		SEP	1	Can
1972	FEB	10	Tau		OCT	26	Leo
	MAR	27	Gem	1978	JAN	26	Can
	MAY	12	Can		APR	10	Leo
	JUN	28	Leo		JUN	14	Vir
	AUG	15	Vir		AUG	4	Lib
	SEP	30	Lib		SEP	19	Scp
	NOV	15	Scp		NOV	2	Sag
	DEC	30	Sag		DEC	12	Cap
1973	FEB	12	Cap	1979	JAN	20	Aqu
	MAR	26	Aqu		FEB	27	Pic
	MAY	8	Pic		APR	7	Ari
	JUN	20	Ari		MAY	16	Tau
	AUG	12	Tau		JUN	26	Gem
	OCT	29	Ari		AUG	8	Can
	DEC	24	Tau		SEP	24	Leo
1974	FEB	27	Gem		NOV	19	Vir
	APR	20	Can	1980	MAR	11	Leo
	JUN	9	Leo		MAY	4	Vir
	JUL	27	Vir		JUL	10	Lib
	SEP	12	Lib		AUG	29	Scp
	OCT	28	Scp		OCT	12	Sag
	DEC	10	Sag		NOV	22	Cap
1975	JAN	21	Cap		DEC	30	Aqu
	MAR	3	Aqu	1981	FEB	6	Pic
	APR	11	Pic		MAR	17	Ari
	MAY	21	Ari		APR	25	Tau
	JUL	1	Tau		JUN	5	Gem
	AUG	14	Gem		JUL	18	Can
	OCT	17	Can		SEP	2	Leo
	NOV	25	Gem		OCT	21	Vir
1976	MAR	18	Can		DEC	16	Lib
	MAY	16	Leo	1982	AUG	3	Scp
	JUL	6	Vir		SEP	20	Sag
	AUG	24	Lib		OCT	31	Cap
	OCT	8	Scp		DEC	10	Aqu
	NOV	20	Sag	1983	JAN	17	Pic
1977	JAN	1	Cap		FEB	25	Ari
	FEB	9	Aqu		APR	5	Tau
	MAR	20	Pic		MAY	16	Gem
	APR	27	Ari		JUN	29	Can

	AUG	13	Leo	1990	JAN	29	Cap
	SEP	30	Vir		MAR	11	Aqu
	NOV	18	Lib		APR	20	Pic
1984	JAN	11	Scp		MAY	31	Ari
	AUG	17	Sag		JUL	12	Tau
	OCT	5	Cap		AUG	31	Gem
	NOV	15	Aqu		DEC	14	Tau
	DEC	25	Pic	1991	JAN	21	Gem
1985	FEB	2	Ari		APR	3	Can
	MAR	15	Tau		MAY	26	Leo
	APR	26	Gem		JUL	15	Vir
	JUN	9	Can		SEP	1	Lib
	JUL	25	Leo		OCT	16	Scp
	SEP	10	Vir		NOV	29	Sag
	OCT	27	Lib	1992	JAN	9	Cap
	DEC	14	Scp		FEB	18	Aqu
1986	FEB	2	Sag		MAR	28	Pic
	MAR	28	Cap		MAY	5	Ari
	OCT	9	Aqu		JUN	14	Tau
	NOV	26	Pic		JUL	26	Gem
1987	JAN	8	Ari		SEP	12	Can
	FEB	20	Tau	1993	APR	27	Leo
	APR	5	Gem		JUN	23	Vir
	MAY	21	Can		AUG	12	Lib
	JUL	6	Leo		SEP	27	Scp
	AUG	22	Vir		NOV	9	Sag
	OCT	8	Lib		DEC	20	Cap
	NOV	24	Scp	1994	JAN	28	Aqu
1988	JAN	8	Sag		MAR	7	Pic
	FEB	22	Cap		APR	14	Ari
	APR	6	Aqu		MAY	23	Tau
	MAY	22	Pic		JUL	3	Gem
	JUL	13	Ari		AUG	16	Can
	OCT	23	Pic		OCT	4	Leo
	NOV	1	Ari		DEC	12	Vir
1989	JAN	19	Tau	1995	JAN	22	Leo
	MAR	11	Gem		MAY	25	Vir
	APR	29	Can		JUL	21	Lib
	JUN	16	Leo		SEP	7	Scp
	AUG	3	Vir		OCT	20	Sag
	SEP	19	Lib		NOV	30	Cap
	NOV	4	Scp	1996	JAN	8	Aqu
	DEC	18	Sag		FEB	15	Pic

	MAR	24	Ari		MAR	1	Tau
	MAY	2	Tau		APR	13	Gem
	JUN	12	Gem		MAY	28	Can
	JUL	25	Can		JUL	13	Leo
	SEP	9	Leo		AUG	29	Vir
	OCT	30	Vir		OCT	15	Lib
1997	JAN	3	Lib		DEC	1	Scp
	MAR	8	Vir	2003	JAN	17	Sag
	JUN	19	Lib		MAR	4	Cap
	AUG	14	Scp		APR	21	Aqu
	SEP	28	Sag		JUN	17	Pic
	NOV	9	Cap		DEC	16	Ari
	DEC	18	Aqu	2004	FEB	3	Tau
1998	JAN	25	Pic		MAR	21	Gem
	MAR	4	Ari		MAY	7	Can
	APR	13	Tau		JUN	23	Leo
	MAY	24	Gem		AUG	10	Vir
	JUL	6	Can		SEP	26	Lib
	AUG	20	Leo		NOV	11	Sep
	OCT	7	Vir		DEC	25	Sag
	NOV	27	Lib	2005	FEB	6	Cap
1999	JAN	26	Scp		MAR	20	Aqu
	MAY	5	Lib		MAY	1	Pic
	JUL	5	Scp		JUN	12	Ari
	SEP	2	Sag		JUL	28	Tau
	OCT	17	Cap	2006	FEB	17	Gem
	NOV	26	Aqu		APR	14	Can
2000	JAN	4	Pic		JUN	3	Leo
	FEB	12	Ari		JUL	22	Vir
	MAR	23	Tau		SEP	8	Lib
	MAY	3	Gem		OCT	23	Scp
	JUN	16	Can		DEC	6	Sag
	AUG	1	Leo	2007	JAN	16	Cap
	SEP	17	Vir		FEB	25	Aqu
	NOV	4	Lib		APR	6	Pic
	DEC	23	Scp		MAY	15	Ari
2001	FEB	14	Sag		JUNE	24	Tau
	SEP	8	Cap		AUG	7	Gem
	OCT	27	Aqu		SEP	28	Can
	DEC	8	Pic		DEC	31	Gem*
2002	JAN	18	Ari				

*Repeat means planet is retrograde.

JUPITER SIGNS 1901–2007

1901	JAN	19	Cap		1930	JUN	26	Can
1902	FEB	6	Aqu		1931	JUL	17	Leo
1903	FEB	20	Pic		1932	AUG	11	Vir
1904	MAR	1	Ari		1933	SEP	10	Lib
	AUG	8	Tau		1934	OCT	11	Scp
	AUG	31	Ari		1935	NOV	9	Sag
1905	MAR	7	Tau		1936	DEC	2	Cap
	JUL	21	Gem		1937	DEC	20	Aqu
	DEC	4	Tau		1938	MAY	14	Pic
1906	MAR	9	Gem			JUL	30	Aqu
	JUL	30	Can			DEC	29	Pic
1907	AUG	18	Leo		1939	MAY	11	Ari
1908	SEP	12	Vir			OCT	30	Pic
1909	OCT	11	Lib			DEC	20	Ari
1910	NOV	11	Scp		1940	MAY	16	Tau
1911	DEC	10	Sag		1941	MAY	26	Gem
1913	JAN	2	Cap		1942	JUN	10	Can
1914	JAN	21	Aqu		1943	JUN	30	Leo
1915	FEB	4	Pic		1944	JUL	26	Vir
1916	FEB	12	Ari		1945	AUG	25	Lib
	JUN	26	Tau		1946	SEP	25	Scp
	OCT	26	Ari		1947	OCT	24	Sag
1917	FEB	12	Tau		1948	NOV	15	Cap
	JUN	29	Gem		1949	APR	12	Aqu
1918	JUL	13	Can			JUN	27	Cap
1919	AUG	2	Leo			NOV	30	Aqu
1920	AUG	27	Vir		1950	APR	15	Pic
1921	SEP	25	Lib			SEP	15	Aqu
1922	OCT	26	Scp			DEC	1	Pic
1923	NOV	24	Sag		1951	APR	21	Ari
1924	DEC	18	Cap		1952	APR	28	Tau
1926	JAN	6	Aqu		1953	MAY	9	Gem
1927	JAN	18	Pic		1954	MAY	24	Can
	JUN	6	Ari		1955	JUN	13	Leo
	SEP	11	Pic			NOV	17	Vir
1928	JAN	23	Ari		1956	JAN	18	Leo
	JUN	4	Tau			JUL	7	Vir
1929	JUN	12	Gem			DEC	13	Lib

1957	FEB	19	Vir	1974	MAR	8	Pic
	AUG	7	Lib	1975	MAR	18	Ari
1958	JAN	13	Scp	1976	MAR	26	Tau
	MAR	20	Lib		AUG	23	Gem
	SEP	7	Scp		OCT	16	Tau
1959	FEB	10	Sag	1977	APR	3	Gem
	APR	24	Scp		AUG	20	Can
	OCT	5	Sag		DEC	30	Gem
1960	MAR	1	Cap	1978	APR	12	Can
	JUN	10	Sag		SEP	5	Leo
	OCT	26	Cap	1979	FEB	28	Can
1961	MAR	15	Aqu		APR	20	Leo
	AUG	12	Cap		SEP	29	Vir
	NOV	4	Aqu	1980	OCT	27	Lib
1962	MAR	25	Pic	1981	NOV	27	Scp
1963	APR	4	Ari	1982	DEC	26	Sag
1964	APR	12	Tau	1984	JAN	19	Cap
1965	APR	22	Gem	1985	FEB	6	Aqu
	SEP	21	Can	1986	FEB	20	Pic
	NOV	17	Gem	1987	MAR	2	Ari
1966	MAY	5	Can	1988	MAR	8	Tau
	SEP	27	Leo		JUL	22	Gem
1967	JAN	16	Can		NOV	30	Tau
	MAY	23	Leo	1989	MAR	11	Gem
	OCT	19	Vir		JUL	30	Can
1968	FEB	27	Leo	1990	AUG	18	Leo
	JUN	15	Vir	1991	SEP	12	Vir
	NOV	15	Lib	1992	OCT	10	Lib
1969	MAR	30	Vir	1993	NOV	10	Scp
	JUL	15	Lib	1994	DEC	9	Sag
	DEC	16	Scp	1996	JAN	3	Cap
1970	APR	30	Lib	1997	JAN	21	Aqu
	AUG	15	Scp	1998	FEB	4	Pic
1971	JAN	14	Sag	1999	FEB	13	Ari
	JUN	5	Scp		JUN	28	Tau
	SEP	11	Sag		OCT	23	Ari
1972	FEB	6	Cap	2000	FEB	14	Tau
	JUL	24	Sag		JUN	30	Gem
	SEP	25	Cap	2001	JUL	14	Can
1973	FEB	23	Aqu	2002	AUG	1	Leo

2003	AUG	27	Vir	2006	NOV	24	Sag
2004	SEP	24	Lib	2007	DEC	17	Cap
2005	OCT	26	Scp				

SATURN SIGNS 1903–2007

1903	JAN	19	Aqu		SEP	22	Ari
1905	APR	13	Pic	1940	MAR	20	Tau
	AUG	17	Aqu	1942	MAY	8	Gem
1906	JAN	8	Pic	1944	JUN	20	Can
1908	MAR	19	Ari	1946	AUG	2	Leo
1910	MAY	17	Tau	1948	SEP	19	Vir
	DEC	14	Ari	1949	APR	3	Leo
1911	JAN	20	Tau		MAY	29	Vir
1912	JUL	7	Gem	1950	NOV	20	Lib
	NOV	30	Tau	1951	MAR	7	Vir
1913	MAR	26	Gem		AUG	13	Lib
1914	AUG	24	Can	1953	OCT	22	Scp
	DEC	7	Gem	1956	JAN	12	Sag
1915	MAY	11	Can		MAY	14	Scp
1916	OCT	17	Leo		OCT	10	Sag
	DEC	7	Can	1959	JAN	5	Cap
1917	JUN	24	Leo	1962	JAN	3	Aqu
1919	AUG	12	Vir	1964	MAR	24	Pic
1921	OCT	7	Lib		SEP	16	Aqu
1923	DEC	20	Scp		DEC	16	Pic
1924	APR	6	Lib	1967	MAR	3	Ari
	SEP	13	Scp	1969	APR	29	Tau
1926	DEC	2	Sag	1971	JUN	18	Gem
1929	MAR	15	Cap	1972	JAN	10	Tau
	MAY	5	Sag		FEB	21	Gem
	NOV	30	Cap	1973	AUG	1	Can
1932	FEB	24	Aqu	1974	JAN	7	Gem
	AUG	13	Cap		APR	18	Can
	NOV	20	Aqu	1975	SEP	17	Leo
1935	FEB	14	Pic	1976	JAN	14	Can
1937	APR	25	Ari		JUN	5	Leo
	OCT	18	Pic	1977	NOV	17	Vir
1938	JAN	14	Ari	1978	JAN	5	Leo
1939	JUL	6	Tau		JUL	26	Vir

1980	SEP	21	Lib	1994	JAN	28	Pic
1982	NOV	29	Scp	1996	APR	7	Ari
1983	MAY	6	Lib	1998	JUN	9	Tau
	AUG	24	Scp		OCT	25	Ari
1985	NOV	17	Sag	1999	MAR	1	Tau
1988	FEB	13	Cap	2000	AUG	10	Gem
	JUN	10	Sag		OCT	16	Tau
	NOV	12	Cap	2001	APR	21	Gem
1991	FEB	6	Aqu	2003	JUN	3	Can
1993	MAY	21	Pic	2005	JUL	16	Leo
	JUN	30	Aqu	2007	SEP	2	Vir

CHAPTER 7

Your Rising Sign Tells Where the Action Is

You can learn much about a person by the signs and interactions of the sun, moon, and planets in the horoscope, but you can't tell where in that person's life the activity will take place. Knowing the rising sign, which is based on the exact moment in time of an event such as a birth, will provide information that enables the astrologer to make predictions. For example, you might know that a person has Mars in Aries, which will describe that person's dynamic fiery energy. But if you also know that the person has a Capricorn rising sign, this Mars will fall in the fourth house of home and family, so you know where that energy will operate.

Your rising sign is the degree of the zodiac ascending over the eastern horizon when you were born. (That's why it's often called the ascendant.) It marks the first point in the horoscope, the beginning of the first house, one of twelve divisions of the horoscope, each of which represents a different area of your life. After the rising sign sets up the first house, the other houses parade around the chart in sequence, with the following sign on the house cusp. Due to the earth's rotation, the rising sign changes every two hours, which means that other babies, who may have been born later or earlier on the same day in the same hospital as you were (and will be sure to have most planets in the same signs as you do) may not have the same rising sign and their planets may fall in different houses in the chart.

For instance, if Mars is in Gemini and your rising sign is Taurus, Mars will most likely be active in the second or financial house of your chart. Someone born later in the day when the rising sign is Virgo would have Mars positioned at the top of the chart, energizing the tenth house of career.

Most astrologers insist on knowing the exact time of a client's birth before analyzing a chart. The more accurate your birth time, the more accurately an astrologer can position the planets in your chart. Without a valid rising sign, your collection of planets would have no homes. One would have no idea which area of your life would be influenced by a particular planet.

How Your Rising Sign Can Influence Your Sun Sign

Your rising sign has an important relationship with your sun sign. Some will complement the sun sign; others hide it under a totally different mask, as if playing an entirely different role, making it difficult to guess the person's sun sign from outer appearances. This may be the reason why you might not look or act like your sun sign's archetype. For example, a Leo with a conservative Capricorn ascendant would come across as much more serious than a Leo with a fiery Aries or Sagittarius ascendant.

Though the rising sign usually creates the first impression you make, there are exceptions. When the sun sign is reinforced by other planets in the same sign, this might overpower the impression of the rising sign. For instance, a Leo sun plus a Leo Venus and Leo Jupiter would counteract the more conservative image that would otherwise be conveyed by the person's Capricorn ascendant.

Those born early in the morning when the sun was on the horizon will be most likely to project the image of their sun sign. These people are often called a "double Aries" or a "double Virgo" because the same sun sign and ascendant reinforce each other.

Find Your Rising Sign

Look up your rising sign from the chart at the end of this chapter. Since rising signs change every two hours, it is important to know your birth time as close to the minute as possible. Even a few minutes' difference could change the rising sign and therefore the setup of your chart. If you are unsure about the exact time, but know within a few hours, check the following descriptions to see which is most like the personality you project.

Aries Rising: Alpha Energy

You are the most aggressive version of your sun sign, with boundless energy that can be used productively if it's channeled in the right direction. Watch a tendency to overreact emotionally and blow your top. You come across as openly competitive, a positive asset in business or sports. Be on guard against impatience, which could lead to head injuries. Your walk and bearing could have the telltale head-forward Aries posture. You may wear more bright colors, especially red, than others of your sign. You may also have a tendency to drive your car faster.

Can you see the alpha Aries tendency in Barbra Streisand (a sun-sign Taurus) and Bette Midler (a sun-sign Sagittarius)?

Taurus Rising: Down to Earth

You're slow-moving, with a beautiful (or distinctive) speaking or singing voice that can be especially soothing or melodious. You probably surround yourself with comfort, good food, luxurious environments, and other sensual pleasures. You prefer welcoming others into your home to gadding about. You may have a talent for business, especially in trading, appraising, and real estate. A Taurus ascendant gives a well-padded physique that gains weight easily, like Liza Minnelli. This ascendant can also endow females with a curvaceous beauty.

Gemini Rising: A Way with Words

You're naturally sociable, with lighter, more ethereal mannerisms than others of your sign, especially if you're female.

You love to communicate with people, and express your ideas and feelings easily, like British prime minister Tony Blair. You may have a talent for writing or public speaking. You thrive on variety, a constantly changing scene, and a lively social life. However, you may relate to others at a deeper level than might be suspected. And you will be far more sympathetic and caring than you project. You will probably travel widely, changing partners and jobs several times (or juggle two at once). Physically, your nerves are quite sensitive. Occasionally, you would benefit from a calm, tranquil atmosphere away from your usual social scene.

Cancer Rising: Nurturing Instincts

You are naturally acquisitive, possessive, private, a moneymaker, like Bill Gates or Michael Bloomberg. You easily pick up on others' needs and feelings—a great gift in business, the arts, and personal relationships. But you must guard against overreacting or taking things too personally, especially during full moon periods. Find creative outlets for your natural nurturing gifts, such as helping the less fortunate, particularly children. Your insights would be helpful in psychology. Your desire to feed and care for others would be useful in the restaurant, hotel, or child-care industries. You may be especially fond of wearing romantic old clothes, collecting antiques, and, of course, dining on exquisite food. Since your body may retain fluids, pay attention to your diet. To relax, escape to places near water.

Leo Rising: Diva Dazzle

You may come across as more poised than you really feel. However, you play it to the hilt, projecting a proud royal presence. A Leo ascendant gives you a natural flair for drama, like Marilyn Monroe, and you might be accused of stealing the spotlight. You'll also project a much more outgoing, optimistic, sunny personality than others of your sign. You take care to please your public by always projecting your best star quality, probably tossing a luxuriant mane of hair, sporting a striking hairstyle, or dressing to impress. Females often dazzle with spectacular jewelry. Since you may have a strong parental nature, you could well be the regal family matriarch or patriarch, like George W. Bush.

Virgo Rising: High Standards

Virgo rising masks your inner nature with a practical, analytical outer image. You seem neat, orderly, more particular than others of your sign. Others in your life may feel they must live up to your high standards. Though at times you may be openly critical, this masks a well-meaning desire to have only the best for loved ones. Your sharp eye for details could be used in the financial world, or your literary skills could draw you to teaching or publishing. The healing arts, health care, and service-oriented professions attract many with a Virgo ascendant. You're likely to take good care of yourself, with great attention to health, diet, and exercise, like Madonna. You might even show some hypochondriac tendencies, like Woody Allen. Physically, you may have a very sensitive digestive system.

Libra Rising: The Charmer

Libra rising gives you a charming, social public persona, like Bill Clinton. You tend to avoid confrontations in relationships, preferring to smooth the way or negotiate diplomatically rather than give in to an emotional reaction. Because you are interested in all aspects of a situation, you may be slow to reach decisions. Physically, you'll have good proportions and symmetry. You will move with natural grace and balance. You're likely to have pleasing, if not beautiful, facial features, with a winning smile, like Cary Grant. You'll show natural good taste and harmony in your clothes and home decor. Legal, diplomatic, or public relations professions could draw your interest.

Scorpio Rising: An Air of Mystery

You project an intriguing air of mystery with this ascendant, as the Scorpio secretiveness and sense of underlying power combines with your sun sign. As with Jackie O, there's more to you than meets the eye. You seem like someone who is always in control and who can move comfortably in the world of power. Your physical look comes across as intense. Many of you have remarkable eyes, with a direct, penetrating gaze. But you'll never reveal your private agenda, and you tend to keep your true feelings under wraps (watch a tendency toward paranoia). You may have an interesting romantic history with secret love affairs, like Grace Kelly. Many of you heighten your air of mystery by wearing black. You're happiest near water and should provide yourself with a seaside retreat.

Sagittarius Rising: The Explorer

You travel with this ascendant. You may also be a more outdoor, sportive type, with an athletic, casual, outgoing air. Your moods are camouflaged with cheerful optimism or a philosophical attitude. Though you don't hesitate to speak your mind, like Ted Turner, who was called the Mouth of the South, you can also laugh at your troubles or crack a joke more easily than others of your sign. A Sagittarius ascendant can also draw you to the field of higher education or to spiritual life. You'll seem to have less attachment to things and people, and may explore the globe. Your strong, fast legs are a physical bonus.

Capricorn Rising: Serious Business

This rising sign makes you come across as serious, goal-oriented, disciplined, and careful with cash. You are not one of the zodiac's big spenders, though you might splurge occasionally on items with good investment value. You're the traditional, conservative type in dress and environment, and you might come across as quite normal and business-like, like Rupert Murdoch. You'll function well in a structured or corporate environment where you can climb to the top. (You are always aware of who's the boss.) In your personal life, you could be a loner or a single parent who is "father and mother" to your children.

Aquarius Rising: One of a Kind

You come across as less concerned about what others think and could even be a bit eccentric. You're more at ease with groups of people than others in your sign, and you may be attracted to public life, like Jay Leno. Your appearance may be unique, either unconventional or unimportant to you. Those of you whose sun is in a water sign (Cancer, Scorpio, Pisces) may exercise your nurturing qualities with a large group, an extended family, or a day-care or community center.

Pisces Rising: Romantic Roles

Your creative, nurturing talents are heightened and so is your ability to project emotional drama. And, like Antonio Banderas, your dreamy eyes and poetic air bring out the protective instinct in others. You could be attracted to the arts, especially theater, dance, film, and photography, or to psychology, spiritual practice, and charity work. You are happiest when you are using your creative ability to help others. Since you are vulnerable to mood swings, it is especially important for you to find interesting, creative work where you can express your talents and heighten your self-esteem. Accentuate the positive. Be wary of escapist tendencies, particularly involving alcohol or drugs to which you are supersensitive, like Whitney Houston.

RISING SIGNS—A.M. BIRTHS

	1 AM	2 AM	3 AM	4 AM	5 AM	6 AM	7 AM	8 AM	9 AM	10 AM	11 AM	12 NOON
Jan 1	Lib	Sc	Sc	Sc	Sag	Sag	Cap	Cap	Aq	Aq	Pis	Ar
Jan 9	Lib	Sc	Sc	Sag	Sag	Sag	Cap	Cap	Aq	Pis	Ar	Tau
Jan 17	Sc	Sc	Sc	Sag	Sag	Cap	Cap	Aq	Aq	Pis	Ar	Tau
Jan 25	Sc	Sc	Sag	Sag	Sag	Cap	Cap	Aq	Pis	Ar	Tau	Tau
Feb 2	Sc	Sc	Sag	Sag	Cap	Cap	Aq	Pis	Pis	Ar	Tau	Gem
Feb 10	Sc	Sag	Sag	Sag	Cap	Cap	Aq	Pis	Ar	Tau	Tau	Gem
Feb 18	Sc	Sag	Sag	Cap	Cap	Aq	Pis	Pis	Ar	Tau	Gem	Gem
Feb 26	Sag	Sag	Sag	Cap	Aq	Aq	Pis	Ar	Tau	Tau	Gem	Gem
Mar 6	Sag	Sag	Cap	Cap	Aq	Pis	Pis	Ar	Tau	Gem	Gem	Can
Mar 14	Sag	Cap	Cap	Aq	Aq	Pis	Ar	Tau	Tau	Gem	Gem	Can
Mar 22	Sag	Cap	Cap	Aq	Pis	Ar	Ar	Tau	Gem	Gem	Can	Can
Mar 30	Cap	Cap	Aq	Pis	Pis	Ar	Tau	Tau	Gem	Can	Can	Can
Apr 7	Cap	Cap	Aq	Pis	Ar	Ar	Tau	Gem	Gem	Can	Can	Leo
Apr 14	Cap	Aq	Aq	Pis	Ar	Tau	Tau	Gem	Gem	Can	Can	Leo
Apr 22	Cap	Aq	Pis	Ar	Ar	Tau	Gem	Gem	Gem	Can	Leo	Leo
Apr 30	Aq	Aq	Pis	Ar	Tau	Tau	Gem	Can	Can	Can	Leo	Leo
May 8	Aq	Pis	Ar	Ar	Tau	Gem	Gem	Can	Can	Leo	Leo	Leo
May 16	Aq	Pis	Ar	Tau	Gem	Gem	Can	Can	Can	Leo	Leo	Vir
May 24	Pis	Ar	Ar	Tau	Gem	Gem	Can	Can	Leo	Leo	Leo	Vir
June 1	Pis	Ar	Tau	Gem	Gem	Can	Can	Can	Leo	Leo	Vir	Vir
June 9	Ar	Ar	Tau	Gem	Gem	Can	Can	Leo	Leo	Leo	Vir	Vir
June 17	Ar	Tau	Gem	Gem	Can	Can	Can	Leo	Leo	Vir	Vir	Vir
June 25	Tau	Tau	Gem	Gem	Can	Can	Leo	Leo	Leo	Vir	Vir	Lib
July 3	Tau	Gem	Gem	Can	Can	Can	Leo	Leo	Vir	Vir	Vir	Lib
July 11	Tau	Gem	Gem	Can	Can	Leo	Leo	Leo	Vir	Vir	Lib	Lib
July 18	Gem	Gem	Can	Can	Can	Leo	Leo	Vir	Vir	Vir	Lib	Lib
July 26	Gem	Gem	Can	Can	Leo	Leo	Leo	Vir	Vir	Vir	Lib	Lib
Aug 3	Gem	Can	Can	Can	Leo	Leo	Vir	Vir	Vir	Lib	Lib	Sc
Aug 11	Gem	Can	Can	Leo	Leo	Leo	Vir	Vir	Lib	Lib	Lib	Sc
Aug 18	Can	Can	Can	Leo	Leo	Vir	Vir	Vir	Lib	Lib	Sc	Sc
Aug 27	Can	Can	Leo	Leo	Leo	Vir	Vir	Lib	Lib	Lib	Sc	Sc
Sept 4	Can	Can	Leo	Leo	Leo	Vir	Vir	Lib	Lib	Lib	Sc	Sc
Sept 12	Can	Leo	Leo	Leo	Vir	Vir	Lib	Lib	Lib	Sc	Sc	Sag
Sept 20	Leo	Leo	Leo	Vir	Vir	Vir	Lib	Lib	Sc	Sc	Sc	Sag
Sept 28	Leo	Leo	Leo	Vir	Vir	Lib	Lib	Lib	Sc	Sc	Sag	Sag
Oct 6	Leo	Leo	Vir	Vir	Vir	Lib	Lib	Sc	Sc	Sc	Sag	Sag
Oct 14	Leo	Vir	Vir	Vir	Lib	Lib	Lib	Sc	Sc	Sag	Sag	Cap
Oct 22	Leo	Vir	Vir	Lib	Lib	Lib	Sc	Sc	Sc	Sag	Sag	Cap
Oct 30	Vir	Vir	Vir	Lib	Lib	Sc	Sc	Sc	Sag	Sag	Cap	Cap
Nov 7	Vir	Vir	Lib	Lib	Lib	Sc	Sc	Sc	Sag	Sag	Cap	Cap
Nov 15	Vir	Vir	Lib	Lib	Sc	Sc	Sc	Sag	Sag	Cap	Cap	Aq
Nov 23	Vir	Lib	Lib	Lib	Sc	Sc	Sag	Sag	Sag	Cap	Cap	Aq
Dec 1	Vir	Lib	Lib	Sc	Sc	Sc	Sag	Sag	Cap	Cap	Aq	Aq
Dec 9	Lib	Lib	Lib	Sc	Sc	Sag	Sag	Sag	Cap	Cap	Aq	Pis
Dec 18	Lib	Lib	Sc	Sc	Sc	Sag	Sag	Cap	Cap	Aq	Aq	Pis
Dec 28	Lib	Lib	Sc	Sc	Sag	Sag	Sag	Cap	Aq	Aq	Pis	Ar

RISING SIGNS—P.M. BIRTHS

	1 PM	2 PM	3 PM	4 PM	5 PM	6 PM	7 PM	8 PM	9 PM	10 PM	11 PM	12 MIDNIGHT
Jan 1	Tau	Gem	Gem	Can	Can	Can	Leo	Leo	Vir	Vir	Vir	Lib
Jan 9	Tau	Gem	Gem	Can	Can	Leo	Leo	Leo	Vir	Vir	Vir	Lib
Jan 17	Gem	Gem	Can	Can	Can	Leo	Leo	Vir	Vir	Vir	Lib	Lib
Jan 25	Gem	Gem	Can	Can	Leo	Leo	Leo	Vir	Vir	Lib	Lib	Lib
Feb 2	Gem	Can	Can	Can	Leo	Leo	Vir	Vir	Vir	Lib	Lib	Sc
Feb 10	Gem	Can	Can	Leo	Leo	Leo	Vir	Vir	Lib	Lib	Lib	Sc
Feb 18	Can	Can	Can	Leo	Leo	Vir	Vir	Vir	Lib	Lib	Sc	Sc
Feb 26	Can	Can	Leo	Leo	Leo	Vir	Vir	Lib	Lib	Lib	Sc	Sc
Mar 6	Can	Leo	Leo	Leo	Vir	Vir	Vir	Lib	Lib	Sc	Sc	Sc
Mar 14	Can	Leo	Leo	Vir	Vir	Vir	Lib	Lib	Lib	Sc	Sc	Sag
Mar 22	Leo	Leo	Leo	Vir	Vir	Lib	Lib	Lib	Sc	Sc	Sc	Sag
Mar 30	Leo	Leo	Vir	Vir	Vir	Lib	Lib	Sc	Sc	Sc	Sag	Sag
Apr 7	Leo	Leo	Vir	Vir	Lib	Lib	Lib	Sc	Sc	Sc	Sag	Sag
Apr 14	Leo	Vir	Vir	Vir	Lib	Lib	Sc	Sc	Sc	Sag	Sag	Cap
Apr 22	Leo	Vir	Vir	Lib	Lib	Lib	Sc	Sc	Sc	Sag	Sag	Cap
Apr 30	Vir	Vir	Vir	Lib	Lib	Sc	Sc	Sc	Sag	Sag	Cap	Cap
May 8	Vir	Vir	Lib	Lib	Lib	Sc	Sc	Sag	Sag	Sag	Cap	Cap
May 16	Vir	Vir	Lib	Lib	Sc	Sc	Sc	Sag	Sag	Cap	Cap	Aq
May 24	Vir	Lib	Lib	Lib	Sc	Sc	Sag	Sag	Sag	Cap	Cap	Aq
June 1	Vir	Lib	Lib	Sc	Sc	Sc	Sag	Sag	Cap	Cap	Aq	Aq
June 9	Lib	Lib	Lib	Sc	Sc	Sag	Sag	Sag	Cap	Cap	Aq	Pis
June 17	Lib	Lib	Sc	Sc	Sc	Sag	Sag	Cap	Cap	Aq	Aq	Pis
June 25	Lib	Lib	Sc	Sc	Sag	Sag	Sag	Cap	Cap	Aq	Pis	Ar
July 3	Lib	Sc	Sc	Sc	Sag	Sag	Cap	Cap	Aq	Aq	Pis	Ar
July 11	Lib	Sc	Sc	Sag	Sag	Sag	Cap	Cap	Aq	Pis	Ar	Tau
July 18	Sc	Sc	Sc	Sag	Sag	Cap	Cap	Aq	Aq	Pis	Ar	Tau
July 26	Sc	Sc	Sag	Sag	Sag	Cap	Cap	Aq	Pis	Ar	Tau	Tau
Aug 3	Sc	Sc	Sag	Sag	Cap	Cap	Aq	Aq	Pis	Ar	Tau	Gem
Aug 11	Sc	Sag	Sag	Sag	Cap	Cap	Aq	Pis	Ar	Tau	Tau	Gem
Aug 18	Sc	Sag	Sag	Cap	Cap	Aq	Pis	Pis	Ar	Tau	Gem	Gem
Aug 27	Sag	Sag	Sag	Cap	Cap	Aq	Pis	Ar	Tau	Tau	Gem	Gem
Sept 4	Sag	Sag	Cap	Cap	Aq	Pis	Pis	Ar	Tau	Gem	Gem	Can
Sept 12	Sag	Sag	Cap	Aq	Aq	Pis	Ar	Tau	Tau	Gem	Gem	Can
Sept 20	Sag	Cap	Cap	Aq	Pis	Pis	Ar	Tau	Gem	Gem	Can	Can
Sept 28	Cap	Cap	Aq	Aq	Pis	Ar	Tau	Tau	Gem	Gem	Can	Can
Oct 6	Cap	Cap	Aq	Pis	Pis	Ar	Ar	Tau	Gem	Gem	Can	Leo
Oct 14	Cap	Aq	Aq	Pis	Ar	Tau	Tau	Gem	Gem	Can	Can	Leo
Oct 22	Cap	Aq	Pis	Ar	Ar	Tau	Gem	Gem	Can	Can	Leo	Leo
Oct 30	Aq	Aq	Pis	Ar	Tau	Tau	Gem	Can	Can	Can	Leo	Leo
Nov 7	Aq	Aq	Pis	Ar	Tau	Tau	Gem	Can	Can	Can	Leo	Leo
Nov 15	Aq	Pis	Ar	Tau	Gem	Gem	Can	Can	Can	Leo	Leo	Vir
Nov 23	Pis	Ar	Ar	Tau	Gem	Gem	Can	Can	Leo	Leo	Leo	Vir
Dec 1	Pis	Ar	Tau	Gem	Gem	Can	Can	Can	Leo	Leo	Vir	Vir
Dec 9	Ar	Tau	Tau	Gem	Gem	Can	Can	Leo	Leo	Leo	Vir	Vir
Dec 18	Ar	Tau	Gem	Gem	Can	Can	Can	Leo	Leo	Vir	Vir	Vir
Dec 28	Tau	Tau	Gem	Gem	Can	Can	Leo	Leo	Vir	Vir	Vir	Lib

CHAPTER 8

Learn the Glyphs and Read Your Own Chart!

If you get to a certain point in astrology, you'll want to read your own chart (or someone else's). Or perhaps you'll have a reading and be given a copy of your chart by an astrologer. In either case, you'll be confronted by a circular chart covered with mysterious symbols—unreadable except by someone who has learned these glyphs.

Breaking into astrology requires cracking the ancient code that is a type of picture writing universally understood by astrologers. It's well worth the effort to learn these symbols. You'll not only be able to read a chart, but you will be able to make use of free charts available on any number of Internet sites and astrology software programs. This year, you can even take astrology with you on your PDA and read a chart on the go. But almost none of these programs show the planetary positions written in plain English, so you'll miss out if you don't learn the glyphs.

Each little symbol has built-in clues to help you decipher not only which sign or planet it represents, but what the object means in a more esoteric sense. Actually the physical act of writing the symbol is a mystical experience in itself, a way to invoke the deeper meaning of the sign or planet through age-old visual elements that have been with us since time began.

Since there are only twelve signs and ten planets (not counting a few asteroids and other space objects some astrologers use), it's a lot easier than learning to read a foreign language. Here's a code cracker for the glyphs, beginning with the glyphs for the planets. To those who already know their glyphs, don't just skim over the chapter.

These familiar graphics have hidden meanings you will discover!

The Glyphs for the Planets

The glyphs for the planets are easy to learn. They're simple combinations of the most basic visual elements: the circle, the semicircle or arc, and the cross. However, each component of a glyph has a special meaning in relation to the other parts of the symbol.

The circle, which has no beginning or end, is one of the oldest symbols of spirit or spiritual forces. Early diagrams of the heavens—spiritual territory—are shown in circular form. The never-ending line of the circle is the perfect symbol for eternity. The semicircle or arc is an incomplete circle, symbolizing the receptive, finite soul, which contains spiritual potential in the curving line.

The vertical line of the cross symbolizes movement from heaven to earth. The horizontal line describes temporal movement, here and now, in time and space. Combined in a cross, the vertical and horizontal planes symbolize manifestation in the material world.

The Sun Glyph ☉

The sun is always shown by this powerful solar symbol, a circle with a point in the center. The center point is you, your spiritual center, and the symbol represents your infinite personality incarnating (the point) into the finite cycles of birth and death.

The sun has been represented by a circle or disk since ancient Egyptian times when the solar disk represented the sun god, Ra. Some archaeologists believe the great stone circles found in England were centers of sun worship. This particular version of the symbol was brought into common use in the sixteenth century after German occultist and scholar Cornelius Agrippa (1486–1535) wrote a book called *Die Occulta Philosophia*, which became accepted as the authority in the field. Agrippa collected many medieval astrological and magical symbols in this book, which have been used by astrologers since then.

The Moon Glyph ☽

The moon glyph is the most recognizable symbol on a chart, a left-facing arc stylized into the crescent moon. As part of a circle, the arc symbolizes the potential fulfillment of the entire circle, the life force that is still incomplete. Therefore, it is the ideal representation of the reactive, receptive, emotional nature of the moon.

The Mercury Glyph ☿

Mercury contains all three elemental symbols: the crescent, the circle, and the cross in vertical order. This is the "Venus with a hat" glyph (compare with the symbol of Venus). With another stretch of the imagination, can't you see the winged cap of Mercury the messenger? Think of the upturned crescent as antennae that tune in and transmit messages from the sun, reminding you that Mercury is the way you communicate, the way your mind works. The upturned arc is receiving energy into the spirit or solar circle, which will later be translated into action on the material plane, symbolized by the cross. All the elements are equally sized because Mercury is neutral; it doesn't play favorites! This planet symbolizes objective, detached, unemotional thinking.

The Venus Glyph ♀

Here the relationship is between two components: the circle of spirit and the cross of matter. Spirit is elevated over matter, pulling it upward. Venus asks, "What is beautiful? What do you like best? What do you love to have done to you?" Consequently, Venus determines both your ideal of beauty and what feels good sensually. It governs your own allure and power to attract, as well as what attracts and pleases you.

The Mars Glyph ♂

In this glyph, the cross of matter is stylized into an arrow-head pointed up and outward, propelled by the circle of spirit. With a little imagination, you can visualize it as the shield and spear of Mars, the ancient god of war. You can deduce that Mars embodies your spiritual energy projected into the outer world. It's your assertiveness, your initiative, your aggressive drive, what you like to do to others, your temper. If you know someone's Mars, you know whether they'll blow up when angry or do a slow burn. Your task is to use your outgoing Mars energy wisely and well.

The Jupiter Glyph ♃

Jupiter is the basic cross of matter, with a large stylized crescent perched on the left side of the horizontal, temporal plane. You might think of the crescent as an open hand, because one meaning of Jupiter is "luck," what's handed to you. You don't have to work for what you get from Jupiter; it comes to you, if you're open to it.

The Jupiter glyph might also remind you of a jumbo jet plane, with a huge tail fin, about to take off. This is the planet of travel, mental and spiritual, of expanding your horizons via new ideas, new spiritual dimensions, and new places. Jupiter embodies the optimism and enthusiasm of the traveler about to embark on an exciting adventure.

The Saturn Glyph ♄

Flip Jupiter over, and you've got Saturn. This might not be immediately apparent because Saturn is usually stylized into an "h" form like the one shown here. The principle it expresses is the opposite of Jupiter's expansive tendencies. Saturn pulls you back to earth: the receptive arc is pushed down underneath the cross of matter. Before there are any rewards or expansion, the duties and obligations of the material world must be considered. Saturn says, "Stop, wait, finish your chores before you take off!"

Saturn's glyph also resembles the sickle of old "Father Time." Saturn was first known as Chronos, the Greek god of time, for time brings all matter to an end. When it was the most distant planet (before the discovery of Uranus), Saturn was believed to be the place where time stopped. After the soul departed from earth, it journeyed back to the outer reaches of the universe and finally stopped at Saturn, or at "the end of time."

The Uranus Glyph ♅

The glyph for Uranus is often stylized to form a capital *H* after Sir William Herschel, who discovered the planet. But the more esoteric version curves the two pillars of the H into crescent antennae, or "ears," like satellite disks receiving signals from space. These are perched on the horizontal material line of the cross of matter and pushed from below by the circle of the spirit. To many sci-fi fans, Uranus looks like an orbiting satellite.

Uranus channels the highest energy of all, the white electrical light of the universal spiritual force that holds the cosmos together. This pure electrical energy is gathered from all over the universe. Because Uranus energy doesn't follow any ordinary celestial drumbeat, it can't be controlled or predicted (which is also true of those who are strongly influenced by this eccentric planet). In the symbol, this energy is manifested through the balance of polarities (the two opposite arms of the glyph) like the two polarized wires of a lightbulb.

The Neptune Glyph ♆

Neptune's glyph is usually stylized to look like a trident, the weapon of the Roman god Neptune. However, on a more esoteric level, it shows the large upturned crescent of the soul pierced through by the cross of matter. Neptune nails down, or materializes, soul energy, bringing impulses from the soul level into manifestation. That is why Neptune is associated with imagination or "imagining in," making an image of the soul. Neptune works through feelings, sensitivity, and the mystical capacity to bring the divine into the earthly realm.

The Pluto Glyph ♀

Pluto is written two ways. One is a composite of the letters *PL,* the first two letters of the word Pluto and coincidentally the initials of Percival Lowell, one of the planet's discovers. The other, more esoteric symbol is a small circle above a large open crescent that surmounts the cross of matter. This depicts Pluto's power to regenerate. Imagine a new little spirit emerging from the sheltering cup of the soul. Pluto rules the forces of life and death. After this planet has passed a sensitive point in your chart, you are transformed, reborn in some way.

Sci-fi fans might visualize this glyph as a small satellite (the circle) being launched. It was shortly after Pluto's discovery that we learned how to harness the nuclear forces that made space exploration possible. Pluto rules the transformative power of atomic energy, which totally changed our lives and from which there is no turning back.

The Glyphs for the Signs

On an astrology chart, the glyph for the sign will appear after that of the planet. For example, when you see the moon glyph followed first by a number and then by another glyph representing the sign, this means that the moon was passing over a certain degree of that astrological sign at the time of the chart. On the dividing lines between the houses on your chart, you'll find the symbol for the sign that rules the house.

Because sun sign symbols do not contain the same basic geometric components of the planetary glyphs, we must look elsewhere for clues to their meanings. Many have been passed down from ancient Egyptian and Chaldean civilizations with few modifications. Others have been adapted over the centuries.

In deciphering many of the glyphs, you'll often find that the symbols reveal a dual nature of the sign, which is not always apparent in the usual sun sign descriptions. For instance, the Gemini glyph is similar to the Roman numeral for two, and reveals this sign's longing to discover a twin soul. The Cancer glyph may be interpreted as resembling either the nurturing breasts or the self-protective claws of a crab, both symbols associated with the contrasting qualities of this sign. Libra's glyph embodies the duality of the spirit balanced with material reality. The Sagittarius glyph shows that the aspirant must also carry along the earthly animal nature in his quest. The Capricorn sea goat is another symbol with dual emphasis. The goat climbs high, yet is always pulled back by the deep waters of the unconscious. Aquarius embodies the double waves of mental detachment, balanced by the desire for connection with others, in a friendly way. Finally, the two fishes of Pisces, which are forever tied together, show the duality of the soul and the spirit that must be reconciled.

The Aries Glyph ♈

Since the symbol for Aries is the Ram, this glyph is obviously associated with a ram's horns, which characterize one aspect of the Aries personality—an aggressive, me-first, leaping-headfirst attitude. But the symbol can be interpreted in other ways as well. Some astrologers liken it to a fountain of energy, which Aries people also embody. The first sign of the zodiac bursts on the scene eagerly, ready to go. Another analogy is to the eyebrows and nose of the human head, which Aries rules, and the thinking power that is initiated by the brain.

One theory of this symbol links it to the Egyptian god Amun, represented by a ram in ancient times. As Amun-Ra, this god was believed to embody the creator of the universe, the leader of all the other gods. This relates easily to the position of Aries as the leader (or first sign) of the zodiac, which begins at the spring equinox, a time of the year when nature is renewed.

The Taurus Glyph ♉

This is another easy glyph to draw and identify. It takes little imagination to decipher the bull's head with long curving horns. Like its symbol the Bull, the archetypal Taurus is slow to anger but ferocious when provoked, as well as stubborn, steady, and sensual. Another association is the larynx (and thyroid) of the throat area (ruled by Taurus) and the eustachian tubes running up to the ears, which coincides with the relationship of Taurus to the voice, song, and music. Many famous singers, musicians, and composers have prominent Taurus influences.

Many ancient religions involved a bull as the central figure in fertility rites or initiations, usually symbolizing the victory of man over his animal nature. Another possible origin is in the sacred bull of Egypt, who embodied the incarnate form of Osiris, god of death and resurrection. In early Christian imagery, the Taurus Bull represented St. Luke.

The Gemini Glyph ♊

The standard glyph immediately calls to mind the Roman numeral for two (II) and the Twins symbol, as it is called, for Gemini. In almost all drawings and images used for this sign, the relationship between two persons is emphasized. Usually one twin will be touching the other, which signifies communication, human contact, the desire to share.

The top line of the Gemini glyph indicates mental communication, while the bottom line indicates shared physical space.

The most famous Gemini legend is that of the twin sons, Castor and Pollux, one of whom had a mortal father while the other was the son of Zeus, king of the gods. When it came time for the mortal twin to die, his grief-stricken brother pleaded with Zeus, who agreed to let them spend half the year on earth in mortal form and half in immortal life, with the gods on Mount Olympus. This reflects a basic duality of humankind, which possesses an immortal soul yet is also subject to the limits of mortality.

The Cancer Glyph ♋

Two convenient images relate to the Cancer glyph. It is easiest to decode the curving claws of the Cancer symbol, the Crab. Like the crab's, Cancer's element is water. This sensitive sign also has a hard protective shell to protect its tender interior. The crab must be wily to escape predators, scampering sideways and hiding under rocks. The crab also responds to the cycles of the moon, as do all shellfish. The other image is that of two female breasts, which Cancer rules, showing that this is a sign that nurtures and protects others as well as itself.

In ancient Egypt, Cancer was also represented by the scarab beetle, a symbol of regeneration and eternal life.

The Leo Glyph ♌

Notice that the Leo glyph seems to be an extension of Cancer's glyph, with a significant difference. In the Cancer glyph, the lines curve inward protectively. The Leo glyph expresses energy outwardly. And there is no duality in the symbol, the Lion, or in Leo, the sign.

Lions have belonged to the sign of Leo since earliest times. It is not difficult to imagine the king of beasts with his sweeping mane and curling tail from this glyph. The upward sweep of the glyph easily describes the positive energy of Leo: the flourishing tail, their flamboyant qualities. Anther analogy, perhaps a stretch of the imagination, is that of a heart leaping up with joy and enthusiasm, also very typical of Leo, which also rules the heart. In early Christian imagery, the Leo Lion represented St. Mark.

The Virgo Glyph ♍

You can read much into this mysterious glyph. For instance, it could represent the initials of "Mary Virgin," or a young woman holding a staff of wheat, or stylized female genitalia, all common interpretations. The M shape might also remind you that Virgo is ruled by Mercury. The cross beneath the symbol reveals the grounded, practical nature of this earth sign.

The earliest zodiacs link Virgo with the Egyptian goddess Isis, who gave birth to the god Horus after her husband Osiris had been killed, in the archetype of a miraculous conception. There are many ancient statues of Isis nursing her baby son, which are reminiscent of medieval Virgin and Child motifs. This sign has also been associated with the image of the Holy Grail, when the Virgo symbol was substituted with a chalice.

The Libra Glyph ♎

It is not difficult to read the standard image for Libra, the Scales, into this glyph. There is another meaning, however, that is equally relevant: the setting sun as it descends over the horizon. Libra's natural position on the zodiac wheel is the descendant, or sunset position (as the Aries natural position is the ascendant, or rising sign). Both images relate to Libra's personality. Libra is always weighing pros and cons for a balanced decision. In the sunset image, the sun (male) hovers over the horizontal earth (female) before setting. Libra is the space between these lines, harmonizing yin and yang, spiritual and material, male and female; ideal and real worlds. The glyph has also been linked to the kidneys, which are ruled by Libra.

The Scorpio Glyph ♏

With its barbed tail, this glyph is easy to identify as the Scorpion for the sign of Scorpio. It also represents the male sexual parts, over which the sign rules. From the arrowhead, you can draw the conclusion that Mars was once its ruler. Some earlier Egyptian glyphs for Scorpio represent it as an erect serpent, so the Serpent is an alternate symbol.

Another symbol for Scorpio, which is not identifiable in this glyph, is the Eagle. Scorpios can go to extremes, either in soaring like the eagle or self-destructing like the scorpion. In early Christian imagery, which often used zodiacal symbols, the Scorpio Eagle was chosen to symbolize the intense apostle St. John the Evangelist.

The Sagittarius Glyph ♐

This is one of the easiest to spot and draw: an upward pointing arrow lifting up a cross. The arrow is pointing skyward, while the cross represents the four elements of the material world, which the arrow must convey. Elevating materiality into spirituality is an important Sagittarius quality, which explains why this sign is associated with higher learning, religion, philosophy, travel—the aspiring professions. Sagittarius can also send barbed arrows of frankness in the pursuit of truth, so the Archer symbol for Sagittarius is apt. (Sagittarius is also the sign of the supersalesman.)

Sagittarius is symbolically represented by the centaur, a mythological creature who is half man, half horse, aiming his arrow toward the skies. Though Sagittarius is motivated by spiritual aspiration, it also must balance the powerful appetites of the animal nature. The centaur Chiron, a figure in Greek mythology, became a wise teacher who, after many adventures and world travels, was killed by a poisoned arrow.

The Capricorn Glyph ♑

One of the most difficult symbols to draw, this glyph may take some practice. It is a representation of the sea goat: a mythical animal that is a goat with a curving fish's tail. The goat part of Capricorn wants to leave the waters of the emotions and climb to the elevated areas of life. But the fish tail is the unconscious, the deep chaotic psychic level that draws the goat back. Capricorn is often trying to escape the deep, feeling part of life by submerging himself in work, steadily ascending to the top. To some people, the glyph represents a seated figure with a bent knee, a reminder that Capricorn governs the knee area of the body.

An interesting aspect of this glyph is the contrast of the sharp pointed horns—which represent the penetrating, shrewd, conscious side of Capricorn—with the swishing tail—which represents its serpentine, unconscious, emotional force. One Capricorn legend, which dates from Roman times, tells of the earthy fertility god, Pan, who tried to save himself from uncontrollable sexual desires by jumping into the Nile. His upper body then turned into a goat, while the lower part became a fish. Later, Jupiter gave him a safe haven as a constellation in the skies.

The Aquarius Glyph ♒

This ancient water symbol can be traced back to an Egyptian hieroglyph representing streams of life force. Symbolized by the Water Bearer, Aquarius is distributor of the waters of life—the magic liquid of regeneration. The two waves can also be linked to the positive and negative charges of the electrical energy that Aquarius rules, a sort of universal wavelength. Aquarius is tuned in intuitively to higher forces via this electrical force. The duality of the glyph could also refer to the dual nature of Aquarius, a sign that runs hot and cold and that is friendly but also detached in the mental world of air signs.

In Greek legends, Aquarius is represented by Ganymede, who was carried to heaven by an eagle in order to become the cupbearer of Zeus and to supervise the annual flooding of the Nile. The sign later became associated with aviation and notions of flight.

The Pisces Glyph $\mathcal{H}$

Here is an abstraction of the familiar image of Pisces, two Fishes swimming in opposite directions yet bound together by a cord. The Fishes represent the spirit—which yearns for the freedom of heaven—and the soul—which remains attached to the desires of the temporal world. During life on earth, the spirit and the soul are bound together. When they complement each other, instead of pulling in opposite directions, they facilitate the Pisces creativity. The ancient version of this glyph, taken from the Egyptians, had no connecting line, which was added in the fourteenth century.

In another interpretation, it is said that the left fish indicates the direction of involution or the beginning of a cycle, while the right fish signifies the direction of evolution, the way to completion of a cycle. It's an appropriate grand finale for Pisces, the last sign of the zodiac.

CHAPTER 9

Astrology on Your Computer: Where to Find Software That Suits Your Budget and Ability

Once you've learned the basics of astrology, you'll be ready to practice reading charts. It's great fun to start out by analyzing the charts of friends and family so you can see how the planets manifest in real life. If you have a computer, there's no easier way than to use astrology software, which can calculate a chart in seconds and even help you interpret it.

When it comes to astrology software, there are endless options. How do you make the right choice? First, define your goals. Do you want to do charts of friends and family, study celebrity charts, or check the aspects every day on your Palm Pilot? Do you want to invest in a more comprehensive program that adapts to your changing needs as you learn astrology?

The good news is that there's a program for every level of interest in all price points—starting with free. For the dabbler, there are the affordable Winstar Express and the Astroscan shareware. For the serious student, there are Astrolog (free), Solar Fire, Kepler, Winstar Plus—software that does every technique on planets and gives you beautiful chart printouts. You can do a chart of someone you've just met on your PDA with Astracadabra. If you're a Mac user, you'll be satisfied with the wonderful IO and Time Passages software.

However, since all the programs use the astrology symbols, or glyphs, for planets and signs, rather than written words, you should learn the glyphs before you purchase your software. Our chapter on the glyphs in this book will help you do just that. Here are some software options for you to explore.

Easy for Beginners

Time Passages

Designed for either a Macintosh or Windows computer, Time Passages is straightforward and easy to use. It allows you to generate charts and interpretation reports for yourself or friends and loved ones at the touch of a button. If you haven't yet learned the astrology symbols, this might be the program for you; just roll your mouse over any symbol of the planets, signs, or house cusps, and you'll be shown a description in plain English below the chart. Then click on the planet, sign, or house cusp and up pops a detailed interpretation. It couldn't be easier. A new basic edition, under fifty dollars at this writing, is bargain priced and ideal for beginners.

Time Passages
(866) 772-7876 (866-77-ASTRO)
Web site: www.astrograph.com

Growth Opportunities

Astrolabe

Astrolabe is one of the top astrology software resources. Check out the latest version of their powerful Solar Fire software for Windows. A breeze to use, it will grow with your increasing knowledge of astrology to the most sophisticated levels. This company also markets a variety of programs for all levels of expertise and a wide selection of computer-generated astrology readings. This is a good resource for innovative software as well as applications for older computers.

The Astrolabe Web site is a great place to start your astrology tour of the Internet. Visitors to the site are greeted with a chart of the time you log on. And you can get your chart calculated, also free, with an interpretation e-mailed to you.

Astrolabe
Box 1750-R
Brewster, MA 02631
Phone: (800) 843-6682
Web site: www.alabe.com

Matrix Software

You'll find a wide variety of software at student and advanced levels in all price ranges, demo disks, and lots of interesting readings. Check out Winstar Express, a powerful but reasonably priced program suitable for all skill levels. The Matrix Web site offers lots of fun activities for Web surfers, such as free readings from the *I Ching,* the runes, and the tarot. There are many free desktop backgrounds with astrology themes. Go here to connect with news groups and online discussions. Their online almanac helps you schedule the best day to sign on the dotted line, ask for a raise, or plant your tomatoes.

Matrix Software
126 South Michigan Ave.
Big Rapids, MI 49307
Phone: (800) 752-6387
Web site: www.astrologysoftware.com

Astro Communications Services (ACS)

Books, software for Mac and IBM compatibles, individual charts, and telephone readings are offered by this California company. Their freebies include astrology greeting cards and new moon reports. Find technical astrology materials here, such as *The American Ephemeris* and PC atlases. ACS will calculate and send charts to you, a valuable service if you do not have a computer.

ACS Publications
P.O. box 1646
El Cajon, CA 72022-1646
Phone: (800) 514-5070
Fax: (619) 631-0185
Web site: www.astrocom.com

Air Software

Here you'll find powerful, creative astrology software, and current stock market analysis. Financial astrology programs for stock market traders are a specialty. There are some interesting freebies at this site; check out the maps of eclipse paths for any year and a free astrology clock program.

Air Software
115 Caya Avenue
West Hartford, CT 06110
Phone: (800) 659-1247
Web site: www.alphee.com

Kepler: State of the Art

Here's a program that has everything. Gorgeous graphic images, audio-visual effects, and myriad sophisticated chart options are built into this fascinating software. It's even got an astrological encyclopedia, plus diagrams and images to help you understand advanced concepts. This program is expensive, but if you're serious about learning astrology, it's an investment that will grow with you! There's a cheaper scaled-down version called Pegasus for those who don't want all the features. Check out its features at www.astrologysoftwareshop.com.

Time Cycles Research: For Mac Users

Here's where Mac users can find astrology software that's as sophisticated as it gets. If you have a Mac, you'll love their beautiful graphic IO Series programs.

Time Cycles Research
P.O. Box 797
Waterford, CT 06385
Web site: www.timecycles.com

Shareware and Freeware: The Price Is Right!

Halloran Software: A Super Shareware Program

Check out Halloran Software's Web site (www.halloran. com), which offers several levels of Windows astrology software. Beginners should consider their Astrology for Windows shareware program, which is available in unregistered demo form as a free download and in registered form for a very reasonable price.

Astrolog

If you're computer-savvy, you can't go wrong with Walter Pullen's amazingly complete Astrolog program, which is offered absolutely free at the site. The Web address is www.astrolog.org/astrolog.htm.

Astrolog is an ultrasophisticated program with all the features of much more expensive programs. It comes in versions for all formats—DOS, Windows, Mac, UNIX—and has some cool features, such as a revolving globe and a constellation map. If you are looking for astrology software with bells and whistles that doesn't cost big bucks, this program has it all!

Astroscan

Surf to www.astroscan.ca for a free program called Astroscan. Stunning graphics and ease of use make this basic program a winner. Astroscan has a fun list of celebrity charts you can call up with a few clicks.

Programs for the Pocket PDA and Palm Pilot

Would you like to have astrology at your fingertips everywhere you go? No need to drag along your laptop. You can check the chart of the moment or of someone you've just met on your pocket PDA or Palm Pilot. As with most other programs, you'll need to know the astrological symbols in order to read the charts.

For the pocket PC that has the Microsoft Pocket PC 2002 or the Microsoft Windows Mobile 2003 operating system, there is the versatile Astracadabra, which can interchange charts with the popular Solar Fire software. It can be ordered at www.leelehman.com or www.astrologysoftwareshop.com.

For the Palm OS5 and compatible handheld devices, there is Astropocket from www.yves.robert.org/features.html. This is a shareware program, which allows you to use all the features free. However, you cannot store more than one chart at a time until you pay a mere twenty-eight-dollar registration fee for the complete version.

CHAPTER 10

How to Connect with Astrology Fans Around the Globe

Are you interested in connecting with other astrology fans? How about expanding your knowledge by studying with a famous astrologer or by attending international lectures and conferences, even astrological workshops in exotic places? The astrological community is ready to welcome you.

You need only type the word astrology into any Internet search engine and watch hundreds of listings of astrology-related sites pop up. There are local meetings and international conferences where you can connect with other astrologers, and books and tapes to help you study at home.

To help you sort out the variety of options available, here are our top picks of the Internet and the astrological community at large.

Nationwide Astrology Organizations and Conferences

National Council for Geocosmic Research (NCGR)

Whether you'd like to know more about such specialties as financial astrology or techniques for timing events, or if you'd prefer the psychological or mythological approach, you'll meet the top astrologers at conferences sponsored by the National Council for Geocosmic Research. NCGR is dedicated to providing quality education, bringing astrologers and astrology fans together at conferences, and promoting fellowship. Their course structure provides a systematized study of the many facets of astrology. The organization sponsors educational workshops, taped lectures, conferences, and a directory of professional astrologers. For an annual membership fee, you get their excellent publications and newsletters, plus the opportunity to network with other astrology buffs at local chapter events. (At this writing there are chapters in twenty-six states and four countries.)

To join NCGR for the latest information on upcoming events and chapters in your city, consult their Web site: www.geocosmic.org.

American Federation of Astrologers (AFA)

Established in 1938, this is one of the oldest astrological organizations in the United States. AFA offers conferences, conventions, and a thorough correspondence course. If you are looking for a reading, their interesting Web site will refer you to an accredited AFA astrologer.

AFA
P.O. Box 22040
Tempe, AZ 85285-2040
Phone: (888) 301-7630 or (480) 838-1751
Fax: (480) 838-8293
Web site: www.astrologers.com

Association for Astrological Networking (AFAN)

Did you know that astrologers are still being harassed for practicing astrology? AFAN provides support and legal information and works toward improving the public image of astrology. AFAN's network of local astrologers links with the international astrological community. Here are the people who will go to bat for astrology when it is attacked in the media. Everyone who cares about astrology should join!

AFAN
8306 Wilshire Boulevard
PMB 537
Beverly Hills, CA 90211
Phone: (800) 578-2326
E-mail: info@afan.org
Web site: www.afan.org

International Society for Astrology Research (ISAR)

An international organization of professional astrologers dedicated to encouraging the highest standards of quality in the field of astrology with an emphasis on research. Among ISAR's benefits are a quarterly journal, a weekly e-mail newsletter, frequent conferences, and a free membership directory.

ISAR
P.O. Box 38613
Los Angeles, CA 90038
Fax: (805) 933-0301
Web site: www.isarastrology.com

Astrology Magazines

In addition to articles by top astrologers, most of these have listings of astrology conferences, events, and local happenings.

Horoscope Guide
Kappa Publishing Group
Dept. 4
P.O. Box 2085
Marion, OH 43306-8121

Dell Horoscope
P.O. Box 54097
Boulder, CO 80322-4907

The Mountain Astrologer

A favorite magazine of astrology fans! *The Mountain Astrologer* also has an interesting Web site featuring the latest news from an astrological point of view, plus feature articles from the magazine.

The Mountain Astrologer
P.O. Box 970
Cedar Ridge, CA 95924
Phone: (800) 247-4828
Web site: www.mountainastrologer.com

Astrology College

Kepler College of Astrological Arts and Sciences

A degree-granting college, which is also a center of astrology, has long been the dream of the astrological community and is a giant step forward in providing credibility to the profession. Therefore, the opening of Kepler College in 2000 was a historical event for astrology. It is the only college in the western hemisphere authorized to issue B.A. and M.A. degrees in Astrological Studies. Here is where to study with the best scholars, teachers, and communicators in the field. A long-distance study program is available for those interested.

For more information, contact:

Kepler College of Astrological Arts and Sciences
4630 200th Street SW
Suite A-1
Lynnwood, WA 98036
Phone: (425) 673-4292
Fax: (425) 673-4983
Web site: www.kepler.edu

Our Favorite Web Sites

Of the thousands of astrological Web sites that come and go on the Internet, these have stood the test of time and are likely to still be operating when this book is published.

Astrodienst (www.astro.com)

Don't miss this fabulous international site that has long been one of the best astrology resources on the Internet. It's also a great place to view and download your own astrology chart. The world atlas on this site will give you the accurate longitude and latitude of your birthplace for setting up your horoscope. Then you can print out your free chart in a range of easy-to-read formats. Other attractions: a list of famous people born on your birth date, a feature that helps you choose the best vacation spot, plus articles by world-famous astrologers.

AstroDatabank (www.astrodatabank.com)

When the news is breaking, you can bet this site will be the first to get accurate birthdays of the headliners. The late astrologer Lois Rodden was a stickler for factual information and her meticulous research is being continued, much to the benefit of the astrological community. The Web site specializes in charts of current newsmakers, political figures, and international celebrities. You can also participate in discussions and analysis of the charts and see what some of the world's best astrologers have to say about them. Their AstroDatabank program, which you can purchase at the site, provides thousands of verified birthdays sorted into categories. It's an excellent research tool.

StarIQ (www.stariq.com)

Find out how top astrologers view the latest headlines at the must-see StarIQ site. Many of the best minds in astrology comment on the latest news, stock market ups and downs, political contenders. You can sign up to receive e-mail forecasts at the most important times keyed to your individual chart. (This is one of the best of the many online forecasts.)

Astrology Books (www.astroamerica.com)

The Astrology Center of America sells a wide selection of books on all aspects of astrology, from the basics to the most advanced, at this online bookstore. Also available are many hard-to-find and recycled books.

Astrology Scholars' Sites

See what one of astrology's great teachers, Robert Hand, has to offer on his site: www.robhand.com. A leading expert on the history of astrology, he's on the cutting edge of the latest research.

The Project Hindsight group of astrologers is devoted to restoring the astrology of the Hellenistic period, the primary source for all later Western astrology. There are fascinating articles for astrology fans on this site, www.project hindsight.com.

Financial Astrology Sites

Financial astrology is a hot specialty, with many tipsters, players, and theorists. There are online columns, newsletters, specialized financial astrology software, and mutual funds run by astrology seers. One of the more respected financial astrologers is Ray Merriman, whose column on www.stariq.com is a must read for those following the bulls and bears. Other top financial astrologers offer tips and forecasts at the www.afund.com and www.alphee.com sites.

CHAPTER 11

Got a Big Question? A Personal Reading Might Give You the Answer

Life can sometimes leave you feeling bewitched, bothered, and bewildered, as the song goes. Whether you're faced with a seemingly insurmountable problem or would simply like an objective opinion, it might be helpful to consult a professional astrologer who will take all the facets of your astrological chart into consideration. A good reading can give you peace of mind by confirming those mysterious intuitive feelings that you can't quite identify. It can give you insights on your situation that will lead you to better choices, perhaps ones that have been blocked by a blind spot.

A reading can answer some very practical questions as well, such as setting the perfect date for a wedding, a crucial job interview, or a real estate closing. If a partnership is turning sour, insights from a reading might help you put the relationship back on track. Or, after a reading, you might understand the compromises and adjustments needed to make it work. For example, one astrologically minded business team has charts done to help them work well together. Charts for family members might be done to help improve home life or figure out some complicated family dynamics.

Another good reason for a reading is to improve your personal knowledge of astrology by consulting someone who has years of experience analyzing charts. You might choose someone with a special technique that intrigues you. Armed with the knowledge of your chart that you have acquired so far, you can learn to interpret subtle nuances or gain perspective on your talents and abilities.

But what kind of reading should you have? Besides one-on-one readings with a professional astrologer, there are personal readings by mail, telephone, Internet, and tape. Well-advertised computer-generated reports and celebrity-sponsored readings are sure to attract your attention.

Done by a qualified astrologer, the personal reading can be an empowering experience if you want to reach your full potential, size up a lover or business situation, or find out what the future has in store. There are astrologers who are specialists in certain areas such as finance or medical astrology. And, unfortunately, there are many questionable practitioners who range from streetwise gypsy fortune-tellers to unscrupulous scam artists.

The following basic guidelines can help you sort out your options to find the reading that's right for you.

One-on-One Consultations with a Professional Astrologer

Nothing compares to a one-on-one consultation with a professional astrologer who has analyzed thousands of charts and can pinpoint the potential in yours. During your reading, you can get your specific questions answered. For instance, how to get along better with your mate or coworker. There are many astrologers who now combine their skills with training in psychology and are well-suited to help you examine your alternatives.

To give you an accurate reading, an astrologer needs certain information from you: the date, time, and place where you were born. (A horoscope can be cast about anyone or anything that has a specific time and place.) Most astrologers will then enter this information into a computer, which will calculate a chart in seconds. From the resulting chart, the astrologer will do an interpretation.

If you don't know your exact birth time, you can usually locate it at the Bureau of Vital Statistics at the city hall or county seat of the state where you were born. If you still have no success in getting your time of birth, some astrologers can estimate an approximate birth time by using past events in your life to determine the chart. This technique is called *rectification*.

How to Find an Astrologer

Choose your astrologer with the same care as you would any trusted adviser such as a doctor, lawyer, or banker. Unfortunately, anyone can claim to be an astrologer—to date, there is no licensing of astrologers or universally established professional criteria. However, there are nationwide organizations of serious, committed astrologers that can help you in your search.

Good places to start your investigation are organizations such as the American Federation of Astrologers (AFA) or the National Council for Geocosmic Research (NCGR), which offer a program of study and certification. If you live near a major city, there is sure to be an active NCGR chapter or astrology club in your area; many are listed in astrology magazines available at your local newsstand. In response to many requests for referrals, both the AFA and the NCGR have directories of professional astrologers listed on their Web sites; these directories include a glossary of terms and an explanation of specialties within the astrological field. Contact the NCGR and AFA headquarters for information (see chapter 10 in this book).

Warning Signals

As a potentially lucrative freelance business, astrology has always attracted self-styled experts who may not have the knowledge or the counseling experience to give a helpful reading. These astrologers can range from the well-meaning amateur to the charlatan or street-corner gypsy who has for many years given astrology a bad name. Be very wary of astrologers who claim to have occult powers or who make pretentious claims of celebrated clients or miraculous achievements. You can often tell from the initial phone conversation if the astrologer is legitimate. He or she should ask for your birthday time and place, then conduct the conversation in a professional manner. Any astrologer who gives a reading based only on your sun sign is highly suspect.

When you arrive at the reading, the astrologer should be prepared. The consultation should be conducted in a private, quiet place. The astrologer should be interested in your problems of the moment. A good reading involves feedback on your part. So if the reading is not relating to your concerns, you should let the astrologer know. You should feel free to ask questions and get clarifications of technical terms. The more you actively participate, rather than expecting the astrologer to carry the reading or come forth with oracular predictions, the more meaningful your experience will be. An astrologer should help you validate your current experience and be frank about possible negative happenings, but also suggest a positive course of action.

In their approach to a reading, some astrologers may be more literal, others more intuitive. Those who have had counseling training may take a more psychological approach. Though some astrologers may seem to have an almost psychic ability, extrasensory perception or any other parapsychological talent is not essential. A very accurate picture can be drawn from the data in your horoscope chart.

An astrologer may do several charts for each client, including one for the time of birth and a *progressed chart,* showing the evolution from birth to the present time. According to your individual needs, there are many other possibilities, such as a chart for a different location if you are contemplating a change of place. Relationships between any two people, things, or events can be interpreted with a chart that compares one partner's horoscope with the other's. A composite chart, which uses the midpoint between planets in two individual charts to describe the relationship, is another commonly used device.

An astrologer will be particularly interested in transits, those times when cycling planets activate the planets or sensitive points in your birth chart. These indicate important events in your life.

Many astrologers offer tape-recorded readings, another option to consider, especially if the astrologer you choose lives at a distance. In this case, you'll be mailed a taped reading based on your birth chart. This type of reading is more personal than a computer printout and can give you valuable insights, though it is not equivalent to a live dialogue with the astrologer when you can discuss your specific interests and issues of the moment.

The Telephone Reading

Telephone readings come in two varieties: a dial-in taped reading, usually recorded in advance by an astrologer, or a live consultation with an "astrologer" on the other end of the line. The taped readings are general daily or weekly forecasts, applied to all members of your sign and charged by the minute. The quality depends on the astrologer. One caution: Be aware that these readings can run up quite a telephone bill, especially if you get into the habit of calling every day. Be sure that you are aware of the per-minute cost of each call beforehand.

Live telephone readings also vary with the expertise of the astrologer. Ideally, the astrologer at the other end of the line enters your birth date into a computer, which then quickly calculates your chart. This chart will be referred to during the consultation. The advantage of a live telephone reading is that your individual chart is used and you can ask about a specific problem. However, before you invest in any reading, be sure that your astrologer is qualified and that you fully understand in advance how much you will be charged. There should be no unpleasant financial surprises later.

Computer-Generated Reports

Companies that offer computer programs (such as ACS, Matrix, Astrolabe) also offer a variety of computer-generated horoscope readings. These can be quite comprehensive, offering a beautiful printout of the chart plus many pages of detailed information about each planet and aspect of the chart. You can then study it at your convenience. Of course, the interpretations will be general, since there is no personal input from you, and may not cover your immediate concerns. Since computer-generated horoscopes are much lower in cost than live consultations, you might consider one as either a supplement or a preparation for an eventual live reading. You'll then be more familiar with your chart and able to plan specific questions in advance. They also make terrific gifts for astrology fans. There are several companies, listed in chapter 9, that offer computerized readings prepared by reputable astrologers.

Whichever option you decide to pursue, may your reading be an empowering one!

CHAPTER 12

Your Pet-scope for 2007: How to Choose Your Best Friend for Life

With both Jupiter, the planet of luck and expansion, and powerful Pluto in the animal-loving sign of Sagittarius, this is sure to be a year of pets and a great time to bring joy into your life by adopting an animal friend. At this writing, 63 percent of all American households have at least one pet, according to a recent survey by the American Pet Product Manufacturers Association. And we spend billions of dollars on the care and feeding of our beloved pets. Our pets are counted as part of the family, often sharing our beds and accompanying us on trips.

Whether you choose to adopt an animal from a local shelter or buy a thoroughbred from a breeder, try for an optimal time of adoption and the sun sign of your new friend. If you're rescuing an animal, however, it's difficult to know the sun sign of the animal, but you can adopt on a day when the moon is compatible with yours, which should bless the emotional relationship. Using the moon signs listed in the daily forecasts in this book, choose a day when the moon is in your sign, a sign of the same element, or a compatible element. This means fire and air signs should go for a day when the moon is in fire signs—Aries, Leo, Sagittarius—or air signs—Gemini, Libra, or Aquarius. Water and earth signs should choose a day when the moon is in water signs—Cancer, Scorpio or Pisces—or earth signs—Taurus, Virgo, or Capricorn. If possible, aim for a new moon, good for beginning a new relationship.

Here are some sign-specific tips for adopting an animal that will become your best friend for life.

Aries: The Rescuer

Aries gets special pleasure from rescuing animals in distress and rehabing them, so check your local shelters if you're thinking of adopting an animal. As an active fire sign, you'd be happiest with a lively animal, and you might do well with a rescue animal, such as a German shepherd or Labrador retriever. You'd also enjoy training such an animal. Otherwise look for intelligence, alertness, playfulness, and obedience in your friend. Since Aries tend to have an active life, look for a sleek, low-maintenance coat on your dog or cat. Cat lovers would enjoy the more active breeds such as the Siamese or Abyssinian.

An Aries sun-sign dog or cat would be ideal. Aries animals have a brave, energetic, rather combative nature. They can be mischievous, so the kittens and puppies should be monitored for safety. They'll dare to jump higher, run faster, and chase more animals than their peers. They may require stronger words and more obedience training than other signs. Give them plenty of toys and play active games with them often.

Taurus: The Toucher

Taurus is a touchy-feely sign; this tendency extends to your animal relationships. Look for a dog or cat that enjoys being petted and groomed, is affectionate, and adapts well to family life. As one of the great animal-loving signs, Taurus is likely to have several pets, so it is important that they all get along together. Give each one its own special safe space to minimize turf wars.

Taurus animals are calm and even tempered, but do not like being teased and could retaliate, so be sure to instruct children how to handle and play with their pet. Since this sign has strong appetites and tends to put on weight easily, be careful not to overindulge the animals in high-calorie treats and table snacks.

Taurus female animals are excellent mothers and make good breeders. They tend to be clean and less destructive of home furnishings than other animals.

Gemini: The Companion

A bright, quick-witted sign like yours requires an equally interesting and communicative pet. Choose a social animal that adapts well to different environments, since you may travel or have homes in different locations.

Gemini animals can put up with noise, telephones, music, and people coming and going. They'll want to be part of the action, so place a pillow or roost in a public place. They do not like being left alone. If you will be away for long periods, find them an animal companion to play with. You might consider adopting two Gemini pets from the same litter.

Animals born under this sign are easy to teach and some enjoy doing tricks or retrieving. They may be more vocal than other animals, especially if they are confined without companionship.

Cancer: The Nurturer

Cancer enjoys a devoted, obedient animal who demonstrates loyalty to its master. An affectionate home-loving dog or cat that welcomes you and sits on your lap would be ideal. The emotional connection with your pet is most important; therefore, you may depend on your powerful psychic powers when choosing an animal. Wait until you feel a strong bond of psychic communication. The moon sign of the day you adopt is very important for moon-ruled Cancer, so choose a water sign, if possible.

Cancer animals need a feeling of security; they don't like changes of environment or too much chaos at home. If you intend to breed your animal, the Cancer pet makes a wonderful and fertile mother.

Leo: The Prideful Owner

The Leo owner may choose a pet that reminds you of your own physical characteristics, such as similar coloring or build. You will be proud of your pet, will keep the animal groomed to perfection, and will choose the most spectacular example of the breed. Noble animals with a regal attitude, beautiful fur, or striking markings are often preferred, such as the Himalayan or the red tabby Persian cat, the standard poodle or the chow chow. An attention getter is a must.

Under the sign of the king of beasts, Leo-born animals have proud noble natures. They usually have a cheerful, magnanimous disposition and rule their domains regardless of their breed, holding their heads with pride and walking with great authority. They enjoy being groomed, like to show off, and enjoy the attention of fans. Leo animals thrive in the spotlight.

Virgo: The Caregiver

Virgo owners will be very particular about their pets, paying special attention to requirements for care and maintenance. You need a pet who is clean, obedient, intelligent, yet rather quiet. A highly active, barking or meowing pet that might get on your nerves is a no-no.

Cats are usually very good pets for Virgo. Choose one of the calm breeds, such as a Persian. Though this is a high-maintenance cat, its beauty and personality will be rewarding. You are compassionate with animals in need, and you might find it rewarding to volunteer at a local shelter or veterinary clinic or to train service dogs.

Virgo animals can be fussy eaters and very particular about their environment. They are gentle and intelligent; they respond to kind words and quiet commands, never harsh treatment. Virgo is an excellent sign for dogs that are trained to do service work, since they seem to enjoy being useful and are intelligent enough to be easily trained.

Libra: The Beautifier

The Libra owner responds to beauty and elegance in your pet. You require a well-mannered, but social companion, who can be displayed in all of nature's finery. An exotic variety such as a graceful curly-haired Devon Rex cat would be a show stopper. Libra often prefers the smaller varieties, such as a miniature schnauzer, a mini greyhound, or a teacup poodle.

Pets born under Libra are usually charming and well-mannered. They tend to be more careful than those of other signs. They'll avoid confrontations and harsh sounds, but respond to words of love and gentle corrections.

Scorpio: The Powerful

Scorpios enjoy a powerful animal with a strong character. They enjoy training animals and do well with service dogs, guard dogs, or police animals. Some Scorpios enjoy exotic, edgy pets, such as hairless Sphynx cats or Chinese Chin dogs. Rescuing animals in dire circumstances and finding them new homes are especially rewarding for Scorpios, as Matthew McConaughey did during Hurricane Katrina.

Animals born under this sign tend to be one-person pets, very strongly attached to their owners and extremely loyal and possessive. They are natural guard animals that will take extreme risks to protect their owners. They are best ruled by love and with consistent behavior training. They need to respect their owners and will return their love with great devotion.

Sagittarius: The Jovial Freedom Lover

Sagittarius is a traveler and one of the great animal lovers of the zodiac. The horse is especially associated with your sign, and you could well be a horse whisperer. You generally respond most to large, active animals. If a small animal, like a chihuahua, steals your heart, be sure it's one that travels well or tolerates your absence. Outdoor dogs like hunting dogs, retrievers, and border collies would be good companions on your outdoor adventures.

Sagittarius animals are freedom-loving, jovial, happy-go-lucky types. They may be wanderers, however, so be sure they have the proper identification tags and consider embedded microchip identification. These animals tend to be openly affectionate, companionable, and untemperamental. They enjoy socializing and playing with humans and other animals and are especially good with active children.

Capricorn: The Thoroughbred

Capricorn is a discriminating owner, with a great sense of responsibility toward your animal. You will be concerned with maintenance and care; you will rarely neglect or overlook any health issues with your pet. You will also discipline your pet wisely, not tolerating any destructive or outrageous antics. You will be attracted to good breeding, good manners, and deep loyalty from your pet.

The Capricorn pet tends to be more quiet and serious than other pets, perhaps a lone wolf who prefers the company of its owner rather than a sociable or mischievous type. This is another good sign for a working dog, such as a herder, because Capricorn animals enjoy this outlet for their energy.

Aquarius: The Independent Original

Aquarius owners tend to lead active, busy lives and need an animal who can either accompany them cheerfully or who won't make waves. Demanding or high-maintenance dogs are not for you. You might prefer unusual or oddball pets, such as dressed-up chihuahuas that travel in your tote bag or scene-stealing, rather shocking hairless cats. Or you will acquire a group of animals that can play with one another when you are pursuing outside activities. You can relate to the independence of cats.

Aquarius animals are not loners. They enjoy the companionship of humans or groups of other animals. They tend to be more independent and may require more training to follow the house rules.

Pisces: The Soul-Mate

This is the sign that can talk to the animals. Pisces owners enjoy deep communication with their pets, love having their animals accompany them, sleep with them, and show affection. Pisces will often rescue an animal in distress or adopt an animal from a shelter. Tropical fish are often recommended as a Pisces pet, and they seem to have a natural tranquilizing effect on this sign. However, Pisces may require an animal that shows more affection than do their fish friends.

Pisces animals are creative types; they can be sensually seductive and mysterious, mischievous and theatrical. They make fine house pets, do not usually like to roam far from their owners, and have winning personalities, especially with the adults in the home. Naturally sensitive and seldom vicious, they should be treated gently and given much praise and encouragement.

CHAPTER 13

Your Baby-scope: Children Born in 2007

Will the babies born this year be easy to raise or will they require a time-out mat or supernanny? Astrology answers these questions by looking beyond sun signs to the planets that describe a whole generation.

Children born this year will belong to one of the most spiritual generations in history. The three outer planets—Uranus, Neptune, and Pluto, which stay in a sign for at least seven years—are the ones that most affect each generation. Now passing through Pisces, Aquarius, and Sagittarius respectively, the three most visionary signs are sure to imprint the children of 2007.

In the past century, Uranus in Pisces coincided with enormous creativity, which should impact this year's children. Neptune in Aquarius and Pluto in Sagittarius are bringing a time of dissolving barriers, of globalization, of interest in religion and spirituality . . . breaking away from the materialism of the last century. In contrast, the members of this generation will truly be children of the world, searching for deeper meanings to existence.

Astrology can be an especially helpful tool that can be used to design an environment that will enhance and encourage each child's positive qualities. Some parents start before conception, planning the birth of their child as far as possible to harmonize with the signs of other family members. However, each baby has its own schedule, so if yours arrives a week early or late, or elects a different sign than you'd planned, recognize that the new sign may be more in line with the mission your child is here to accomplish. In other words, if you were hoping for a Libra child and he arrives during Virgo, that Virgo energy may be just what is needed to stimulate or complement your family. Remember that there are many astrological elements besides the sun sign that indicate strong family ties. Usually each child will share a particular planetary placement, an emphasis on a particular sign or house, or a certain chart configuration with his parents and other family members. Often there is a significant planetary angle that will define the parent-child relationship, such as family sun signs that form a T-square or a triangle.

One important thing you can do is to be sure the exact moment of birth is recorded. This will be essential in calculating an accurate astrological chart. The following descriptions can be applied to the sun or moon sign (if known) of a child—the sun sign will describe basic personality and the moon sign indicates the child's emotional needs.

The Aries Child

Baby Aries is quite a handful! This energetic child will walk—and run—as soon as possible and perform daring feats of exploration. Caregivers should be vigilant. Little Aries seems to know no fear (and is especially vulnerable to head injuries). Many Aries children, in their rush to get on with life, seem hyperactive and are easily frustrated when they can't get their own way. Violent temper tantrums and dramatic physical displays are par for the course with these children, necessitating a time-out chair.

The very young Aries should be monitored carefully, since he is prone to take risks and may injure himself. An Aries loves to take things apart and may break toys easily, but with encouragement, the child will develop formidable coordination. Aries's bossy tendencies should be molded into leadership qualities, rather than bullying. Otherwise, the me-first Aries will have many clashes with other strong-willed youngsters. Encourage these children to take out aggressions and frustrations in active, competitive sports, where they usually excel. When a young Aries learns to focus his energies long enough to master a subject and learns consideration for others, the indomitable Aries spirit will rise to the head of the class.

Aries born in 2007 will benefit from the jovial rays of Jupiter in Sagittarius until December of that year, which should give this child a sunny, optimistic personality.

The Taurus Child

This is a cuddly, affectionate child who eagerly explores the world of the senses, especially the senses of taste and touch. The Taurus child can be a big eater and will put on weight easily if not encouraged to exercise. Since this child likes comfort and gravitates to beauty, try coaxing little Taurus to exercise to music or take him outdoors for hikes or long walks. Though Taurus may be a slow learner, this sign has an excellent retentive memory and generally masters a subject thoroughly. Taurus is interested in results and will see each project patiently through to completion, continuing long after others have given up.

Choose Taurus toys carefully to help develop innate talents. Construction toys, such as blocks or erector sets, appeal to their love of building. Paints or crayons develop their sense of color. Many Taurus have musical talents and love to sing, which is apparent at a young age.

This year's Taurus will want a pet or two and a few plants of his own. Give little Taurus a minigarden and watch the natural green thumb develop. This child has a strong sense of acquisition and an early grasp of material value. After filling a piggy bank, Taurus graduates to a savings account, before other children have started to learn the value of money. Jupiter in their house of joint ventures this year should give Taurus another edge in financial matters.

The Gemini Child

Little Gemini will talk as soon as possible, filing the air with questions and chatter. This is a friendly child who enjoys social contact, seems to require company, and adapts quickly to different surroundings. Geminis have quick minds that easily grasp the use of words, books, and telephones and will probably learn to talk and read at an earlier age than most. Though they are fast learners, Gemini may have a short attention span, darting from subject to subject. Projects and games that help focus the mind could be used to help them concentrate. Musical instruments, typewriters, and computers help older Gemini children combine mental with manual dexterity. Geminis should be encouraged to finish what they start before they go on to another project. Otherwise, they can become jack-of-all-trade types who have trouble completing anything they do. Their dispositions are usually cheerful and witty, making these children popular with their peers and delightful company at home.

This year's Gemini baby should go to the head of the class. Uranus in Pisces could inspire Gemini to make an unusual career choice, perhaps in a high-tech field. When he grows up, this year's Gemini may change fields several times before he finds a job that satisfies his need for stimulation and variety.

The Cancer Child

This emotional, sensitive child is especially influenced by patterns set early in life. Young Cancers cling to their first memories as well as their childhood possessions. They thrive in calm emotional waters, with a loving, protective mother, and usually remain close to her (even if their relationship with her was difficult) throughout their lives. Divorce, death—anything that disturbs the safe family unit—are devastating to Cancers, who may need extra support and reassurance during a family crisis.

They sometimes need a firm hand to push the positive, creative side of their personality and discourage them from getting swept away by emotional moods or resorting to emotional manipulation to get their way. Praised and encouraged to find creative expression, Cancer will be able to express his positive side consistently on a firm, secure foundation.

This year's Cancer child should be more grounded and practical, thanks to Jupiter in Sagittarius. This also brings the blessing of good health!

The Leo Child

Leo children love the limelight and will plot to get the lion's share of attention. These children assert themselves with flair and drama and can behave like tiny tyrants to get their way. But in general, they have sunny, positive dispositions and are rarely subject to blue moods. At school, they're the ones who are voted most popular, head cheerleader, or homecoming queen. Leo is sure to be noticed for personality, if not for stunning looks or academic work; the homely Leo will be a class clown and the unhappy Leo may be the class bully.

Above all, a Leo child cannot tolerate being ignored for long. Drama or performing-arts classes, sports, and school politics are healthy ways for Leo to be a star. But Leos must learn to take lesser roles occasionally, or they will have some painful put-downs in store. Usually, the popularity of Leos is well earned; they are hard workers who try to measure up to their own high standards—and usually succeed.

The Leo baby born this year is likely to be more serious than the typical Leo, thanks to the taskmaster planet Saturn finishing up its two-year stay in Leo. This endows the child with self-discipline and the ability to function well in structured situations. With enhanced focusing ability, little Leo can be a high achiever.

The Virgo Child

The young Virgo can be a quiet, rather serious child, with a quick, intelligent mind. Early on, little Virgo shows far more attention to detail and concern with small things than other children do. Little Virgo has a built-in sense of order and a fascination with how things work. It is important for these children to have a place of their own, which they can order as they wish and where they can read or busy themselves with crafts and hobbies.

This child's personality can be very sensitive. Little Virgo may get hyper and overreact to seemingly small irritations, which can take the form of stomach upsets or delicate digestive systems. But this child will flourish where there is mental stimulation and a sense of order. Virgos thrive in school, especially in writing or language skills, and seem truly happy when buried in books. Chances are, young Virgo will learn to read ahead of classmates. Hobbies that involve detail work or that develop fine craftsmanship are especially suited to young Virgos.

Baby Virgo of 2007 is likely to be an especially active, intelligent child, since there are at least five planets in mutable signs during this period. With Saturn, also in Virgo beginning on September 2, he should respond to discipline. However, there should be plenty of mental and social stimulation in his environment to tame his restless nature.

The Libra Child

The Libra child learns early about the power of charm and appearance. This is often a very physically appealing child with an enchanting dimpled smile, who is naturally sociable and enjoys the company of both children and adults. It is a rare Libra child who is a discipline problem, but when their behavior is unacceptable, they respond better to calm discussion than displays of emotion, especially if the discussion revolves around fairness. Because young Libras without a strong direction tend to drift with the mood of the group, these children should be encouraged to develop their unique talents and powers of discrimination so they can later stand on their own.

In school, this child is usually popular and will often have to choose between social invitations and studies. In the teen years, social pressures mount as the young Libra begins to look for a partner. This is the sign of best friends, so Libra's choice of companions can have a strong effect on his future direction. Beautiful Libra girls may be tempted to go steady or have an unwise early marriage. Chances are, both sexes will fall in and out of love several times in their search for the ideal partner.

Little Libra of 2007 should have a way with words, thanks to Jupiter and Pluto in Sagittarius, which will enhance verbal and communications skills. This is an especially social, talkative child, who gets along well with siblings and classmates. Later in life, this Libra could choose a career in writing or the communication field.

The Scorpio Child

The Scorpio child may seem quiet and shy, but will surprise others with intense feelings and formidable willpower. Scorpio children are single-minded when they want something and intensely passionate about whatever they do. One of a caregiver's tasks is to teach this child to balance activities and emotions, yet at the same time to make the most of his or her great concentration and intense commitment.

Since young Scorpios do not show their depth of feelings easily, parents will have to learn to read almost imperceptible signs that troubles are brewing beneath the surface. Both Scorpio boys and girls enjoy games of power and control on or off the playground. Scorpio girls may take an early interest in the opposite sex, masquerading as tomboys, while Scorpio boys may be intensely competitive and loners. When their powerful energies are directed into work, sports, or challenging studies, Scorpio is a superachiever, focused on a goal. With trusted friends, young Scorpio is devoted and caring—the proverbial friend through thick and thin, loyal for life.

Jupiter and Pluto in Sagittarius should give this year's baby Scorpio a more carefree personality plus a flair for finance. There's lots of water in their horoscope, with Pisces and Cancer planets endowing these babies with plenty of imagination and creativity to be developed. Mars in Cancer will ignite a spirit of adventure and a love of water sports. Long journeys could be in the future.

The Sagittarius Child

This restless, athletic child will be out of the playpen and off on adventures as soon as possible. Little Sagittarius is remarkably well-coordinated, attempting daredevil feats on any wheeled vehicle from scooters to skateboards. These natural athletes need little encouragement to channel their energies into sports. Their cheerful, friendly dispositions earn them popularity in school, and once they have found a subject where their talent and imagination can soar, they will do well academically. They love animals, especially horses, and will be sure to have a pet or two, if not a home zoo. When they are old enough to take care of themselves, they'll clamor to be off on adventures of their own, away from home, if possible.

This child loves to travel, will not get homesick at summer camp, and may sign up to be a foreign-exchange student or spend summers abroad. Outdoor adventure appeals to little Sagittarius, especially if it involves an active sport, such as skiing, cycling, or mountain climbing. Give them enough space and encouragement, and their fiery spirit will propel them to achieve high goals.

Baby Sagittarius of 2007 is a freedom-loving child with a bonanza of luck and charisma, thanks to potent Pluto and lucky Jupiter in Sagittarius. This child has a natural generosity of spirit and an optimistic, expansive nature. He may need reality checks from time to time, since he may also be a big risk taker. He will also demand a great deal of freedom.

The Capricorn Child

These purposeful, goal-oriented children will work to capacity if they feel this will bring results. They're not ones who enjoy work for its own sake—there must be an end in sight. Authority figures can do much to motivate these children, but once set on an upward path, young Capricorns will mobilize energy and talent and work harder, and with more perseverance, then any other sign. Capricorn has built-in self-discipline that can achieve remarkable results, even if lacking the flashy personality, quick brain power, or penetrating insight of others. Once involved, young Capricorn will stick to a task until it is mastered. These children also know how to use others to their advantage and may well become team captains or class presidents.

A wise parent will set realistic goals for the Capricorn child, paving the way for the early thrill of achievement. Youngsters should be encouraged to express their caring, feeling side to others, as well as their natural aptitude for leadership. Capricorn children may be especially fond of grandparents and older relatives and will enjoy spending time with them and learning from them. It is not uncommon for young Capricorns to have an older mentor or teacher who guides them. With their great respect for authority, Capricorn children will take this influence very much to heart.

The Capricorn born in 2007 will have serious and responsible alliances, thanks to Saturn in the house of mutual ventures. This placement also hints at financial savvy—so give the child a savings account early on. Jupiter in Sagittarius promises a deep inner life and a generous nature.

The Aquarius Child

The Aquarius child has an innovative, well-focused mind that often streaks so far ahead of those of peers that this child seems like an oddball. Routine studies never hold the restless youngster for long; he will look for another, more experimental place to try out his ideas and develop his inventions. Life is a laboratory to the inquiring Aquarius mind. School politics, sports, science, and the arts offer scope for such talents. But if there is no room for expression within approved social limits, Aquarius is sure to rebel. Questioning institutions and religions comes naturally, so these children may find an outlet elsewhere, becoming rebels with a cause. It is better not to force this child to conform, but rather to channel forward-thinking young minds into constructive group activities.

This year's Aquarius will have far-out glamour as well as

charisma, thanks to his ruler, Uranus, in a friendly bond with Neptune. This child could be a rock star, a statesman, or a scientist.

The Pisces Child

Give young Pisces praise, applause, and a gentle, but firm, push in the right direction. Lovable Pisces children may be abundantly talented, but may be hesitant to express themselves, because they are quite sensitive and easily hurt. It is a parent's challenge to help them gain self-esteem and self-confidence. However, this same sensitivity makes them trusted friends who'll have many confidants as they develop socially. It also endows many Pisces with spectacular creative talent.

Pisces adores drama and theatrics of all sorts; therefore, encourage them to channel their creativity into art forms rather than indulging in emotional dramas. Understand that they may need more solitude than other children, as they develop their creative ideas. But though daydreaming can be creative, it is important that these natural dreamers not dwell too long in the world of fantasy. Teach them practical coping skills for the real world. Since Pisces are physically sensitive, parents should help them build strong bodies with proper diet and regular exercise. Young Pisces may gravitate to more individual sports, such as swimming, sailing, and skiing, rather than to team sports. Or they may prefer more artistic physical activities like dance or ice skating.

Born givers, these children are often drawn to the underdog (they fall quickly for sob stories) and attract those who might take advantage of their emphatic nature. Teach them to choose friends wisely and to set boundaries in relationships, to protect their emotional vulnerability—invaluable lessons in later life.

With the planet Uranus now in Pisces, the 2007 baby belongs to a generation of Pisces movers and shakers. This child may have a rebellious streak that rattles the status quo. But this generation also has a visionary nature, which will be much concerned with the welfare of the world at large.

CHAPTER 14

Is This the Right Time to Fall in Love?

Astrology gives you a power tool for discovering why you are attracted to a certain person and how that person might act or react toward you. It also gives you the times when you are at your most attractive to the opposite sex. Although astrology can't guarantee that you'll have a problem-free relationship, it can give you a romantic timetable and road map to guide you over the rough spots and reveal what you might expect in the future with your partner, after the initial glow has given way to day-to-day reality. Working in your favor is the fact that no one totally embodies any one sign; we're a combination of all the signs in different proportions. So there will always be some naturally compatible (as well as incompatible) aspects between two people's charts.

The Right Time to Reunite with an Old Lover or Reignite Passion in Your Current Relationship

An old love might resurface in your life when the planet Mercury, which rules communications, is in retrograde motion, about three times each year. (Check this information in chapter 2.) This planet often brings back people from the past, as well as old issues that should be resolved. It's an ideal time to troubleshoot existing relationships in which passion has cooled and to take action to reignite the flame of love. Heart-to-heart talks about what went wrong could help you understand each other better. Retrograde Venus is another good time to set a relationship back on course; it happens briefly in Virgo this year, from July 27 until September 8, when it turns direct in Leo. Those especially affected will have the sun or moon in Leo or Virgo. It is not a good idea to begin a new romantic relationship when either Venus or Mercury is retrograding.

Take a Chance on Love

Jupiter, the planet of risk, is in the risk-taking sign Sagittarius, which it rules this year. This could inspire fire signs (Aries, Leo, Sagittarius), in particular, to take a chance on love, perhaps choosing someone from a distant land or different culture. The mood of love is adventurous, exciting, daring, flirtatious. You could be swept off your feet, but this is not necessarily a time for long-term monogamous relationships. Jupiter encourages exploration in all areas!

Make the First Move

Venus is the planet that makes others respond favorably to you. When it's in your sun sign or a favorable sign, you have a terrific opportunity to attract the opposite sex, so turn on the charm. Ideally both the sun and Venus in your sun sign make you catnip to others.

Go Out and Meet Someone New

New activities of all kinds are favored during the new moon, especially if it's the new moon in your sun sign (or a sign in the same or complementary element). You'll also want a favorable Mercury (not retrograde) to give you the right words and a good Venus so that hot new prospect gets your message.

When to Break Up

Breaking up may be easier to do during a waning moon, in the last quarter, when we're gearing up for a new cycle. However, some planetary aspects such as eclipses could force emotional issues out into the open and thus cause a breakup. As Mars transits your sun sign, you may become impatient with long-standing irritations in a relationship and be tempted to move on. Check the Mars tables after chapter 6 and the new and full moon list in chapter 2.

Is This Person the Right One?

Here's a three-step technique for determining if your lover is the right one for a lasting relationship.

How to Predict Your Romantic Success

Consider the other planets in your lover's chart, not just the sun sign (you can look up most of them using the charts in this book). Venus will tell what attracts you both. Mars reveals your temper and sex drive, Mercury how you'll communicate, and the moon your emotional nature. (For the moon and Mercury signs, consult one of the free charts available on the Internet. See chapter 10.)

Step One: Size Up the Overall Relationship

To do an instant take on your relationship, compare the elements of the sun, moon, Mercury, Mars, and Venus— each a key planet in compatibility, in both charts. The interaction of elements (earth, air, fire, water) is the fastest way to size up a relationship. Planets of the same element will have the smoothest chemistry.

Earth element: Taurus Virgo, Capricorn
Air element: Gemini, Libra, Aquarius

Fire element: Aries, Leo, Sagittarius
Water element: Cancer, Scorpio, Pisces

When your partner has the same planet in the same element as your planet in question, the energy will flow freely. Complementary elements (fire signs with air signs or earth signs with water signs) also get along easily.

What if many planets are in other combinations? That's where you'll probably have to work at the relationship. There is tension and possible combustion between fire and water signs or earth and air signs. Take the analogies literally. Fire brings water to a boil; earth and air create a dust storm or tornado. If both your Venus signs are clashing, you will probably have very different tastes, something that could adversely affect a long-term relationship. However, challenges can be stimulating as well, adding spice to a relationship, especially when planets of sexual attraction—Mars relating to Venus—are involved.

Step Two: Find Out How the Individual Planets Relate

Find out and compare how each planet operates in both your horoscopes (sun, moon, Mercury, Venus, and Mars) by comparing its quality or mode. Planets in cardinal signs are active, assertive; planets in fixed signs are tenacious, stubborn; planets in mutable signs are adaptable, easily changeable. Two planets of the same quality (but different signs) do not easily relate—there is usually a conflict of interests—but they can challenge each other to be more flexible or they can open up new areas in each other's lives. This is where you have to make compromises to reconcile different points of view. You'll have to be flexible or give in often.

Cardinal signs (active): Aries, Cancer, Libra, Capricorn
Fixed signs (static): Taurus, Leo, Scorpio, Aquarius
Mutable signs (changeable): Gemini, Virgo, Pisces, Sagittarius

Step Three: Rate Your Overall Compatibility

The planets closest to the earth (sun, moon, Mercury, Mars, Venus) are those most likely to affect close relationships. Where possible, look up your planets and those of your partner in this book and grade them as follows. (The more A's and B's, the better! Y's and Z's indicate where you'll have to compromise to work things out.)

Grade A: for the same element (earth, air, fire, water)
Grade B: for complementary elements (air with fire, earth with water)
Grade Y: for challenging elements (air with water, earth with fire)
Grade Z: for the same quality, but different signs

By now, you should have a good idea where your relationship stands astrologically. A further check of the individual planets can answer some all-important questions.

Here's what the individual planets in your charts can reveal about your relationship:

Are you basically attracted? Compare sun signs.

The sun sign gives the big picture. Though it is not the whole story, and can be modified by other factors, the sun sign will always have an overall effect.

Are you emotionally compatible? Check your moon signs.

Emotional compatibility is strong enough to offset many other stressful factors in your horoscopes. Compare moon and sun signs too. There is an especially strong bond if your partner's moon is in your sun sign or vice versa.

How well do you communicate? Check Mercury.

Mercury in the same quality (cardinal, fixed, or mutable) could give you mental stimulation or irritation. Mercury in the same sign or element could be a meeting of minds.

Do you have similar tastes? Check Venus.

An incompatible Venus relationship can be very difficult
over the long run, if other factors do not balance this out,
because it has so much to do with the kind of atmosphere
that makes you happy. One of you likes modern; the other
likes traditional. One of you has an elegant style; the other
is casual. It can be difficult to find the middle ground where
you both win. Sometimes you just don't want to compromise that much.

Sexually sizzling or fizzling? Check Mars.

It is also useful to compare both Mars and Venus signs.
Mars and Venus in the same sign or element is strong
chemistry. Your partner's Mars or Venus in your sun sign
is another big plus. Sometimes if Mars and Venus are in
different modes, it can add sizzle to the relationship.

Will your partner be faithful?

Some sun signs tend to more monogamous than others.
Fixed signs like a steady relationship and tend not to have
multiple lovers. However, if a person with a fixed sign is
unhappy, he will tend to have lovers on the side. The chief
culprit here is Leo, which needs to be treated like royalty
or else it will exercise royal rights elsewhere. Mutable signs
tend to be the least monogamous. Gemini, Sagittarius, and
Pisces are difficult to tie down and more difficult to hold.
Sharing common interests and providing a stable home base
can be a big help here, especially with Gemini.

Where can you meet the sign of your dreams?

If you have a sun sign in mind, here are places where they
are likely to be (and like to go):

Aries: Try a sports event, martial arts display, action
movie, cooking school, adventure sports vacation, the
trendy new hot spot in town, the jogging or bike path.

Taurus: Meet them at a gourmet restaurant, auction house, farm or place where there are animals, flower show, garden shop, art classes, stores—especially food or jewelry stores.

Gemini: Meet them working for a newspaper or radio station, at parties or social events, writing courses, lectures, watering holes where there's good talk.

Cancer: Family dinners, boating or boat shows, cruises, on the beach, at seafood dinners, fishing, cooking schools, gourmet food stores, photography classes, art exhibits.

Leo: Big parties, country clubs, golfing, tanning salons, acting classes, theatrical events, movies, dancing, nightclubs, fine department stores, classy restaurants, VIP lounges at the airport, first-class hotels and travel.

Virgo: Craft stores, craft shows, flea markets, adult education courses, your local college, libraries, book stores, health food stores, doctors' offices, your local hospital or medical centers, health lectures, concerts, fine art events.

Libra: Art shows, fine restaurants, shopping centers, tennis matches, social events, parties and entertainment, the most fashionable stores, exhibits of beautiful objects, antique shows, decorating centers, ballet and the theater.

Scorpio: In banks, tax-preparation offices, police stations, sports events, motorcycle rallies, at the beach or swimming pool, doing water sports, at the gym, at action movies or mysteries, psychic fairs, ghostbusting.

Sagittarius: At a comedy club or laugh-a-minute film, at horse races or horse shows, pet stores or animal breeders, walking your dog, taking night courses at your local college, at a political debate, traveling to an exotic place, at a car show, mountain climbing, jogging, skiing, discussion group.

Capricorn: At a country music show, decorator show house, investment seminar, prestigious country club, exclusive resort, mountain climbing, party for a worthy cause, self-improvement course.

Aquarius: At a political rally, sci-fi convention, restaurant off the beaten path, union meeting, working for a worthy cause, campaigning for your candidate, fund-raising, flying lessons or airport.

Pisces: At any waterside place, at the theater or acting class, arts class, dancing, ballet, swimming pool, seafood restaurant, psychic event, church or other spiritual gathering, visiting at a hospital, at your local watering hole.

For your sun sign's compatibility with every other sign, see chapter 21.

How to Keep Your Relationship Sizzling

The Aries Lover

To keep your Aries mate red-hot, be sure to maintain your own energy level. This is one sign that shows little sympathy for aches, pains, and physical complaints. Curb any tendency toward self-pity—whining is one sure Aries turnoff (water signs take note). This is an open, direct sign. Don't expect your lover to probe your innermost needs. Intense psychological discussions that would thrill a Cancer or Scorpio only make Aries restless. Aries is not the stay-at-home type. This sign is sure to have plenty of activities going on at once. Share them (or they'll find someone else who will)!

Always be a bit of a challenge to your Aries mate—this sign loves the chase almost as much as the conquest. So don't be too easy or accommodating—let them feel a sense of accomplishment when they've won your heart.

Stay up-to-date in your interests and appearance. You

can wear the latest style off the fashion show runway with an Aries, especially if it's bright red. Aries is a pioneer, an adventurer, always ahead of the pack. Play up your frontier spirit. Present the image of the two of you as an unbeatable team that can conquer the world, and you'll keep this courageous sign at your side.

Since they tend to idealize their lovers, Aries partners are especially disillusioned when their mates flirt. So tone down your roving eye to make sure they always feel like number one in your life.

The Taurus Lover

Taurus is an extremely sensual, affectionate, nurturing lover, but can be quite possessive. Taurus likes to own you. Don't hold back with them or play power games. If you need more space in the relationship, be sure to set clear boundaries, letting them know exactly where they stand. When ambiguity in a relationship makes Taurus uneasy, they may go searching for someone more solid and substantial. A Taurus romance works best where the limits are clearly spelled out.

Taurus needs physical demonstrations of affection—don't hold back on hugs. Together you should create an atmosphere of comfort, good food, and beautiful surroundings. In fact, Taurus is often seduced by surface physical beauty alone. Their five senses are highly susceptible, so find ways to appeal to all of them! Your home should be a restful haven from the outside world. Get a great sound system and some comfortable furniture to sink into and keep the refrigerator stocked with treats. Most Taurus would rather entertain on their own turf than gad about town, so it helps if you're a good host or hostess.

Taurus likes a calm, contented, committed relationship. This is not a sign to trifle with. Don't flirt or tease if you want to please. Don't rock the boat or try to make this sign jealous. Instead, create a steady, secure environment with lots of shared pleasures.

The Gemini Lover

Keeping Gemini faithful is like walking a tightrope. This sign needs stability and a strong home base to accomplish their goals. But they also require a great deal of personal freedom.

A great role model is Barbara Bush, a Gemini married to another Gemini. This is a sign that loves to communicate. Sit down and talk things over. Don't interfere: Be interested in your partner's doings, but have a life of your own and ideas to contribute. Since this is a social sign, don't insist on quiet nights at home when your Gemini is in a party mood.

Gemini needs plenty of rope but a steady hand. Focus on common goals and abstract ideals. Gemini likes to share—be a twin soul and do things together. Keep up on their latest interests. Stay in touch mentally and physically. Use both your mind and your hands to communicate.

Variety is the spice of life to this flirtatious sign. Guard against jealousy—it is rarely justified. Provide a stimulating sex life—this is a very experimental sign—to keep them interested. Be a bit unpredictable. Don't let lovemaking become a routine. Most of all, sharing lots of laughs can make Gemini take your relationship very seriously.

The Cancer Lover

This is probably the water sign that requires the most TLC. Cancers tend to be very private people who may take time to open up. They are extremely self-protective and will rarely tell you what is truly bothering them. They operate indirectly, like the movements of the crab. You may have to divine problems by following subtle clues. Draw them out gently and try to voice any criticism in the most tactful, supportive way possible.

Family ties are especially strong for Cancer. They will rarely break a strong family bond. Create an intimate family atmosphere, with an emphasis on food and family get-togethers. You can get valuable clues to Cancer appeal from their mothers and their family situation. Whatever you do, don't compete with a mother! Get her to teach you the favorite family recipes; take her out to dinner. If your lover's early life was unhappy, it's important that Cancer feels there is a close family with you.

Encouraging creativity can counter Cancer's moodiness,

which is also a sure sign of emotional insecurity. Find ways to distract them from negative moods. Calm them with a good meal or a trip to the seashore. Cancers are usually quite nostalgic and attached to the past. So be careful not to throw out their old treasures or photos.

The Leo Lover

Whether the Leo is a sunny, upbeat partner or reveals cat-like claws could depend on how you handle the royal Leo pride. A relationship is for two people—a fact that ego-centered Leo can forget. You must gently remind them. Appearances are important to Leo, so try to always look your best.

Leo thinks big—so don't you be petty or miserly—and likes to live like a king. Remember special occasions with a beautifully wrapped gift or flowers. Make an extra effort to treat them royally. Keep a sense of fun and playfulness and loudly applaud Leo's creative efforts. React, respond, and be a good audience! If Leo's ignored, this sign will seek a more appreciative audience fast! Cheating Leos are almost always looking for an ego boost.

Be generous with compliments. You can't possibly overdo here. Always accentuate the positive. Make them feel important by asking for advice and consulting them often. Leo enjoys a charming sociable companion, but be sure to make them the center of attention in your life. If you have a demanding job or outside schedule, make a point to pull out all the stops once in a while, to create special events that keep romance alive.

The Virgo Lover

Virgo may seem cool and conservative on the surface, but underneath, you'll find a sensual romantic. Think of Raquel Welch, Sophia Loren, Jacqueline Bisset, and Garbo! It's amazing how seductive this practical sign can be!

They are idealists, however, looking for someone who meets their high standards. If you've measured up, they'll do anything to serve and please you. Virgos love to feel needed, so give them a job to do in your life. They are great fixer-uppers. Take their criticism as a form of love and caring, of noticing what you do. Bring them out socially—they're often very shy. Calm their nerves with good food, a healthy environment, and trips to the country.

Mental stimulation is a turn-on to this Mercury-ruled sign. An intellectual discussion could lead to romantic action, so stay on your toes and keep well-informed. This sign often mixes business with pleasure, so it helps if you share the same professional interests—you'll get to see more of your busy mate. With Virgo, the couple who works as well as plays together stays together.

The Libra Lover

Libra enjoys life with a mate and needs the harmony of a steady relationship. Outside affairs can throw them off balance. However, members of this sign are natural charmers who love to surround themselves with admirers, and this can cause a very possessive partner to feel insecure. Most of the time, Libras, who love to be the belles of the ball, are only testing their allure with harmless flirtations and will rarely follow through, unless they are not getting enough attention or there is an unattractive atmosphere at home.

Mental compatibility is what keeps Libra in tune. Unfortunately this sign, like Taurus, often falls for physical beauty or someone who provides an elegant lifestyle, rather than someone who shares their ideals and activities, which is the kind of sharing that will keep you together in the long run.

Do not underestimate Libra's need for beauty and harmony. To keep them happy, avoid scenes. Opt for calm, impersonal discussion of problems (or a well-reasoned debate) over an elegant dinner. Pay attention to the niceties of life. Send little gifts on Valentine's Day and don't forget birthdays and anniversaries. Play up the romance to the hilt—with all the lovely gestures and trimmings—but tone down intensity and emotional drama (Aries and Scorpio take note). Libra needs to be surrounded by a physically tasteful atmosphere—elegant, well-designed furnishings, calm colors, good manners, and good grooming at all times.

The Scorpio Lover

Scorpios are often deceptively cool and remote on the outside, but don't be fooled. This sign always has a hidden agenda and feels very intense about most things. The disguise is necessary because Scorpio does not trust easily; but when they do, they are devoted and loyal. You can lean on this very focused sign. The secret is in first establishing that basic trust through mutual honesty and respect.

Scorpio is fascinated by power and control in all its forms. They don't like to compromise—it's all or nothing. Therefore they don't trust or respect anything that comes too easily. Be a bit of a challenge and keep them guessing. Maintain your own personal identity, in spite of Scorpio's desire to probe your innermost secrets.

Sex is especially important to those under this sign. They will demand fidelity from you though they may not plan to deliver it themselves, so communication on this level is critical. Explore Scorpio's fantasies together. Scorpio is a detective—watch your own flirtations—don't play with fire. This is a jealous and vengeful sign, so you'll live to regret it. Scorpios rarely flirt for the fun of it themselves. There is usually a strong motive behind their actions.

Scorpio has a fascination with the dark, mysterious side of life. If unhappy, they are capable of carrying on a secret affair. So try to emphasize the positive, constructive side of life with them. Don't fret if they need time alone to sort out problems. They may also prefer time alone with you to socializing with others, so plan romantic getaways together to a private beach or a secluded wilderness spot.

The Sagittarius Lover

Be a mental and spiritual traveling companion. Sagittarius is a footloose adventurer whose ideas know no boundaries. So don't try to fence them in! Sagittarius resents restrictions of any kind. For a long relationship, be sure you are in harmony with their ideals and spiritual beliefs. They like to feel that their lives are constantly being elevated and taken to a higher level. Since down-to-earth matters often get put aside by Sagittarius schemes of things, get finances under control (money matters upset more relationships with Sagittarius than any other problems), but try to avoid becoming the stern disciplinarian in this relationship (find a good accountant to do this chore).

Sagittarius is not generally a homebody (unless there are several homes). Be ready and willing to take off on the spur of the moment, or they'll go without you. Sports, outdoor activities, and physical fitness are important. Stay in shape with some of Sagittarius Jane Fonda's tapes. Dress with flair and style. It helps if you look especially good in sportswear. Sagittarius men like beautiful legs, so play up yours. And this is one of the great animal lovers, so try to get along with the dog, cat, or horse.

The Capricorn Lover

These people are ambitious, even if they are the stay-at-home partner in your relationship. They will be extremely active, have a strong sense of responsibility to their partner, and take commitments seriously. However, they might look elsewhere if the relationship becomes too dutiful. They also need romance, fun, lightness, humor, and adventure!

Generation gaps are not unusual in Capricorn romances, where the older Capricorn partner works hard all through life and seeks pleasurable rewards with a young partner, or the young Capricorn gets a taste of luxury and instant status from an older lover. This is one sign that grows more interested in romance with age! Younger Capricorns often tend to put business way ahead of pleasure.

Capricorn is impressed by those who entertain well, have class, and can advance their status in life. Keep improving yourself and cultivate important people. Stay on the conservative side. Extravagant or frivolous loves don't last. Capricorn keeps an eye on the bottom line. Even the wildest Capricorns, such as Elvis Presley, Rod Stewart, and David Bowie, show a conservative streak in their personal lives. It's also important to demonstrate a strong sense of loyalty to your family, especially to older members. This reassures Capricorn, who'll be happy to grow old along with you!

The Aquarius Lover

Aquarius is one of the most independent, least domestic signs. Finding time alone with this sign may be one of your greatest challenges. The are everybody's buddy, usually surrounded by people they collect, some of whom may be old lovers. However, it is unlikely that old passions will be rekindled if you become their best friend as well as lover, and if you get actively involved in other important aspects of their lives, such as the political or charitable causes they believe in.

Aquarius needs a supportive backup person who encourages them, but is not overpossessive when their natural charisma attracts admirers by the dozen. Take a leaf from Joanne Woodward, whose marriage to perennial Aquarius heartthrob Paul Newman has lasted more than thirty years. Encourage them to develop their original ideas. Don't rain on their parade if they decide suddenly to market their spaghetti sauce and donate the proceeds to their favorite charity, or drive racing cars. Share their goals and be their fan, or you'll never see them otherwise.

You may be called on to give them grounding where needed. Aquarius needs someone who can keep track of their projects. But always remember, it's basic friendship—with the tolerance and common ideals that implies—that will hold you together.

The Pisces Lover

To keep a Pisces hooked, don't hold the string too tight! This is a sensitive, creative sign that may appear to need someone to manage life or point the direction out of their Neptune fog; but if you fall into that role, expect your Pisces to rebel against any strong-arm tactics. Pisces is more susceptible to a play for sympathy than a play for power. They are suckers for a sob story, the most empathetic sign of the zodiac. More than one Pisces has been seduced and held by someone who plays the underdog role.

They are great fantasists and extremely creative lovers, so use your imagination to add drama and spice to your time together. You can let your fantasies run wild with this sign, and they'll go you one better! They enjoy variety in lovemaking, so try never to let it become routine.

Long-term relationships work best if you can bring Pisces down to earth and, at the same time, encourage their creative fantasies. Deter them from escapism into alcohol or substance abuse by helping them to get counseling, if needed. Pisces will stay with the lover who gives positive energy, self-confidence, and a safe harbor from the storms of life, as well as one who is a soul mate.

CHAPTER 15

Is There Prosperity in Your Future?

There are big changes in the stars ahead, so projecting astrologically a few years down the line could point your career and investments in the most profitable direction.

For long-term trends, look to the outer planets, which cause major changes as they move into a different sign. Soon there will be a shift in the atmosphere as Pluto, the planet of transformation, moves into Capricorn in 2008 until 2024. (You'll notice a different kind of energy starting a few months in advance.) What's more, Jupiter, the planet of luck and expansion, also moves through Capricorn during 2008, accelerating changes and bringing luck to Capricorn, so expect many of that sign to surge into prominence. Bet on the sea goat (Capricorn's symbol) and areas associated with it. Capricorns should prepare to move into the limelight. ("It's about time," you Capricorns may well say!)

If you're headed for the fast track, set your sights on Capricorn fields, which will be going through radical changes. This will affect Capricorn-associated corporations, big business, government, institutions of all kinds, mining, land speculation, property owners and dealers, builders and building trades, contractors and engineers, civil service, providers of status products. Capricorn-influenced fields are known for function, structure, discipline, and order, so consider careers that have these qualities or can provide them to others.

Everyone Old Is New

Want to cash in on a much-neglected market? Services and care for the aging should be booming with career opportunities, thanks to our elder population explosion. Remember that the generation now entering the aging population was born with Pluto in Leo; it's the rock-and-roll generation, who will resist the idea of aging and retirement as long as possible.

This particular elder population will be highly visible and financially viable. They are big spenders who will be remaining much longer in the workforce. Those who do retire may begin second careers, so the workplace will be rethinking its relationship to grandmas and grandpas and changing to accommodate them. Since America has been a youth-oriented culture, expect a major transformation in advertising, retailing, fashion, housing, and health care.

Since the Pluto in Leo generation is one of the most image-conscious ever, anything that keeps these folks looking and feeling great is sure to succeed. Don't expect your grandma and grandpa to hang around the house. This is a curious, adventurous generation that will welcome opportunities to explore the globe that are especially tailored to their age group and interests.

Cater to Horatio Alger

Capricorn is the Horatio Alger sign of rising through one's own volition and ambition. Self-improvement courses will be booming as we search for more fulfilling careers and try to keep up with new technology.

Do you enjoy helping others fulfill their potential? Career coaching—in fact, coaching in all aspects of life—is a hot field. In the corporate area, human resources is a much-touted area of job growth. You'll need skills in training and in helping other people find jobs. Get involved with helping people adapt to the times and retrain themselves for new careers. Leos, Sagittarius, Virgos, and Aquarius make excellent trainers and teachers. Aries are the supermotivators.

Education, especially high education, will be in for a whole new approach, as gray-haired students decide to complete their educations or simply enjoy expanding their knowledge. College towns will become hot retirement destinations, which provide intellectual stimulation plus an elder-compatible atmosphere.

The demand for teachers will increase and provide a steady stream of jobs. Look into special education, private education of all kinds, and unusual approaches to teaching. The natural teaching signs—Virgo, Leo, Sagittarius, and Aquarius—are winners here.

Since the world has become a smaller place and the trend toward international involvement escalates, demand for language skills also increases. Americans may need to speak several languages including some once considered exotic for the average American, such as Chinese or Arabic. Language teachers, translators, and linguists, especially those with a Gemini emphasis in their charts, should find many opportunities.

Waste Not, Want Not

Capricorn is an intensely practical sign that dislikes waste of any kind, so consider careers in recycling and waste management, antiques, renovation, preserving old buildings, land conservation, and teaching history.

Environment-related careers are hot options, since there will be so much cleaning up of toxic wastes, rebuilding after cataclysmic natural events, and redesigning of equipment. Engineers, attorneys, designers, bankers, and researchers should slant their career search in this direction. Taurus, Scorpio, Libra, Pisces, and Aquarius could make their fortune here.

Keep Treasured Traditions Alive

It looks like a conservative time, when people will be concerned with traditional values. Hospitality businesses can capitalize on this trend by promoting the beloved holidays of all cultures, reviving the old customs and memories. Holiday vacations for the whole family to share, reunions, and celebrations could revitalize the resort and cruise business. Tourism that caters to the needs of the aging, but still adventurous, traveler should thrive.

Head for the Hills

If you're thinking about a change of scene, consider relocating to a Capricorn-influenced place, which should have growth potential now. If you're adventurous, head for Central Europe, especially mountainous regions. The Balkans, Bosnia, Bulgaria, Lithuania, Macedonia, and Albania are Capricorn places. India, Belgium, Hesse and Constance in Germany, Mexico, and New Zealand are also on the Capricorn wavelength.

Health Care for the Antiaging Population

Have you considered the health-care field? Careers in medical services are among the hottest prospects as the nation begins to reform its health-care systems. Physical therapists, nurses, physicians' assistants, and pharmacists, as well as health services administrators, will all be in demand to service the aging population. If you have strong Virgo, Scorpio, or Capricorn placements, which give you a flair for the health field and excellent organizational skills, you should consider this area. Compassionate signs such as Pisces and Cancer make excellent health caregivers.

Consider the Capricorn fields of knee surgery and therapy, bone and joint diseases, chiropractic care, dermatology. New techniques in self-enhancement, such as plastic surgery, dental work, and hair replacement, should also do well for this aging generation who'd love to look and feel forever young.

Therapists specializing in treatment of disabling conditions, optometrists, nursing home operators and managers, and home care for the aged should be thriving.

The Talent Finder

Designers and manufacturers of clothing, furniture and equipment suited to the over-sixty consumer should also do well. Look into this area if you have planets in Capricorn (ruler of old age), Pisces (creativity, compassion), Taurus and Cancer (associated with the home environment and of nurturing), and Aries (pioneering ventures).

Do you thrive on life in the fast lane? Sports and special events are high-visibility careers where salesmanship and flair count, so they're especially suited to fire signs Aries, Leo, and Sagittarius. Good communicators like Gemini and Libra do well in public relations in this market.

Capricorn-favored sports require great discipline and endurance and are luckiest when they take place in the mountains. Rock and mountain climbing, hiking, and skiing are specially favored.

There will be a continuing boom in fitness careers, with the emphasis on well-run health clubs, personal attention, and social atmosphere. As the population ages, there will be more emphasis on weight training and rehabilitation aimed at elder bodies. Virgos, Sagittarius, Leos, and Aries are specially suited to the high-energy demands of this field, while Libras, Geminis, and Pisces provide good communication, diplomacy, and compassion.

We'll be eating more consciously as America slims down (Capricorn is the sign of discipline). Diet-specific restaurants, vegetarian restaurants, diet consultants, and organic food farmers and gardeners should be expanding. We'll be especially concerned with the quality of our meat and seafood. This is a fertile area for Taurus, Virgo, Cancer, Pisces, and Leos with skills in working with agriculture, diet counseling, cooking, restaurant management, organizing farmers' markets, and managing health food stores.

High-Tech Options

Though computer fields should continue to grow, the outsourcing of high-tech service jobs is also likely to continue. The good news is that there will still be a need for software designers, trainers, salespersons, and local repair staff, as computers have become an integral part of our lives. Aquarians are natural in all areas of computer work. Sagittarius and Geminis do well in teaching and sales, while

Capricorns excel in organization, Pisces in creative software design, and Cancers in applying high tech to industry.

Video-related careers can only get bigger in 2010 as Neptune, ruler of film, moves into Pisces, its strongest position. Video stores, cameras, and viewing equipment, new uses of video for education and entertainment, technical experts in production and performing—all should be booming. Pisces, Leo, Sagittarius, and Gemini should find plenty of opportunities in performance, sales, and marketing.

Take these tips from the stars and do your career planning with the planets!

CHAPTER 16

Heath and Diet Makeovers from the Stars

Health spas, fitness resorts, gyms, yoga studios, and sports complexes are multiplying around the country. Vitamin stores and juice bars are opening up in malls. We're buying shelves of diet books. Yet we're still one of the fattest nations on the planet! This year, the stars say we'll have more discipline to make over our bad eating habits and resolve to become as healthy as possible. Astrology can clue you in to the tendencies that contribute to good or ill health (especially when it comes to controlling your appetite). Finding the right diet and health program and having the patience to stick with them over time could be your big challenge this year. So follow these sun-sign tips on how best to lose those extra pounds and make this your healthiest year ever.

Aries Tips: Avoid the Quick Fix

Thanks to your hyperactive Mars-ruled lifestyle, you're sometimes too busy to bother with healthy meals in a calm atmosphere. You're more likely to grab carbohydrate-laden, calorie-packed fast foods for instant energy on the run. You need a regimen that gives you sustained energy, rather than a quick fix or a caffeine-fueled jump start. Aim for frequent small meals and carry healthy snacks with you to recharge your batteries. Protein and fruit smoothies in the morning might provide you with a quick, healthy head start to the day.

Aries is associated with the head, your most vulnerable area, which you should be especially careful to protect by wearing the appropriate headgear during risky activities and sports. Headaches warn you to slow down and take it easy for a while. If you've been stocking up on headache remedies, it might be time to consult a nutritionist for expert dietary advice.

Superbusy, impatient Aries tends to overschedule and stress out when others don't, won't, or can't keep up to your pace. Sports to the rescue! Swatting a ball, cheering on your favorite team, training for a marathon, or just running around the block can be the best remedies for whatever ails an Aries. Sports allow you to let off steam in an atmosphere of excitement and competition where you can feel the joy of winning. Your daring moves and Mars-powered energy should earn you a stellar spot on any team. If you're older, volunteer to coach local youngsters.

Martial arts of any kind appeal to your love of action. The slower, more flowing forms, such as tai chi, can be done throughout life. You don't have to be Jackie Chan or Russell Crowe to show your Aries flair for action heroics. Try racket sports (any sport that involves hitting or working with a swordlike object), fencing, tap dancing, or aerobics if martial arts don't give you a kick. However, remember to take time to check your equipment, warm up, and wait until you're properly conditioned before you jump to expert-level challenges.

Once you've found a sport you love, try not to push yourself too hard. Listen to your body when it tells you it's time to quit (never easy for Aries). Finally, know the difference between well-exercised, fatigued muscles and the pain that signals trouble.

Taurus Tips: Downsize Portions

Taurus loves all kinds of food in large quantities—especially rich, creamy desserts and fried goodies. (Once you start eating rich food, you find it almost impossible to stop.) Deprivation in any form is not going to work for you, so find a diet that allows you healthy variations of the foods you love most. Aim for smaller portions and fill up on skinny foods like salads. First, raid your refrigerator and eliminate any foods that are not on your diet. If it's there, you'll find it and eat it. The techniques for weight loss in Cher's diet books might inspire you.

Pleasure is the key to your exercise routine. You need an attractive place to work out, not a sweaty gym. Why not plan your workout to take place in one of the scenic areas of your town? Jogging or biking along a river or through a park, exploring the woodlands and seashore in your area with long nature hikes, or horseback riding along a scenic trail can make you look forward to exercising. Or plant an extensive garden that requires lots of active maintenance. If you live in an appropriate setting, get a dog that requires lots of exercise. Working with animals can also be a joy for Taurus.

Pay special attention to the Taurus area of the body: the neck. Yoga exercises, head rolls, the proper pillow, and a good masseur can make a big difference here. Though Taurus is a hardy sign with great stamina and endurance, you can become sluggish if you're overweight or if you have a thyroid problem. So, if you can barely drag yourself off the couch, be sure to check your thyroid. If you're not getting enough sleep, it could be due to tension in your neck. Try changing your pillow to one specially designed to support your neck.

Massage is one way to soothe the raging bull in you, especially if tension is lodging in your neck. Try shiatsu massage targeted to the acupressure points in the neck area. Neck massages are a sybaritic way to release tension and promote restful sleep.

Gemini Tips: Make a Game of It

Gemini is an on-the-go sign that does not usually have a weight problem, as long as you keep moving. If life circumstances force you to be sedentary, however, you may eat out of boredom and watch the pounds pile on. Your active social life can also sabotage your weight with sumptuous party buffets and restaurant meals where you have to sample everything. Your challenge is to find a healthy eating system with enough variety so you won't get bored. Develop a strategy for eating out—at parties or restaurants—and fill up the buffet plates with salad or veggies before you sample the desserts. Sociable Geminis on a diet can benefit from group support in a system like Weight Watchers. Find a diet twin who'll support you and have fun losing weight together.

Gemini is associated with the nervous system, our body's lines of communications. If your nerves are on edge, you may be trying to do too many things at once, leaving no time for fun and laughter. When you overload your circuits, it's time to get together with friends and go out to parties. Investigate natural tension relievers, such as yoga or meditation. Doing things with your hands—playing the piano, typing, craftwork—is also helpful.

Gemini is also associated with the lungs, which are especially sensitive. If you smoke, consider quitting. Yoga, which incorporates deep breathing into physical exercise, brings oxygen into your lungs. Among its many benefits are the deep relaxation and tranquillity so needed by your sign.

Combine healthful activities with social get-togethers for fun and plenty of fringe benefits for everyone. Include friends in your exercise routines; join an exercise class or jogging club. Gemini excels at sports that require good timing and manual dexterity as well as communication with others, like tennis or golf. Those who jog may want to add hand weights or upper-body exercises, which will benefit the Gemini-ruled arms and hands. If you spend long hours at the computer, try an ergonomic keyboard for comfort and protection against carpal tunnel syndrome.

Cancer Tips: Get the Emotional Support You Need

Dieting can be difficult for Cancers, who love good cuisine, find emotional solace with goodies, and fill up with comfort foods in tough times. There are sure to be conflicts in the Cancer who wants to be fashionably thin, but also to please the family with Grandma's favorite dishes. Cancer food conflicts sometimes lead to eating disorders, as with Princess Diana. Remember that you must be nurtured emotionally as well as physically. A diet-therapy group might help you deal with issues surrounding food and give you the support you need to stick to a diet. Find nonfood ways to baby yourself, such as a visit to a spa, walks along the beach, or beauty treatments to help you feel good about yourself while you lose weight.

Get the family behind you when you diet. You'll never lose weight if they insist on eating caloric favorites in front of you. Challenge yourself to create diet-conscious variations of family recipes so the whole family can eat healthy.

Your natural water-sign element is also your best therapy. Sometimes just a walk by a pond or a brief stop by a fountain can do wonders to relieve emotional stress and tension. You will be more likely to stick to an exercise routine if it's in or near water. Pool aerobics, swimming, fishing, sailing, and all other all water sports provide ideal ways for you to stay fit.

Health-wise, Cancer is associated with the breasts. Have regular checkups, according to your age and family health history of breast-related illness, and be sure to wear the proper supportive bra. Cancer is also prone to digestive difficulties, especially gastric ulcers and eating disorders. When emotionally caused digestive problems from those stomach-knotting insecurities crop up, baby yourself with extra pampering. If you're feeling blue, a visit with loved ones, old friends, and family could provide the support you need. Plan special family activities that bring everyone close together.

Leo Tips: The Downside of the Good Life

Leo's diet downfall might be your preference for the finer things in life, like dining on gourmet food at the best restaurants. And a Leo that is not getting the love and attention you need can easily turn to food for consolation. Give yourself the royal treatment in nonfood ways and imagine how great you'll look in that sexy gold dress.

Like your lion namesake, Leos often tend to be carnivores, so a low-carbohydrate, high-protein diet might work best for you, such as the Perricone or Atkins diet. If you're having trouble getting started on your diet, give yourself a jump start with a spa vacation. Some extra pampering, plus expert advice, could see you through the first difficult week and get you on the road to healthy eating.

Leo is associated with the spine and heart, two important areas to guard throughout your life. Be sure you have a good mattress to support the vulnerable Leo spine. Learn some therapeutic exercises to strengthen and protect your back. Aerobic exercises that benefit the heart and lungs are also musts for Leo.

Ruled by the sun, you're one sign that usually loves to tan. However, considering the permanent damage sun exposure can cause, you may elect to remain porcelain pale like Madonna or to use a spray-on tanning product. Don't leave for the beach without a big hat, umbrella, and sunblock formulated for your skin type. Many makeup foundations now come with a sunblock added, a good idea for Leo ladies.

Leos are proud of your body and usually take excellent care of it. Like the archetypal Leo male, Arnold Schwarzenegger, you can summon up great discipline and determination to maintain your public image. To make your body worthy of the spotlight, consider a bodybuilding regimen in which you're supervised by a personal trainer. Be sure any exercise routine you choose emphasizes good posture. The way you carry yourself can make the most of your figure type and dramatically affect your energy level. Get that regal bearing!

Virgo Tips: Find a Diet Coach

Since Virgo is associated with the digestive system, you can make quite an issue of food quality, preparation, and diet. Many of you will select a very detailed special diet to promote health, such as a macrobiotic diet. Potassium-rich vegetables are especially important, as is your relationship to whole grains. The mind-body connection to overweight has been emphasized by Virgo diet coach, Dr. Phil MacGraw. If you become overweight, it usually comes from coping with emotional or work-related stress. To counteract this tendency, add activities to your life that promote peace of mind. Exercises that use mental as well as physical techniques could help you stay with your program.

As one of the most health-conscious signs in the zodiac, caring for the health of yourself and others is usually a high priority with Virgos. Many great doctors, nurses, and dieticians were born under Virgo, such as the noted heart surgeon Dr. Michael DeBakey.

You tend to troubleshoot your health, scheduling medical exams and appropriate diagnostic tests promptly. You have probably learned that running your life efficiently does much to eliminate health-robbing stress. It's a great comfort to know you've got a smooth health-maintenance routine in place to back you up.

Virgos benefit from exercises that stress the relationship of the mind and body, such as yoga or tai chi. Sports that require a certain technical skill to master can also challenge Virgo. The key factor in Virgo-appealing exercises is to offer self-improvement on several levels simultaneously, not just a boring or repetitive routine.

Libra Tips: Resist Sweet Temptations

One of the most famous diet doctors, Dr. Robert Atkins, was a Libra. A well-spoken gentleman with a liking for sweets, he fit your sign's profile. At first, the low-carbohydrate diet he advocated was vilified by nutritional experts. In recent years, however, he has been vindicated, and the effectiveness of the Atkins diet proven. It could be the perfect diet for Libras who often put on too much weight from indulging in sweets. Because your sign rules the kidneys, it's no surprise that this diet advocates drinking plenty of water to cleanse the system as you reduce. Since you are one of the most social signs, you may entertain or be entertained often. Plan your food choices before you go out, so you'll know exactly what to eat. Then you'll be more likely to resist sweet temptations. Dieting with your mate or a group of friends could provide the support you need and keep you on track when you go out to dinner.

Restoring and maintaining equilibrium is the Libra key to health. Balance in all things should be your mantra. If you have been working too hard or taking life too seriously, a dose of culture, art, or music or perhaps some social activity will balance your scales. Make time to entertain friends, be romantic with the one you love, and enjoy the artistic life of your city.

Since Libra is associated with the kidneys and lower back, watch these areas for misalignment or health problems. Consider yoga, spinal adjustments, or a detoxification program if your body is out of balance. Working out in a gym may be unappealing to aesthetic Libras. Since yours is the sign of relationships, you may enjoy exercising with a partner or with loved ones. Make morning walks or weekend hikes family affairs. Take a romantic bicycle tour, picnic in the autumn countryside. Libra is also the sign of grace, so any kind of dancing may appeal. Dancing combines art, music, romance, relaxation, graceful movement, social contact, and exercise.

Put more beauty in all areas of your life, and you'll be healthier and happier.

Scorpio Tips: Diet for Self-Transformation

Scorpios never do anything halfway, so they need to be fully committed to their diets. Some Scorpios will go to great lengths to transform themselves, even resorting to extreme means like stomach stapling or gastric bypass, as Roseanne Barr did. You are gifted with amazing focus and discipline and can stick with any diet, once you have made up your mind. The trick is to eliminate self-destructive food habits. Finding a diet plan you can live with for long periods, such as the South Beach Diet, which worked for Hillary Clinton, will help you avoid the yo-yo diet syndrome.

Though Scorpio usually has a strong constitution that can literally rise from the ashes of extreme illness or misfortune, resist the temptation to take this for granted or sabotage your health with self-destructive habits. Try to curb excessive tendencies in any area of your life. Know when to quit and when to seek help; don't hesitate to ask for help when you need it.

Your sign is associated with regenerative and eliminative organs. Therefore, it follows that sexual activity can be a source of good or ill health for Scorpio. It is important to examine your attitudes about sex, to follow safe-sex practices, and to seek balance in sex, as in all other areas of your life.

It's no accident that Scorpio's month coincides with football season, which reminds us that sports are a very healthy way to defuse emotions. If you enjoy winter sports, be sure to prepare ahead of time for the ski slopes or the ice rinks. Be sure to warm up your muscles before you go all out. Water sports are a terrific outlet for Scorpio, so sign up for pool aerobics or competitive swimming and be sure to treat yourself to a vacation at a spectacular tropical beach resort. Somehow, just being near a saltwater environment can restore your equilibrium.

Sagittarius Tips: Aim for Long-Range Benefits

Dieting is something Sagittarius does with great difficulty. There has to be more to it than just getting thin. Therefore, an eating plan that is part of a spiritually oriented lifestyle, such as vegetarianism, might have more appeal. Aim for long-range benefits by balancing a sane, practical eating plan with plenty of exercise. Beware of fad diets that promise instant results and come with a high-pressure sales pitch. Avoid gimmicks, pills, or anything instant; these solutions are especially tempting to impatient Sagittarius. Exercise is the greatest antidote to overeating for your sports-loving sign, so follow your guru (Jane Fonda), go for the burn, and work off those calories.

Good health for Sagittarius is often a matter of motivation. If you set a fitness goal, it will be much easier to stay motivated than if you exercise or diet haphazardly, so aim for the best you can be and then set a plan to achieve it. Once you've decided on a course of action, get going. Being on the move and physically active keeps you in the best of health, improves your circulation, and protects your arteries. Problems could come from injuries to the hip or thigh areas, as well as arterial problems, so protect yourself with the proper equipment for your sports activity and don't push yourself beyond your capacity.

Exercise is your greatest antidote to stress. Your sign loves working out in groups, so combine socializing with athletic activities and team sports. Touch football, biking, hikes, and long walks with your dog are fun as well as healthy. Let others know that you'd like a health-promoting birthday gift, such as sports equipment, a gym membership, or an exercise video. In your workouts, concentrate on Sagittarius-ruled areas—the hips, legs, and thighs.

If you're already in shape, try out Sagittarius sports such as downhill or cross-country skiing, Rollerblading, and basketball. Since you like to travel, plan an exercise routine that can be done anywhere. Isometric exercises, which use muscle resistance and can be done in a car or plane seat, are a good travel option. If you are always on the road, investigate equipment that fits easily in your suitcase, such as water-filled weights, home gym devices, elastic exercise bands. Locate hotels with well-equipped gyms or parks nearby where you can jog.

Capricorn Tips: Disciplined Dieting

It was a Capricorn hostess and decorator, Lady Elsie de Wolfe Mendl, who introduced dieting to America, via the 1920s health guru Gayelord Hauser. Lady Mendl served very small portions of exquisitely prepared health food at her elegant dinner parties, a good tip for you who may need to downsize portions. One of the skinny signs, Capricorn has amazing self-discipline, a big help in maintaining weight loss. Exercise or active sports should help you keep the pounds off without strenuous dieting. Food and mood are linked with Capricorn, so avoid eating to console or comfort yourself; instead, choose upbeat relaxed companions. Since you are likely to mix business with pleasure, plan your work-related lunches and dinners in advance so you won't be led astray by the dessert tray.

As a Capricorn, you naturally take good care of yourself, getting regular medical checkups and tending toward moderation in your lifestyle. You're one of the signs that ages well and remains physically active in your senior years. But Capricorn's fast-paced, action-packed life can be stressful, so here are some ways to unwind and put the spring back into your step.

Since Capricorn is associated with the bone structure, you need to watch for signs of osteoporosis and take preventive measures. Good posture and stretching exercises such as yoga are essential to remain flexible. You might practice yoga, as Christy Turlington does. Another way to counteract osteoporosis is by adding weight-bearing exercise to your routine. If your knees or joints are showing signs of arthritis, calcium supplements may be helpful. For those who enjoy strenuous sports, remember to protect your knees by doing special exercises to strengthen this area, and always warm up beforehand.

Capricorn's natural self-discipline is a big help in maintaining good health. Keep a steady, even pace for lasting results. Remember to balance workouts with pleasurable activities in your self-care program. Grim determination can be counterproductive, especially if one of your exercise goals is to relieve tension. Take up a sport for pure enjoyment, not necessarily to become a champion.

Since you probably spend much of your life in an office, check your working environment for hidden health saboteurs like poor air quality, bad lighting, and uncomfortable seating. Get an ergonomically designed chair to protect your back, or buy a specially designed back-support cushion if your chair is uncomfortable. If you work at a computer, adjust your keyboard and the height of the computer screen for ergonomic comfort.

Capricorn, the sign of Father Time, brings up the subject of aging. If sags and wrinkles are keeping you from looking as young as you feel, investigate plastic surgery to give you a younger look and psychological lift. Teeth are also associated with your sign, a reminder to have regular dental cleanings and checkups.

Aquarius Tips: The Diet Trendsetter

Aquarius is a sign of reaching out to others, a cue to make your diet program a social one. Sharing your diet with friends might keep you interested and prevent boredom. It worked for Oprah Winfrey, an Aquarius whose yo-yo weight gains and losses became media events. If you know you'll be going public for a party or wedding, you'll be motivated to look your best. The trick is to segue from dieting to an ongoing healthy lifestyle. Otherwise you'll be back up the scale again. Try to find a flexible plan that adapts to individual personalities rather than one that imposes a rigid diet structure. Keep a diet diary or online blog to help monitor yourself, a tip from Oprah.

Clean air is top priority for a health-wise air sign especially vulnerable to airborne allergies and viruses. The effects of air pollution might influence where you choose to live. If you life in a polluted environment, get an air purifier, ionizer, or humidifier. Aquarius tends to travel a lot (or may fly your own plane, as John Travolta and Lorenzo Lamas do). Protect yourself from infections that flourish in the enclosed environments of trains, buses, and planes.

Since Aquarius is associated with the circulatory system, you especially benefit from a therapeutic massage. Find your local day spa and schedule one of their relaxing hands-on treatments. New Age treatments are favored by experimental Aquarius, so consider alternative approaches to health and fitness. Perhaps the Ayurvedic approach from India or Chinese massage therapies might work for you. Calves and ankles are also Aquarius territory, which should be emphasized in your exercise program. Be sure your ankles are well supported. Be careful of sprains and strains, especially if you're a jogger.

You'll follow a fitness routine only if you can make your own rules and exercise at a convenient time, which could mean odd moments. If your schedule makes it difficult to get to the gym or if you dislike the routine of regular exercise classes, videos might solve your problem. There is a vast selection of exercise videos to choose from. Exercising with friends could make staying fit more fun. Try several different kinds of exercise so you can vary your routine from yoga to kick-boxing when you get bored. Or set up a gym at home with portable home exercise equipment. (You're the type who will combine your treadmill sessions with a telephone conversation or TV news show.)

Pisces Tips: The Addictive Eater

Pisces is a sign of no boundaries, one of the most difficult to discipline diet-wise. You can get hooked on a fattening food like French fries (or alcohol), a habit like coffee with lots of sugar and a roll, and easily gain weight. Your water-sign body may have a tendency to bloat, holding water weight at certain times, especially around the full moon. The key for you, as with so many others, is commitment and support. Don't try to go it alone. Get a partner, a doctor, a group, or one of the online diet-related sites to help. Since you're influenced by the atmosphere around you, choose to be with slim healthy friends and those who will support your efforts. Avoid those seemingly well-meaning diet saboteurs who say just one cookie won't do any harm. A seafood-based diet, like the Perricone diet, could be the right one for you. Your Pisces sisters—Queen Latifah, Liza Minnelli, Camryn Manheim, and Elizabeth Taylor—have slimmed down, and so can you!

Health-wise, supersensitive Pisces, associated with the lymphatic system, reacts strongly to environmental toxins and emotional stress. It's no accident that we often do spring cleaning during the Pisces months. Start your birthday off right by detoxing your system with a liquid diet or supervised fast. This may also help with water retention, a common Pisces problem. Lympathic drainage massage is especially relaxing and beneficial to Pisces.

The feet are Pisces territory. Consider how often you take your feet for granted and how miserable life can be when your feet hurt. Since our feet reflect and affect the health of the entire body, devote some time to pampering them. Check your walking shoes or buy ones designed for your kind of exercise. Investigate custom-molded orthotic inserts if your arches are high. They could make a big difference in your comfort and performance.

Just as the sign of Pisces contains traces of all the previous signs, the soles of our feet contain nerve endings that connect with all other parts of our body. This is the theory behind reflexology, a therapeutic foot massage that treats all areas of the body by massaging the soles of the feet. For the sake of your feet, as well as your entire body, consider treating yourself to a session with a local practitioner of this technique.

Exercise is not a favorite Pisces activity, unless it is a creative activity like dance or ice-skating, or is related to your water element, such as water aerobics or swimming. A caring exercise instructor who gives you personal attention can also make a difference in your motivation. Walking regularly releases tension, gets you outdoors, and can be a way to socialize with friends away from the temptation of food and drink. Try doing local errands on foot, if you live in a city, or find a local park where you can take a daily hike. Invite someone you love or would like to get to know better to share this time with you, or get an adorable dog to accompany you.

CHAPTER 17

Discover Your Sagittarius Personality

Did you know that your Sagittarius sun sign colors all areas of your life? What and whom you like, how you behave as a parent, your attitude toward your career—all have a strong Sagittarius influence. The more you know about the Sagittarius in you, the better you can use your personal solar power to help you make good decisions, from something as basic as what to wear today to deeper psychological issues such as what compromises you might need to make in order to get along with a difficult boss or new lover. Your sun sign provides a time-honored guide to what's right for you, so why not turn to it when you're at a crossroads in your career, choosing a new hue for your walls, or deciding whether or not to pursue a romantic relationship? Let the following chapters empower you with the confidence that you're moving in harmony with your natural inclinations.

The basic characteristics of a Sagittarius are determined by blending several ingredients. First, there's your Sagittarius element: fire. Fire signs are passionate go-getters, full of energy and ambition. Sagittarius functions in a mutable way; it's flexible and changeable. Then there's your sign's polarity, which adds a positive, masculine, yang dimension. Let's not forget your planetary ruler: Jupiter, the planet of expansion, travel, luck. Add your sign's place in the zodiac: ninth—the place of travel, big ideas, philosophy, religion, broad vision. Finally, stir in your symbol, the aspiring archer, aiming his arrow high at a distant goal.

This recipe influences everything we say about Sagittarius. A mover-and-shaker fire sign ruled by expansive Jupiter is sure to be a risk taker and possibly a gambler. You're sure to love travel, sports, and animals. Surely, you prefer to work independently and value your freedom. You're a visionary, an idealist who thinks big. But remember that your individual astrological personality contains a blend of many other planets, colored by the signs they occupy, plus factors such as the sign coming over the horizon at the exact moment of your birth. The more Sagittarius planets in your horoscope, the more likely you'll follow your sun sign's prototype. On the other hand, if many planets are grouped together in a different sign, they will color your horoscope accordingly, sometimes toning down a dynamic sun sign. So if the Sagittarius traits mentioned here don't describe you, there could be other factors flavoring your cosmic stew. (Look up your other planets in the tables in this book to find out what they might be!)

The Sagittarius Man: The Spin Master

"Nothing ventured, nothing gained" could be the motto of the Sagittarius man, a gambler who understands that life's potentialities are unlimited. You'll go for broke when the occasion demands, with touching faith that luck (or the force of the universe) is on your side. "Luck is a lady" for you, and you can conjure up dreams that keep you going until the next big deal.

More often than not, your enthusiasm for all that inspires you is contagious and your dreams catch on. Like film-maker Steven Spielberg, you spin fantasies that touch us deeply and that bring you fame and fortune. You're a moti-vator who makes others reach beyond what they thought was possible. As such, you can be an inspiring speaker, a world-class salesperson, a teacher par excellence.

As a freewheeling Sagittarius, you have great faith in yourself, knowing your attitude is likely to save the day, for you can always sell your ideas. Though your main interest is moving ahead, sometimes you don't know quite where you're going. Or you may know your destination, but not how to get there. You'll trust to luck (or higher forces) to put you on the fast track rather than stick to a preplanned strategy. Somehow, planning ahead seems to take the fun out of it for you.

Physical and mental risks are challenges to you. Most Sagittarius are superb athletes, and some have a daredevil streak. You can also be the clown, full of practical jokes, with a boyish sense of humor and a love of games that endear you to others. You're the upbeat companion, the jovial daddy, the good sportsman, the great buddy who has personal friends from all walks of life. You tend to be very male-oriented, taking love lightly and making a fast getaway if someone tries to tie you down, like Frank Sinatra in his "Rat Pack" days.

To reach your Sagittarius potential, you must find a way to help others reach theirs, imparting high ideals of honesty, fairness, and love of truth. Teach others to roll with the punches (by the way, you've probably thrown a few yourself) and to take a philosophical view of life's ups and downs.

Your style is charming but confrontational, as Phil Donahue, William F. Buckley, and Winston Churchill have demonstrated. You thoroughly enjoy a good debate and are very articulate when challenged. But sometimes you may be overly direct when you feel compelled to say exactly what you think, regardless of the correct timing. Confrontations can be fiery, especially when you discount the consequences of your words. However, you rarely hold a grudge.

Since it can be difficult for Sagittarius to take direction, you do best working independently, where you can express your visionary views freely, and where your wise and honest words have more opportunity to be heard.

In a Relationship

You tend to be very idealistic and optimistic about marriage, looking for a fun-loving, cheerful companion (with great legs) who shares your basic philosophy of life. But marital realities can bog you down or cause you to bolt when you discover that marriage involves more intense commitment and heavier responsibilities than you antici-

193

pated. It is not easy to establish a stable home if it is merely to be a base of operations for outside activities, a clubhouse, or a comfortable place to relax between trips. You can surmount the sense of restriction that marriage entails if you establish honest communication with your mate, set common goals to hold your relationship together, and include your mate in trips, in work, and in outside interests. Though not known for fidelity, you'll come home to someone who accepts you as you are and gives you plenty of rope.

The Sagittarius Woman: Lady Luck

Sagittarius is the natural cheerleader of the zodiac, spurring others on to make the most of themselves. Like Jane Fonda, you're at your best and are most successful when you're inspiring and motivating others. You'd much rather give orders than take them, and you can run your own business with flair and style. You have the ability to sell others on your schemes and dreams, whether it's an exciting promotional campaign, an all-female wrestling team, or buying up a whole town, as actress Kim Basinger once did. Many Sagittarius women become professional athletes who enjoy the competition and the chance to stretch themselves, like Chris Evert, Suzy Chaffee, and Tracy Austin.

You're not afraid to think big. Once an idea appeals to you, you can promote it to a mass market, spreading the word with contagious optimism and enthusiasm. These same qualities are naturally suited to a career in politics, sales, public relations, or teaching. You're better off delegating routine chores. Otherwise, you might neglect the repetitive but important day-to-day responsibilities, leaving others holding the bag. A good support system is the key to your success!

Though generally blessed with good fortune (your breezy, positive attitude attracts it!), you can get into trouble if you make promises you can't deliver, or if you run rampant over the feelings of others. Though you feel compelled to tell it like it is, you can make your point without alienating others if you lace your truth telling with side-splitting humor (like the "Divine Miss M," Bette Midler) and always leave 'em in an upbeat mood—if not rolling on the floor.

In a Relationship

The Sagittarius woman usually has no problem juggling career and home life, as long as you find a good backup staff to handle finances and routine chores while you pursue outside interests. This also assumes you have found a liberated partner who is unthreatened by your public personality and enjoys gadding about with you (or has a demanding career of his own). He should appreciate a woman with a fine mind, well-toned body, boundless energy, and strong opinions. You'll be sure to pull your own weight in the marriage, cope with constant changes, and manage a large active family.

Sagittarius in the Family

The Sagittarius Parent

Children bring out the jovial, fun-loving child within you, and you welcome the challenge of raising them. But sometimes the responsibilities of parenting turn out to be more than you bargained for. Sagittarius is not a sign that welcomes dependency of any sort. You may resent parental obligations, as they cut into your outside activities. Though very young children can tie you to the home, you'll think of some ingenious ways to get out and about and to stay involved in community activities. A large family car or van, equipped with child seats, offers one way to take the kids along with you.

Sagittarius often discovers that helping young minds to grow and to explore life's adventures can be more interesting than gadding about. You'll discover that you're a born coach who can make learning fun. You know when to lighten up with a joke, and you understand children's restless antics. Once your children get past the dependent stage, you're one of the most enthusiastic parents.

The Sagittarius Stepparent

Stepchildren are the biggest challenge to spouse number two. But the Sagittarius roll-with-the-punches, upbeat, positive attitude comes to the rescue. With your breezy, casual attitude, you find it easier to adjust to being a stepparent than many other signs. Your sense of humor will stand you in good stead when awkward situations crop up. Your honest, direct approach will help get problems out in the open. Since you allow your mate plenty of space, there will be little rivalry with the children. You'll enjoy planning outdoor activities for everyone to share. In time, you'll be a good friend to the children, one who encourages any effort to expand their horizons and who supports their growth toward independence.

The Sagittarius Grandparent

Lucky is the child with a fun-loving Sagittarius grandparent. Sagittarius stays young at heart right through the senior years. You'll enjoy the independence you now have, which gives you the chance to travel or pursue your interests. You may continue to work in some capacity, perhaps as a writer or teacher. You'll keep informed of global happenings, or at least what's happening outside of the home. This may be a time when you offer spiritual support and leadership in religious life.

You'll enjoy the company of your grandchildren, and you'll have the energy to play right along with them. You'll encourage their educational progress, and perhaps even finance higher studies. You'll pass on your hard-won wisdom, thrilling them with tales of youthful adventures and inspiring them to follow their dreams. Best of all, you're a grandparent who laughs with them and teaches them to look on the bright side of life.

CHAPTER 18

Sagittarius Stellar Style: The Fashion Trends, Home Decor, Colors, and Getaways That Suit Sagittarius Best

Whether you're ready for an extreme makeover or simply want to update your wardrobe, look to your sun sign for the trends and colors that will harmonize with your Sagittarius personality.

Sagittarius Chic

There's something about the way you look, the way you wear your hat, that makes a memorable statement. You love to have fun with fashion and be a bit edgy, so you're usually up to the minute on the latest trends. You also need clothes that travel well, move with your body, and yet have flair and style. Stay away from fussy ruffles or demure patterns! You're naturally better suited to well-cut sports clothes and skirts that show off your fabulous legs. Go all-out for the most sensational jogging suits and workout wear, especially if you're in great shape, like Teri Hatcher, Tyra Banks, or Jennifer Connolly. Get a stock of great stockings and beautiful shoes (from Sagittarius designer Monolo Blahnik). Versatile, packable knits in bold colors are made especially for you!

Your look is sometimes a bit shocking but always full of interesting ideas. Like Anna Nicole Smith or Daryl Hannah, you know how to steal and hold the spotlight. Showing a little—or a lot—of flesh is often part of your strategy. The low-rise jeans of Britney Spears and the daring exposure of "Dirty Grrrl" Christina Aguilera are prime examples.

Sagittarius designers like Thierry Mugler understand how to use bright colors, bold jewelry, and dramatic lines. You'll be hip to the latest trends and know how to adapt them to your lifestyle. Because sports are usually a big part of your life, active sportswear often goes from the playing field to your working life.

Sagittarius men are often fashion trendsetters, such as Brad Pitt and Don Johnson, who redefined men's fashion with his combination of T-shirts and pastel Versace suits in the hit show *Miami Vice*. And who can forget the way Frank Sinatra wore his hat or the spiffy Rat Pack tailoring that exemplified the swinger of the fifties. With many of the looks of that decade now being revived, expect fashions to show new versions of the Sinatra look.

Sagittarius models Milla Jovovich, Shalom Harlow, and Bridget Hall strut the runways in the latest high-fashion styles.

Time for a Home Makeover? Bring Sagittarius into Every Room!

A Sagittarius home is often a base to which you return from outside activities. You'd be happiest in a colorful, stylish, yet low-maintenance atmosphere. Skip the fussy details. Get comfortable, easy-care furniture and rugs. Go casual rather than formal. Many Sagittarius prefer the strong statement of ultramodern architecture or the clean-lined look of the 1950s.

For drama, highlight exotic souvenirs picked up on your travels. Even if you are the rare Sagittarius who has never traveled, you are sure to collect some form of exotica, books, athletic trophies, or sporting pictures. Collectors of your sign love vivid artwork and stunning sculpture.

You'll be unhappy in any room with a closed-in feeling, so find a home with plenty of space and a big fireplace, if possible. Since you're sure to have at least one animal companion (often a large dog), look for pet-proof furniture to accommodate your animal pals. Since many Sagittarius get involved with horses, you could decorate with a western or equestrian theme, with hunter green walls, plaid upholstery, and horse prints.

Sagittarius colors should uplift yourself and your family and reflect your exuberant spirit. Don't be afraid to use color with flair, including purple, fiery red, orange, and royal blue. The bolder, the better. The brilliant colors of Mexico and the contrasting red and black of Spain have special resonance for Sagittarius.

Sagittarius is known as the great sports lover of the zodiac and likes to stay in shape. You may have a home gym, TV's tuned to the sports channels, and plenty of room to entertain buddies. A powerful vacuum cleaner and ample storage space for your travel bags and athletic equipment will complete your list of "must haves."

Your Sagittarius Sound Track

Sagittarius music tastes can be as exotic and varied as your travels! Your gypsy soul soars in Latin rhythms, flamenco guitar, and tango. Religious music uplifts your spirits. Sagittarius Frank Sinatra, Noël Coward, Puccini, and George Gershwin speak your musical language. Two of today's most popular singers, Christina Aguilera and Britney Spears, have the bubbling blonde looks and personality of your sign. Other Sagittarius singers Sinead O'Connor, Tina Turner, Bette Midler, and Dionne Warwick are on your wavelength.

Sagittarius Away from Home

If you're a typical Sagittarius, travel is therapy for you. A car gives you a wonderful feeling of freedom and independence, and you probably drive more often than the rest of your family. Chances are, you enjoy a road trip whenever you can. Some of you may invest in a camper van for adventurous journeys. The life on wheels definitely appeals to you.

You may want to settle down for a while in a place with great sports facilities, or attend a horse show in Ireland, the Grand Prix in Monaco, or the Olympic Games. Sagittarius likes the challenge of outward-bound expeditions, wilderness camping trips, and exploring the culture of such places as Antarctica, Finland, Spain, Chile, Thailand, Hungary—countries that resonate to your Sagittarius frequency.

Keep a bag packed with items you can't live without (copies of your favorite tapes, video workouts, portable exercise equipment, roller blades). Choose hotels that have fitness equipment, pools, or jogging tracks so you won't miss a workout. Keep a separate notebook for your contacts and favorite haunts in each city so all your relevant numbers will be instantly available.

CHAPTER 19

Your Sagittarius Career Finder

What Does Sagittarius Bring to the Table?

What makes some Sagittarius more successful than others? Sagittarius has a special combination of talents and abilities that make you stand out. By discovering and developing your special sun-sign strengths, you'll not only be likely to find a career you truly enjoy, but you'll be able to channel your efforts to areas where you'll be most successful.

Sagittarius is a natural visionary, so your best job will give you a worthy goal to aim at. You become very ambitious and motivated when you find a job that inspires you. Therefore, avoid stodgy offices and tradition-bound businesses. Don't even think about a desk job or any work that gets bogged down in details or requires great patience. Instead, go for a fast-paced job with lots of challenge and a constant change of scenery.

Where to Find Opportunity

Head straight for a field where your ideas will be recognized and appreciated, where you'll have plenty of room to explore new territory and expand your mind. Consider anything in sales, journalism, travel, and tourism. Or make your athletic skills a profession in the sports or fitness fields. Your philosophical ideals can be expressed in the education, politics, and publishing fields. You might also be drawn to New Age spiritual work. Any profession involving animals, especially horses, or the outdoors is very appealing to Sagittarius. Conservation and environmental-protection work should be right up your alley.

Follow your natural Sagittarius tendencies. Like other fire signs, you often gravitate to careers that require heat, either literally or figuratively. Intense competition that would scorch others actually turns you on! And you'll blaze right through office politics because you thrive under pressure. Chefs with a busy restaurant kitchen, firefighters, iron workers (work that requires a blowtorch), and heating contractors are other hot jobs for Sagittarius.

As one of the zodiac's pioneers, you flourish when developing or promoting new, improved products and services. Though you can be a big money earner, thanks to your tireless work ethic, financial rewards alone are not enough to satisfy your fiery spirit. You must believe in what you're doing and be able to move ahead at your own pace.

The Sagittarius Leader

You're a breezy, informal boss who covers a wide territory. Though you're difficult to pin down, you stay on friendly terms with everybody but rarely stay around long enough to get into office politics, unless someone challenges your territory. Then you'll send them packing fast.

You tell it like it is and expect others to change their tune accordingly and quickly. Even though you may occasionally step on some toes, subordinates know where they stand. However, since organization is not your strong point, your business structure may be unconventional and sometimes nonexistent. You may have to learn the hard way not to trust to luck when you really need solid practical support. You need a well-organized backup team to make your high-flying ideas happen.

If you have dreams of running a business that will bring financial and personal satisfaction, some advice from those who achieved phenomenal success could help you make those dreams a reality. The successful Sagittarius is the one who is inspired and inspiring. Walt Disney made America "wish upon a star" and made dreams come true. By turning dreams into reality, he transformed the entertainment industry into what we know today. He pioneered the fields of animation and found new ways to combine entertainment with education. No small part of Disney's success came from his Sagittarius quality of vision; he tapped into America's past, connected it to the future, and created a separate Disney World, where life is more fun for everyone. Another visionary in the Disney tradition is film director Steven Spielberg. Actress and fitness guru Jane Fonda became rich and famous from her motivational videos and books.

The Sagittarius Team Player

You are a born optimist whose energy and cheerful, positive attitude win you a top place on the team. However, since following orders and playing by someone else's rules are not your strong points, you'll travel ahead faster if you run your own show where you have plenty of freedom and very loose reins. Diplomacy is also not a strong point, which could create problems in a close working situation where there are delicate egos to coddle.

Promote Yourself!

Use your special Sagittarius talents and abilities to bring you the highest return on your investment of time and energy. Look for a job that inspires you and gives you lots of freedom. Then play up your Sagittarius strong points:

- Sales ability
- Personal flair and humor
- Energy and good physical shape
- Honesty
- Enthusiasm and positive attitude
- Decisiveness

CHAPTER 20

Let Sagittarius Celebrities Teach You About Your Sun Sign

It's fun to find out who else was born under Sagittarius, especially if it's one of your favorite celebrities. Someone in the public eye who was born on or near your birthday is sure to have many of the traits you do. You may even have a Sagittarius twin born the same day and year. Notice how your famous sign mates used their Sagittarius qualities for better or for worse, how they rose from obscurity to fame (and vice versa), what helped or hindered their success, even how they dress to play up their Sagittarius star quality. Could this work for you as well?

You've got a host of charismatic Sagittarius to inspire you. Britney Spears, Lucy Liu, and Tyra Banks embody the upbeat Sagittarius style. Your sign's famous sense of humor made stars of Bette Midler, Woody Allen, and John Larroquette. John Kerry and William F. Buckley are Sagittarius politicians with opposite points of view. If you're a tabloid fan, how do your sun-sign mates show their Sagittarius traits as they cope with scandal and reinvent themselves?

If there's someone who intrigues you, go deeper into his life by finding his other planets in the tables in this book. You'll learn more about him as you apply the effects of Venus (turn-ons), Mars (temper), Saturn (fear factor), and Jupiter (luck) to his sun-sign traits. You'll be amazed at how the total planetary picture lights up when you have a living example to refer to.

If you've caught the astrology bug, you can move on to analyze the charts of current newsmakers and match your astrology skills with the experts. Of the many celebrity sites on the Internet, the most accurate source of famous birthdays is www.astrodatabank.com, which has charts of world events and headline makers, plus the observations of amateur and professional astrologers.

Sagittarius Celebrities

Rodney Dangerfield (11/22/21)
Jamie Lee Curtis (11/22/58)
Scarlett Johansson (11/22/84)
Harpo Marx (11/23/1893)
William F. Buckley (11/24/25)
Joe DiMaggio (11/25/14)
Ricardo Montalban (11/25/30)
Kathryn Crosby (11/25/33)
John Larroquette (11/25/47)
John F. Kennedy, Jr. (11/25/60)
Christina Applegate (11/25/71)
Barbara and Jenna Bush (11/25/81)
Little Richard (11/26/38)
Tina Turner (11/26/39)
Bruce Lee (11/27/40)
Jimi Hendrix (11/27/42)
Caroline Kennedy (11/27/57)
Robin Givens (11/27/64)
Jordan Lee (11/27/65)
Randy Newman (11/28/43)
Alexander Godunov (11/28/49)
Ed Harris (11/28/50)
Anna Nicole Smith (11/28/67)
Suzy Chaffee (11/29/46)
Kim Delany (11/29/61)
Mark Twain (11/30/1835)
Winston Churchill (11/30/1874)
G. Gordon Liddy (11/30/30)
Ben Stiller (11/30/65)
Woody Allen (12/1/35)
Bette Midler (12/1/45)
Carol Alt (12/1/60)
Judd Nelson (12/1/60)
Julie Harris (12/2/25)

Gianni Versace (12/2/46)
Steven Baur (12/2/56)
Tracy Austin (12/2/62)
Lucy Liu (12/2/68)
Britney Spears (12/2/81)
Andy Williams (12/3/30)
Daryl Hannah (12/3/60)
Julianne Moore (12/3/61)
Katarina Witt (12/3/66)
Jeff Bridges (12/4/49)
Chelsea Noble (12/4/64)
Marisa Tomei (12/4/64)
Fred Durst (12/4/71)
Tyra Banks (12/4/73)
Walt Disney (12/5/1901)
Don King (12/6/21)
Janine Turner (12/6/62)
Ellen Burstyn (12/7/31)
Harry Chapin (12/7/42)
Jim Morrison (12/8/43)
Kim Basinger (12/8/53)
Denzel Washington (12/8/54)
Teri Hatcher (12/8/64)
Sinead O'Connor (12/8/66)
Kirk Douglas (12/9/16)
Morton Downey, Jr. (12/9/33)
Beau Bridges (12/9/41)
John Malkovich (12/9/53)
Felicity Huffman (12/9/62)
Emily Dickinson (12/10/1830)
Dorothy Lamour (12/10/14)
Susan Dey (12/10/52)
Kenneth Branagh (12/10/60)
Carlo Ponti (12/11/13)
Rita Moreno (12/11/31)
Tom Hayden (12/11/39)
Teri Garr (12/11/49)
Christina Onassis (12/11/50)
Frank Sinatra (12/12/15)
Dionne Warwick (12/12/41)
Cathy Rigby (12/12/52)
Jennifer Connolly (12/12/70)

Mayim Bialik (12/12/75)
Dick Van Dyke (12/13/25)
Ted Nugent (12/13/48)
Steve Buscemi (12/13/57)
Charlie Rich (12/14/32)
Jane Birkin (12/14/44)
Patty Duke (12/14/46)
Michael Ovitz (12/14/46)
Jean Paul Getty (12/15/1892)
Don Johnson (12/15/49)
Noël Coward (12/16/1899)
Liv Ullmann (12/16/39)
Lesley Stahl (12/16/41)
Steven Bochco (12/16/43)
Bob Guccione (12/17/30)
Keith Richards (12/18/43)
Steven Spielberg (12/18/47)
Brad Pitt (12/18/63)
Kiefer Sutherland (12/18/67)
Katie Holmes (12/18/78)
Christina Aguilera (12/18/80)
Edith Piaf (12/19/15)
Janie Fricke (12/19/47)
Robert Urich (12/19/47)
Jennifer Beals (12/19/63)
Alyssa Milano (12/19/72)
Milla Jovovich (12/19/75)
Jake Gyllenhaal (12/19/80)
John Hillerman (12/20/32)
Uri Geller (12/20/46)
Phil Donahue (12/21/35)
Jane Fonda (12/21/37)
Donna Summer (12/21/48)
Chris Evert (12/21/54)
Florence Griffith Joyner (12/21/59)

CHAPTER 21

The Sagittarius Power of Attraction: Your Chemistry with Every Other Sign

Understanding how your sun sign works as part of a couple can help you make wise decisions about your most important relationships: romantic, business, or friendship.

Traditional astrological wisdom holds that signs of the same element (for Sagittarius, that means other fire signs—Leo and Aries) are naturally compatible. So are signs that are in complementary elements, such as fire signs with air signs. In these relationships, communication flows easily, and you'll feel most comfortable with each other.

But do you want comfort at certain times of your life? What happens when you meet someone, sparks fly, and an irresistible magnetic pull draws you together or when disagreements and challenges fuel intrigue, mystery, and passion? (Think of the sexy verbal sparring in Jane Austen's novel *Pride and Prejudice*.) Even though it may end sadly, you'll never forget or regret that passionate encounter. Indeed, many lasting marriages happen between incompatible sun signs, while some ideally matched couples fizzle after a few years.

Once you understand how your partner's sun sign is likely to view yours and what each of you wants from a relationship, you'll be in a much better position to judge whether this combination has happiness potential. Will there be chemistry or challenges where you'll both need to compromise . . . and are you willing to make them?

The celebrity couples can help you visualize each Sagittarius combination. Notice that some are legendary couples, others showed promise but broke up after a few years, and still others existed only in the fantasy world of film or television (but still captured our imagination).

Sagittarius/Aries

GOOD CHEMISTRY:

You're good buddies who love the great outdoors, risk-taking adventures, travel, and a high-action lifestyle. You'll support each other's goals. This works especially well if you share spiritual ideals. You're both independent and understand each other's need for space.

COMPROMISES:

You both tend to be self-involved and may not invest enough time in maintaining the relationship. Common goals may not be enough to keep you together, especially if you lack solid financial backup. Unless you become more available to each other, you may find yourselves heading off in different directions, in search of more ego support.

SIGN MATES:

Sagittarius Kim Basinger and Aries Alec Baldwin
Sagittarius Chris Robinson and Aries Kate Hudson

Sagittarius/Taurus

GOOD CHEMISTRY:

Sagittarius energizes Taurus, and gets this sign to take calculated risks and dare to think big. Taurus provides the solid support and steady income to make Sagittarius ideas happen. Sagittarius will be challenged to produce and have realistic goals, Taurus to stretch and grow.

COMPROMISES:

You are very different types who are not especially sympathetic to each other's needs. Taurus believes in hard work, Sagittarius in luck. Sagittarius is a rolling stone; Taurus is a quiet meadow. Sagittarius appreciates freedom; Taurus appreciates substance. Taurus could weigh you down or fence you in.

SIGN MATES:

Sagittarius Jake Gyllenhaal and Taurus Kirsten Dunst

Sagittarius/Gemini

GOOD CHEMISTRY:

These polar opposites shake each other up happily. Sagittarius helps Gemini see higher truths, to look beyond the life of the party and the art of the deal. Gemini adds mental challenge and flexibility to Sagittarius.

COMPROMISES:

Gemini pokes holes in Sagittarius theories. Sagittarius can brand Gemini as a superficial party animal. Work toward developing nonthreatening, nonjudgmental communication. However, you can't talk away practical financial realities. You need a carefully thought-out financial program to make things happen.

SIGN MATES:

Sagittarius Joe DiMaggio and Gemini Marilyn Monroe
Sagittarius Brad Pitt and Gemini Angelina Jolie

Sagittarius/Cancer

GOOD CHEMISTRY:

Sagittarius gets a sensual partner who will keep the home fires burning and the coffers full, while Cancer gets a strong dose of optimism that could banish the blues. Your Sagittarius carefree, outgoing, outdoor lifestyle expands the sometimes narrow Cancer point of view and gets the sedentary Crab physically fit.

COMPROMISES:

This joyride could reach a dead end if Sagittarius shows little sympathy for the Cancer need for mothering or runs roughshod over sensitive Cancer feelings. Whining gets nowhere with you, nor do guilt trips. Cancer could withdraw into a protective shell or use claws when Sagittarius exercises a free hand with the budget.

SIGN MATES:

Sagittarius Liv Ullmann and Cancer Ingmar Bergman

Sagittarius/Leo

GOOD CHEMISTRY:

Under your Sagittarius optimism and good humor, the Leo luck soars. You both inspire each other and boost each other creatively. If you like the outdoor life, have a spirit of adventure, and love to travel, you're a winning combination that could feel destined to be together.

COMPROMISES:

Sagittarius is not one to pour on the flattery Leo loves. Nor are you as a Sagittarius known for monogamy! When both your fiery tempers explode, Leo roars and Sagittarius heads for the door. Leo must tone down bossiness and give Sagittarius a very long leash. Sagittarius must learn to coddle the Leo ego and keep that blazing temper on hold.

SIGN MATES:

Sagittarius Stuart Townsend and Leo Charlize Theron

Sagittarius/Virgo

GOOD CHEMISTRY:

These two signs can fulfill important needs for each other. Sagittarius inspires Virgo to take risks and win, and brings fun, laughter, and mental stimulation to Virgo life. Virgo supplies a support system, organizing and following through on Sagittarius ideas.

COMPROMISES:

Virgo won't relate to your Sagittarius happy-go-lucky financial philosophy and reluctance to make firm commitments. Sagittarius would rather deal with the big picture, and may resent Virgo preoccupation with details. Sexual fidelity could be a key issue if your Sagittarius casual approach to sex conflicts with Virgo desire to have everything perfect.

SIGN MATES:

Sagittarius Carlo Ponti and Virgo Sophia Loren

Sagittarius/Libra

GOOD CHEMISTRY:

Libra charm smooths the rough spots, while Sagittarius provides lofty goals and a spirit of adventure. This can be a blazing romance, full of action and fun on the town together. Neither of you is a stay-at-home type.

COMPROMISES:

Libra vacillation and Sagittarius wanderlust could keep you from making a firm commitment. You both need to find a solid launching pad (either mutual interests or career goals) to give this relationship structure. Libra needs a partner, but Sagittarius, who travels fastest alone, resents being tied down in any way.

SIGN MATES:

Sagittarius John Kerry and Libra Teresa Heinz Kerry

Sagittarius/Scorpio

GOOD CHEMISTRY:

Sagittarius sees an erotic adventure in Scorpio and doesn't mind playing with fire. Scorpio is impressed with your Sagittarius high ideals, energy, and competitive spirit. Sagittarius humor diffuses Scorpio intensity, while Scorpio provides the focus for Sagittarius to reach those goals.

COMPROMISES:

Scorpio sees through schemes and won't fall for a sales pitch unless it has substance. Sagittarius may object to the Scorpio drive for power rather than for higher goals. You will flee from Scorpio possessiveness or heavy-handed controlling tactics.

SIGN MATES:

Sagittarius Jane Fonda and Scorpio Ted Turner
Sagittarius Phil Donahue and Scorpio Marlo Thomas

Sagittarius/Sagittarius

GOOD CHEMISTRY:

This pair functions best on the road. You share each other's ideals and goals. You are the greatest of traveling companions, never tying each other down.

COMPROMISES:

In the real world, your life together may be like a series of one-night stands. Rarely are you in the same place for long, unless you arrange to travel together. You'll need to make an effort to establish a solid home base (delegate financial matters to a disciplined, responsible third party). Otherwise, you could have no one to come home to.

SIGN MATES:

Sagittarius JFK Jr. and Darryl Hannah or Sagittarius twins Jenna and Barbara Bush

Sagittarius/Capricorn

GOOD CHEMISTRY:

Capricorn has a built-in job organizing Sagittarius. But your Sagittarius challenge of doing something for the greater good could bring Capricorn status and recognition. Sagittarius encourages Capricorn to elevate goals beyond the material and brings out both the spiritual side and the humor of this sign. In return, Sagittarius gets a hard worker who'll translate dreams into positive action.

COMPROMISES:

Optimistic Sagittarius meets pessimistic Capricorn and you cancel each other out! Ultimately, you can't play it for laughs. Capricorn pushes Sagittarius to produce and commit. Then Sagittarius takes off to do your own thing.

SIGN MATES:

Sagittarius Woody Allen and Capricorn Diane Keaton

Sagittarius/Aquarius

GOOD CHEMISTRY:

Aquarius unpredictability and concern for humanitarian causes will mesh with your Sagittarius adventurous spirit and lofty ideals. You'll give each other plenty of freedom, and probably invent a unique, unconventional lifestyle.

COMPROMISES:

Dealing with everyday realities could be problematic. This pair may not be able to get things done. You'll have lots of talk, but little concrete action. Each may go your own way, or look elsewhere for backup support.

SIGN MATES:

Sagittarius Brad Pitt and Aquarius Jennifer Aniston

Sagittarius/Pisces

GOOD CHEMISTRY:

You spark each other creatively and romantically. Pisces imagination and Sagittarius innovation work well on all levels. Variety, mental stimulation, and spiritual understanding plus an appreciation of exotic places could draw and keep you together.

COMPROMISES:

Pisces can turn from a gentle tropical angelfish to a vengeful shark when Sagittarius disregards tender Pisces feelings. Sagittarius goes for direct attacks, and could suspect the self-protective Pisces of hiding truths far beneath the surface.

SIGN MATES:

Sagittarius Frank Sinatra and Pisces Barbara Marx Sinatra

CHAPTER 22

Astrological Overview for Sagittarius in 2007

Welcome to 2007, Sagittarius! It looks like a very good year for you, particularly during the first nine months, when your ruler, expansive Jupiter, is in your sign. Serendipity graces many of your experiences—you're in the right place at the right time!

Pluto is also in your sign, continuing a journey that began in 1995. Your life keeps on changing at fundamental levels, pushing you to try new things, meet new people, and seize opportunities as they arrive.

Neptune, another slow-moving planet, continues its journey through Aquarius and your third house. A relationship with a sibling, another relative or perhaps a neighbor brings new insights into your spirituality and also suffuses your artistic sensibilities with a deeper appreciation for simplicity.

Uranus in Pisces has been moving through the home sector of your chart for a few years and continues to bring unexpected change. If you haven't already moved, you may do so this year. Frequent travel is a possibility. Unusual and often brilliant people continue to enter your life and help you to see yourself in a different light.

The best times for romance this year occur when Venus is moving through Aries and your fifth house, between February 21 and March 16. During this period, Venus is forming a harmonious angle with your sun. Good backup dates for romance happen very late in the year—December 30 and into January of 2008. This certainly gives you the opportunity for a great New Year's Eve!

Mars, symbolic of your sexual and physical energy,

moves through your fifth house between May 15 and June 23, heightening your sexuality. During this period, you're interested in having a good time! Any relationships that begin under this transit may not last forever, but you'll enjoy yourself.

Good career periods this year fall between July 14 and July 27, when Venus moves through your tenth house. Venus means smooth sailing. After July 27, Venus turns retrograde and stays like that until September 8. Even though a Venus retrograde isn't as serious as a Mercury retrograde, its energy becomes dormant. Exert caution during this time, don't begin any new projects or take on more work. The period between September 9 and October 8 also favors career matters.

April 17 features a new moon in Aries in your fifth house. This lunation brings new opportunities and people to your doorstep in the areas of romance, love, and creativity. Each month, there's a new moon in a different sector of your chart and this one and the new moon in your sign on December 9 look especially good.

There are four eclipse dates to watch for this year. Two of them involve Virgo, two involve Pisces. Lunar eclipses tend to bring up emotional issues related to the sign and house in which they fall and solar eclipses tend to reveal something that has been hidden. On March 3, the lunar eclipse in Virgo will bring up an emotional issue connected with your career and your relationship with authority—a parent, a boss, even a government figure. Two weeks later, on March 18, the solar eclipse in Pisces brings to light something that has been hidden from you in your home life or personal environment.

On August 28, there's a lunar eclipse in Pisces. This eclipse hits your career area, so expect an emotional issue to surface in that area. On September 11, the solar eclipse is in Virgo. This eclipse reveals something concerning your career.

Every year, Mercury turns retrograde three times, and during these periods, it's easy to be misunderstood, travel plans often go awry, and computers and other appliances act up. It's a good idea not to negotiate or sign contracts. The times to watch for are:

February 13–March 7—Mercury retrograde in Pisces (your fourth house). This retrograde affects your home life.

June 15–July 9—Mercury retrograde in Cancer (your eighth house). Shared resources are affected. Don't apply for loans or mortgages during this period.

October 11–November 1—Mercury retrograde in Scorpio (your twelfth house). Now is a good time for therapy, dream recall, even a past-life regression.

CHAPTER 23

Eighteen Months of Day-by-Day Predictions—July 2006 to December 2007

Moon sign times are calculated for Eastern Standard Time and Eastern Daylight Time. Please adjust for your local time zone.

JULY 2006

Saturday, July 1 (Moon in Virgo)   Even though it's Saturday, you may be focused on professional or career matters. You could be busy on the telephone with coworkers or writing a report that's due. Any dealings with coworkers will be warm and congenial. Avoid any emotional displays in public.

Sunday, July 2 (Moon in Virgo to Libra 1:07 p.m.)   It's a number 8 day. Think of it as a power day. The focus turns to finances. Be positive and act successful, even if you don't always feel that way. You'll find the universe responding to your needs and desires. It's a day to think big and expect a financial coup.

Monday, July 3 (Moon in Libra)   Spread cheer and positive energy wherever you go today. Take on the role of goodwill ambassador for the universe. Foster harmony in everything you do and say. Ease up on your routines at work. Strive for balance.

Tuesday, July 4 (Moon in Libra)   With Mercury going retrograde in your ninth house, be aware of possible delays and miscommunication related to travel. You miss a connection for a flight or you get stuck in a long line at the check-in counter. There also could be a misunderstanding with a foreign person. Take things one step at a time.

Wednesday, July 5 (Moon in Libra to Scorpio 1:14 a.m.)   It's a number 2 day. To get what you want, act in a cooperative manner, even if it hurts. Be kind and understanding. Partnerships play a key role. But you may take a close look at a relationship.

Thursday, July 6 (Moon in Scorpio)   Jupiter is going direct in your twelfth house today. As a result, you should feel a release of a lot of pent-up energy. Take what you've learned over the last few months and put it to good use.

Friday, July 7 (Moon in Scorpio to Sagittarius 10:14 a.m.) With the moon going into your sign this morning, your thoughts and feelings are aligned. You get recharged for the month ahead. You're feeling physically vital; relations with the opposite sex go well.

Saturday, July 8 (Moon in Sagittarius)   Now you're seeing the big picture better than ever. Travel is indicated. Matters relating to the law or publishing are key to your day. Keep your good humor and don't limit yourself. Go for it all. Sex is in the air!

Sunday, July 9 (Moon in Sagittarius to Capricorn 3:25 p.m.)   It's a number 6 day. Be generous and tolerant. Visit a sick family member or friend on this Sunday. Do a good deed for someone. A domestic adjustment works out for the best. Be understanding with others. Focus on making people happy.

Monday, July 10 (Moon in Capricorn)   Did you read the Declaration of Independence on the Fourth of July? Is it full of eighteenth-century feel-good philosophy or does it truly represent our country's values? Think about it, Sagittarius.

Tuesday, July 11 (Moon in Capricorn to Aquarius 5:46 p.m.)   It's a number 8 day; make a power play. Open your mind to a new approach, which could bring in big money. But keep your goal in mind. Be courageous. Look and feel successful, and you'll attract the experiences that make it so.

Wednesday, July 12 (Moon in Aquarius)   With the moon in your third house, you diligently pursue communications with others and you make your opinions known. Find a new way of expressing yourself. Things go well in a social gathering, especially with relatives and neighbors involved. Keep in mind that what you say or write could be subject to varying interpretations. Matters related to the past could affect your thinking.

Thursday, July 13 (Moon in Aquarius to Pisces 7:00 p.m.)   It's a number 1 day. You get a fresh start today. Stress originality. Trust your hunches. Don't be afraid to turn in a new direction. Make room for a new love, if that's what you're looking for. A flirtation could turn serious.

Friday, July 14 (Moon in Pisces)   Imagination is highlighted today. It's a good day for a creative pursuit. Find time for yourself. Meditate. Focus on deep spirituality, universal knowledge, and eternal truths. Compassion is the key word for the day.

Saturday, July 15 (Moon in Pisces to Aries 8:39 p.m.)   It's a number 3 day. Follow up on what you started yesterday related to a creative project. Your imagination remains keen. Your intuition is highlighted. Your charm and wit prevail. Your popularity is on the rise.

Sunday, July 16 (Moon in Aries)   Your energy flows well. Set out on an adventure. You're feeling vital and energized. Follow your natural inclination toward travel. Alternately, your day may involve pursuing an athletic endeavor or attending a sporting event.

Monday, July 17 (Moon in Aries to Taurus 11:45 p.m.)   It's a number 5 day. It's a good day to take a risk. Freedom of thought and action is emphasized. Release old structures; get a new point of view. Experiment today. The potential is good for a long-term commitment.

Tuesday, July 18 (Moon in Taurus)   With Venus going into your eighth house today, love experiences are more intense than usual. You may have strong feelings regarding shared resources. It's a good time to apply for a mortgage or a loan. Your spouse may be getting a raise. Alternately, a new romance is possible, especially if you meet the person at a gathering related to financial matters.

Wednesday, July 19 (Moon in Taurus)   With the Taurus moon in your sixth house, health, exercise, and diet issues come to a head. Attend to personal health matters. It's a good day to get out and work in the garden or take a hike.

Thursday, July 20 (Moon in Taurus to Gemini 4:39 a.m.)   It's a number 8 day. Business discussions go well. You're being watched by people in power. Unexpected money could come your way. With any luck, you could pull off a financial coup.

Friday, July 21 (Moon in Gemini)   Your energy may be high today, but you have to work hard to keep everything in balance and harmony. Conflict could arise between your professional life and home life. Don't ignore your partner's desires.

Saturday, July 22 (Moon in Gemini to Cancer 11:29 a.m.) With Mars going into your tenth house, your career is energized. New opportunities arise. You may be working hard, putting in overtime. You could feel a strong sexual attraction to a coworker or a boss, and it probably conflicts with your current love life. Sparks fly!

Sunday, July 23 (Moon in Cancer)   The moon is in your eighth house, and matters related to taxes, insurance, and investments might come up. Your experiences are more intense than usual. You may take time to pursue a metaphysical interest.

Monday, July 24 (Moon in Cancer to Leo 8:25 p.m.) It's a number 3 day. Remember a special anniversary or birthday. Spread your good news. Take time for conversation or a hobby. Stay positive and upbeat. Have fun today. Tomorrow may require discipline and focus.

Tuesday, July 25 (Moon in Leo) With the new moon in Leo, you boldly move forward, planting seeds for the coming month. You reevaluate your identity and look for new ways of publicizing yourself. Create a ritual by lighting a candle and writing your hopes and wishes, especially those related to travel or education. Visualize yourself as whole and healthy.

Wednesday, July 26 (Moon in Leo) You relate to people with ease. You relate your interests to the interests of others. You put forth new ideas. The emphasis is on the higher mind or higher education. Foreigners or a foreign country may play a role.

Thursday, July 27 (Moon in Leo to Virgo 7:37 a.m.) It's a number 6 day. It's all about service to others. Be diplomatic in any situation where conflict arises. Make sure you see the big picture. Come to the aid of others, but avoid scattering your energies. Be understanding and helpful, but don't be a doormat.

Friday, July 28 (Moon in Virgo) Mercury is going direct in your tenth house, and you receive great news about your career. Communication problems are cleared up; you can move ahead boldly. Just make sure that you pay attention to details in professional matters.

Saturday, July 29 (Moon in Virgo to Libra 8:28 p.m.) It's a number 8 day, a power day. Play it your way. Open your mind to new approaches, especially ones that could open up opportunities for financial gain. Check your expenses; balance the books.

Sunday, July 30 (Moon in Libra) Romance is highlighted. You seek harmony with those around you. You're feeling sensual and attractive, and you're drawing the attention of others. It's a good day for the theater, a visit to a museum, or a concert. Children may play a role.

Monday, July 31 (Moon in Libra)   Friends play an important role, but you may face a challenge keeping everything in balance. Tensions could rise, and there could be conflict with the opposite sex. A legal matter could be at the center of the conflict. Examine your overall goals and make sure they fit with who you really are.

AUGUST 2006

Tuesday, August 1 (Moon in Libra to Scorpio 9:08 a.m.)   It's a number 8 day, your power day. You can pull the strings. Look for a new approach in business matters. It could result in a raise or a financial coup. An unexpected windfall comes your way. Stay calm; remain in control.

Wednesday, August 2 (Moon in Scorpio)   With the moon in your twelfth house, you withdraw today and work behind the scenes. Investigate, dig deep, and look into secret matters. You're feeling intense and passionate. Avoid going to extremes.

Thursday, August 3 (Moon in Scorpio to Sagittarius 7:14 p.m.)   It's a number 1 day. Don't be afraid to take a new direction, one that is uniquely yours. Stress originality; avoid following well-worn trails. Trust your hunches and keep your distance from people with closed minds. Make room for a new love, but keep in mind what that commitment entails.

Friday, August 4 (Moon in Sagittarius)   The energy initiated yesterday continues as the moon moves into the first house, your sun sign. You get a fresh start and you're more appealing to the public.

Saturday, August 5 (Moon in Sagittarius)   You charge ahead as the moon remains in your sun sign. Your feelings and thoughts are aligned. You're more sensitive to other people's feelings. You may feel somewhat moody, but vitality is strong and relations with the opposite sex work well.

Sunday, August 6 (Moon in Sagittarius to Capricorn 1:20 a.m.) It's a number 4 day. It's a good day to take time to get organized. Be methodical and thorough. When you do so, expect to find something that you've misplaced. Look for a new outlet for creativity.

Monday, August 7 (Moon in Capricorn) Money matters arise today. You're dealing with payments, collections, or both. A bank or financial institution may be involved. You feel emotional about objects you possess or desire. But put off big purchases for a few days.

Tuesday, August 8 (Moon in Capricorn to Aquarius 3:48 a.m.) It's a number 6 day. Dedicate your day to service. Focus on making people happy. How can you help someone in your life? Be diplomatic when dealing with someone with a complaint. Be helpful, but avoid scattering your energies.

Wednesday, August 9 (Moon in Aquarius) Your ability to communicate with others, especially groups, goes well today. Your energy flows smoothly. You help the group's goals and your own. Your wishes and dreams come true. You may promote new ideas that diverge from the accepted way of doing things.

Thursday, August 10 (Moon in Aquarius to Pisces 4:11 a.m.) It's a number 8 day. Pay attention to the signs around you. Listen to what people say and look for hidden meanings. Your intuition pays off. You could find yourself in a position for sudden financial gain. However, stay grounded. Avoid self-deception.

Friday, August 11 (Moon in Pisces) You return to your foundations today. Find time to retreat to a private place to recharge your batteries. Meditation leads to creative expansion. Your imagination is highlighted.

Saturday, August 12 (Moon in Pisces to Aries 4:23 a.m.)
With Venus moving into Leo, you could make known your
intentions related to a matter of the heart. Dress in something that attracts attention. You may find yourself surrounded by admirers. It's a great day to initiate a new
love relationship.

Sunday, August 13 (Moon in Aries)   Your energy flows
smoothly today. Your thoughts and feelings are in harmony. You feel vital and energized. You could participate
in a sport or attend a sporting event. Look for adventure,
but avoid reckless behavior.

*Monday, August 14 (Moon in Aries to Taurus 6:01
a.m.)*   It's a number 3 day. Expect an invitation from a
friend or loved one. Your popularity is on the rise. Your
charm, wit, and curiosity work in your favor. Remain flexible; listen to your intuition. Your imagination is particularly
keen today.

Tuesday, August 15 (Moon in Taurus)   With the moon
in your sixth house of health and daily work, health issues
arise. Pay attention to your diet. Take time to exercise;
tend to your garden. Attend to details, handle practical
matters, and stay grounded. In order to cultivate new ideas,
you need to avoid stubborn resistance to change.

*Wednesday, August 16 (Moon in Taurus to Gemini 10:08
a.m.)*   It's a number 5 day. Your mind may be wander-
ing today. You're ready to accept change and variety. Let
go of the restrictions holding you back. Take a risk. Freedom of thought and action prevails. Your physical desires
may be driving you to act.

Thursday, August 17 (Moon in Gemini)   You may be
experiencing some challenges related to a partnership.
Your energy level is probably high today, you're mentally
alert, and you can accomplish a great deal. However, you
need to find harmony with a business partner or your
spouse before you can move ahead.

Friday, August 18 (Moon in Gemini to Cancer 5:04 p.m.)   It's a number 7 day. That means you may be dealing with secrets, a mystery, intrigue, or an exploration of the unknown. If you're privy to confidential information, don't reveal it. Maintain emotional balance.

Saturday, August 19 (Moon in Cancer)   With the moon in your eighth house, your experiences are more intense than usual. An exploration of metaphysical topics, such as life after death, could captivate you. You're particularly sensitive to other people's moods today, and you're probably moody as well.

Sunday, August 20 (Moon in Cancer)   You may be dealing with matters related to taxes, insurance, or investment. Make sure all your papers are ready and in order, if you're seeking a contract. Guard your possessions in any legal dealings. Tend to loved ones. Do something special for your children or spouse.

Monday, August 21 (Moon in Cancer to Leo 2:34 a.m.)   It's a number 1 day, your high cycle. Be creative and original. Don't follow others. Explore and discover. If you're looking for love, you can find it. You get a fresh start, a new outlook.

Tuesday, August 22 (Moon in Leo)   Your energy is strong and meets little resistance. You're feeling passionate, impulsive, and romantic. Any creative project you began yesterday expands today. Look for a foreign or an international connection. It's a good day to plan a long journey.

Wednesday, August 23 (Moon in Leo to Virgo 2:08 p.m.)   A new moon is in Virgo, which means new beginnings. You plant seeds; new ideas that could relate to health issues, a new romance, or possibly a writing project are germinated. Study the details.

Thursday, August 24 (Moon in Virgo)   Stick close to home today, if possible. Tend to details, and seek perfection in all that you pursue, whether it's about cleaning the house or planning healthy meals. Take time to relax and write in a journal. Pose a question to yourself and watch the answers materialize!

Friday, August 25 (Moon in Virgo)   With the moon in your tenth house, professional concerns come into focus. You get along well with fellow workers and could be dealing with bosses. Look for a possible raise or promotion. You're in the public eye today.

Saturday, August 26 (Moon in Virgo to Libra 3:01 a.m.)   It's a number 6 day. Let the music play; find your rhythm for the day. Dance to your own tune. A domestic purchase is highlighted. Be understanding and helpful, but avoid scattering your energies.

Sunday, August 27 (Moon in Libra)   Friends play an important role today. You make deep contact with like-minded individuals. You work well with a group and tend to keep everyone in balance. If there's a disagreement, you're the mediator. Take time for enjoying the arts by attending a play or movie or visiting a museum or art gallery.

Monday, August 28 (Moon in Libra to Scorpio 3:56 p.m.)   It's a number 8 day, your power day. Business negotiations work in your favor. Be courageous; take a chance. Unexpected money may arrive. Open your mind to a new approach that could pay off in a big way.

Tuesday, August 29 (Moon in Scorpio)   It's a good day to investigate a matter that may relate to secret dealings. Dig deep to find out what's going on behind closed doors. Your intuition is heightened today. Expect intense, emotional experiences to arise. You're passionate about what you believe.

Wednesday, August 30 (Moon in Scorpio)   Take time to withdraw from the public view. Work behind the scenes. Use your intuition. Things affecting your past or childhood could come up. You may feel a need to keep your feelings secret. Relations with women may be difficult at this time.

Thursday, August 31 (Moon in Scorpio to Sagittarius 3:00 a.m.) It's a number 2 day. Cooperation is highlighted. You work well with others. It would be a great day to get married! Issues related to a partnership come under scrutiny. Consider where you are going with the partnership and why. Don't make waves today. Be kind and understanding.

SEPTEMBER 2006

Friday, September 1 (Moon in Sagittarius) The moon is in your sun sign. Your feelings and thoughts are aligned, and your relations with the opposite sex work well today. You're feeling physically vital. You may find yourself in a more public position than usual.

Saturday, September 2 (Moon in Sagittarius to Capricorn 10:35 a.m.) It's a number 1 day. Yesterday's high energy surges on. Be independent and creative. Get out and meet new people; have new experiences. Do something you've never done before. Don't be afraid to turn in a new direction.

Sunday, September 3 (Moon in Capricorn) You identify emotionally with whatever you value highly. It could be your values themselves! You feel best when you're surrounded by familiar objects that make you feel comfortable, or when you're surrounded by people who share the same values as you.

Monday, September 4 (Moon in Capricorn to Aquarius 2:15 p.m.) With Pluto going direct in Sagittarius, energy that you've been holding in is released. You can use the powerful energy associated with Pluto. Stay optimistic; remain flexible. Your intuition is strong today. Your attitude determines everything.

Tuesday, September 5 (Moon in Aquarius) Group activities are highlighted. Take a chance; your communication skills are strong. Find a new approach, a new idea for dealing with an old pattern. Let others know that you have a better way than the traditional way something is done.

Wednesday, September 6 (Moon in Aquarius to Pisces 2:57 p.m.) With Venus moving into your tenth house of profession and career, you get along well with your associates in the workplace. You're more emotional, and you feel a special warmth toward colleagues. Be careful, though, not to blur the boundaries between your personal and professional lives.

Thursday, September 7 (Moon in Pisces) With Mars moving into your eleventh house, expect new interest or activity related to advertising, promotion, or any kind of publicity. But make sure that you find the right balance in your message.

Friday, September 8 (Moon in Pisces to Aries 2:24 p.m.) It's a number 7 day. Something secretive comes to light. You may find yourself pursuing a mystery, or embarking on a journey into the unknown. Gather information, but don't make any absolute decisions until tomorrow.

Saturday, September 9 (Moon in Aries) It's a good day for initiating a new project, possibly in your home. Alternately, you might attend a sporting event or embark on an adventure. If there's a mountain to climb, you may be on your way to the summit. However, avoid any reckless behavior.

Sunday, September 10 (Moon in Aries to Taurus 2:31 p.m.) It's a number 9 day, the end of a cycle. Spiritual values arise. Use the day for reflection and expansion. That means letting go of old notions, looking outside the box. Find a universal message. Clear up odds and ends, but don't start anything new.

Monday, September 11 (Moon in Taurus) Find time to get out in nature. Your senses are highly attuned to your surroundings. Listen to music; go for a hike. Health and physical activities are highlighted. Cultivate new ideas, but focus on what's practical and achievable.

Tuesday, September 12 (Moon in Taurus to Gemini 5:00 p.m.) It's a number 2 day. Issues related to marriage, finances, property values, and real estate are on the table. Watch developments as they unfold, but don't make waves. Don't rush or show resentment. The spotlight is on cooperation.

Wednesday, September 13 (Moon in Gemini) The energy related to partnerships continues. You may want to accomplish a great deal, but unless you find harmony with your partner you'll meet resistance, whether that partnership is professional or personal. Confrontations will be more emotional than usual.

Thursday, September 14 (Moon in Gemini to Cancer 10:54 p.m.) It's a number 4 day. Your organizational skills are highlighted. Control your impulses. Stay focused and persevere to get things done. You're building foundations for the future. You may need to tear down in order to rebuild. Rewrite and revise. Emphasize quality.

Friday, September 15 (Moon in Cancer) Experiences at home might be more intense than usual. The focus is on issues related to belongings, things you possess as well as those you share with others. Matters related to taxes, insurance, or investments are also on the table. Alternately, you could be delving into metaphysical matters, which take on added importance.

Saturday, September 16 (Moon in Cancer) It's a good day for a garage sale. Clean out the old. Redecorate and beautify your living environment. You may be feeling somewhat moody and sensitive to other people's moods. It's best to keep things to yourself.

Sunday, September 17 (Moon in Cancer to Leo 8:15 a.m.) It's a number 7 day. Look for the mysterious in the mundane. You may be surprised by what you uncover. Someone may relate secret or confidential information to you. Make sure you see things as they are rather than how you would like them to be. A Virgo or a Pisces plays a distinct or extraordinary role.

Monday, September 18 (Moon in Leo)   Everything feels in harmony today and you're able to accomplish what you set out to do. It's a good day to strut your stuff. Step out into the public view; self-promotion pays off. Let others know what you're doing. You can easily impress.

Tuesday, September 19 (Moon in Leo to Virgo 8:07 p.m.)   It's a number 9 day. Complete projects and make room for the new. Accept whatever comes your way today, but don't start anything. Use the day for reflection and planning. Discard preconceived notions.

Wednesday, September 20 (Moon in Virgo)   With the moon in your tenth house, it's a good day for sales and promotion. Business matters are highlighted. You're in the public view, so make the best of it. There's a good chance for elevating your prestige. People will start looking at you in a new light.

Thursday, September 21 (Moon in Virgo)   Tend to health issues. Watch your diet; don't forget to exercise. Take a yoga class to stretch and relax. Tidy your actual home or your mental abode. Tend to details; seek perfection. Put down your thoughts in a journal.

Friday, September 22 (Moon in Virgo to Libra 9:07 a.m.)   The new moon is in your tenth house; you plant seeds for the future, and they could result in a promotion or an elevation of your prestige within the next month. Seek perfection. Study the details.

Saturday, September 23 (Moon in Libra)   It's a good day for getting together with friends. Seek harmony and peace. Relationships, romance, and sensuality are highlighted. Attending a concert or going to the theater would suit you well today.

Sunday, September 24 (Moon in Libra to Scorpio 9:55 p.m.)   It's a number 5 day. Look for a change of scenery; variety is the spice of life. Take a risk; diversify. Approach the day with an unconventional mind-set. However, be careful not to spread yourself too thin.

232

Monday, September 25 (Moon in Scorpio)   Your intuition is heightened today, and so is your sexuality. Another water sign—a Pisces or a Cancer—may play a role in your day. You may have a tendency to go to extremes. Forgive and forget.

Tuesday, September 26 (Moon in Scorpio)   Investigate. Dig deep for information, especially related to a confidential matter. Control issues surface. Secret meetings come to light. Be aware of possible deception. Things are not necessarily what they appear! Intense and passionate experiences may unfold before your day is over.

Wednesday, September 27 (Moon in Scorpio to Sagittarius 9:17 a.m.)   It's a number 8 day, a money day. You could be dealing with accounting issues, but more likely you'll be focused on a financial coup. Play it your way. Open your mind to a new approach that could turn favorable for your interests.

Thursday, September 28 (Moon in Sagittarius)   The moon is in your sun sign. You're feeling physically vital; relations with the opposite sex go well. You're especially appealing to the public.

Friday, September 29 (Moon in Sagittarius to Capricorn 6:02 p.m.)   It's a number 1 day. The high energy you experienced yesterday flows into your Friday. You get a fresh start, a new beginning. Take the lead on a project and play it your way. Be original. Avoid following others. Exploration, creativity, and discovery are highlighted.

Saturday, September 30 (Moon in Capricorn)   Venus moves into your eleventh house today. That means there's greater warmth and affection among you and friends. You may get together with others who think a lot like you. Also, you put more emotion into thoughts about your wishes and dreams. It's a good day to examine your overall goals.

Sunday, October 1 (Moon in Capricorn to Aquarius 11:25 p.m.) It's a number 1 day. Individuality is stressed. Be independent and creative. Get out and meet new people; have new experiences. Do something you've never done before. If you're ready and willing, make room for a new love.

Monday, October 2 (Moon in Aquarius) You may encounter some misunderstandings today in your communication with others. A minor crisis might arise in your neighborhood. In dealings with relatives, you may be unduly influenced by the past. Take time to record your thoughts and ideas in a journal.

Tuesday, October 3 (Moon in Aquarius) Look beyond the immediate. Play your hunches today. You may feel physically and emotionally energized, even though niggling problems from yesterday might persist, like a burr caught in your sock. Know when to say enough is enough.

Wednesday, October 4 (Moon in Aquarius to Pisces 1:34 a.m.) It's a number 4 day. Think of the four winds, or the four cardinal directions, which orient your place in the world. Work on what's important for building your foundations. You're at the right place at the right time, especially for building a base for a creative outlet.

Thursday, October 5 (Moon in Pisces) With the moon in your fourth house, the energy generated yesterday prevails again. Your work continues related to the foundation of who you are. Today, however, your search turns more inward. Pay attention to your dreams; watch for synchronicities—those uncanny coincidences. Use your imagination. Be compassionate toward others you encounter.

Friday, October 6 (Moon in Pisces to Aries 1:33 a.m.) It's a number 6 day. It's a day that you might dedicate to service. Do a good deed for someone who can use your help. Focus on making people happy. Be understanding, but avoid scattering your energy.

Saturday, October 7 (Moon in Aries)   The moon is in your fifth house. It's a great day for a creative endeavor, especially one dealing with children. Do something original. Get your pets involved! Be protective and nurturing.

Sunday, October 8 (Moon in Aries to Taurus 1:05 a.m.)   It's a number 8 day. Today's energy expands on what you began yesterday. Play it your way. Keep your mind open; find a new approach. Be courageous. Whatever you're pursuing could generate a nice bonus for you, and it could be a financial windfall.

Monday, October 9 (Moon in Taurus)   Don't forget to exercise and watch your diet. Your health and physical activity are emphasized today. You're opinionated and feeling more sensual than usual. You also may be somewhat more stubborn as well.

Tuesday, October 10 (Moon in Taurus to Gemini 2:06 a.m.)   It's a number 1 day. You're at the top of your cycle. It's a good day to take the initiative to start a new project. Get a fresh outlook, a fresh start. Express your opinions dynamically. Avoid people with closed minds or those who may try to discourage you. Creative people play a role.

Wednesday, October 11 (Moon in Gemini)   It's a good day for dealing with communications, legal matters, or possibly marriage. The focus is on partnerships, both personal and professional. Women may play a prominent role in your day. You see both sides of an issue, and as always, Sagittarius, you see the big picture. However, don't allow others to manipulate your feelings.

Thursday, October 12 (Moon in Gemini to Cancer 6:21 a.m.)   It's a number 3 day. Your popularity is on the rise! Your ability to express yourself is enhanced today. You're curious, intuitive, affectionate, and optimistic. Your charm wins over any doubters. You're on your way.

Friday, October 13 (Moon in Cancer)   It's a good day to get off work early and spend time beautifying your home. A new purchase for your home could be the focus for weekend activity. You may be feeling somewhat sensitive and moody. Best to keep that to yourself and tend to loved ones.

Saturday, October 14 (Moon in Cancer to Leo 2:38 p.m.)   It's a number 5 day. On this Saturday, your sense of freedom is enhanced. You may be looking for a new perspective, a change of pace or location. Whatever it is, you want few, if any, restrictions. For whatever you decide on, there's a strong potential for long-term commitment.

Sunday, October 15 (Moon in Leo)   With the moon in your ninth house, which is ruled by your sun sign, you may be considering a long journey to a foreign country or taking a workshop or seminar. You may have an interest in some action related to a big idea, and you'll be placing yourself right at the center of the matter.

Monday, October 16 (Moon in Leo)   The energy ignited yesterday continues into the workweek. You feel passionate about whatever it is that's captivating your attention. Any romantic involvement at this time feels majestic, as if you and your partner are the stars of a great romance and the whole world is watching.

Tuesday, October 17 (Moon in Leo to Virgo 2:16 a.m.)   It's a number 8 day. Your power day has arrived! Go for it. In business matters, you can pull off a financial coup. People in power are watching you, and your efforts will be rewarded. Find a new approach, one that can bring in big bucks!

Wednesday, October 18 (Moon in Virgo)   The moon's in your tenth house, related to profession and career. Stop worrying and fretting. Take time to relax and collect your thoughts. Get your ideas across in writing, and pay attention to all the details. Dig deep for information. Dealing with a boss or bosses goes well. Expect an elevation in prestige, if not an immediate raise.

Thursday, October 19 (Moon in Virgo to Libra 3:20 p.m.) It's a number 1 day. Trust your hunches. Express yourself dynamically. Explore, discover, find your creative self, and extend it into a new realm. The emphasis is on leadership, individuality, and new beginnings.

Friday, October 20 (Moon in Libra) With the moon in your eleventh house, you may be feeling some tension today in regard to relations with groups. It's a good day to find time to step back and examine your overall goals. Make sure that these goals are an expression of who you really are.

Saturday, October 21 (Moon in Libra) Romance is highlighted. Nurture a relationship. Get out and participate in the arts. Go to a concert, a museum, or the theater. You'll be striving for peace and harmony with those around you.

Sunday, October 22 (Moon in Libra to Scorpio 3:55 a.m.) With the new moon in Libra, the energy that started yesterday is recharged. Others may come to you to resolve differences. You can sort out the issues and keep everyone in balance. You act with personal grace and magnetism. You're especially appealing to others.

Monday, October 23 (Moon in Scorpio) With both the moon and Mars in your twelfth house, you're emotionally volatile. A secret love affair could be involved. You're busy behind the scenes. If you're involved in therapy or interested in it, today would be a good day for a session. It's an ideal time for communicating your deepest feelings to another person.

Tuesday, October 24 (Moon in Scorpio to Sagittarius 2:54 p.m.) With Venus moving into your twelfth house, the likelihood is strong that you're involved in a secret affair. Again, as yesterday, you're wrapped up in behind-the-scenes activities. Your intuition is highlighted. Relations with women can be difficult at this time.

Wednesday, October 25 (Moon in Sagittarius)   Today your energy level is high. With the moon in your sun sign, your mental and emotional states are aligned. You're feeling a sense of abundance and prosperity. There's greater passion than usual in a relationship.

Thursday, October 26 (Moon in Sagittarius to Capricorn 11:48 p.m.)   It's a number 8 day, your power day. Unexpected money may fall into your lap. Buy a lottery ticket. Get ready for a windfall. A deal that's been pending pays off.

Friday, October 27 (Moon in Capricorn)   Your ambition and drive to succeed are highlighted. Opportunities arise in your profession or career. It's a good day to pay bills and collect what's owed to you. Something that you lost is recovered. You feel best when you're surrounded by possessions that you value.

Saturday, October 28 (Moon in Capricorn)   Mercury goes retrograde in your twelfth house. Be aware that whatever you communicate to others may be misunderstood. Expect delays and miscommunication. It's not a good time for signing a contract. Work behind the scenes. You may revisit issues that you thought were resolved, such as childhood matters.

Sunday, October 29—Daylight Saving Time Ends (Moon in Capricorn to Aquarius 5:17 a.m.)   It's a number 2 day. Use your intuition to get a sense of your day. The spotlight is on cooperation. Don't make waves. Remain passive and receptive. Take time to process everything that happened yesterday.

Monday, October 30 (Moon in Aquarius)   You express strong opinions when you communicate with others, especially relatives or neighbors. A female relative may question your motives. The best way to handle the situation is to stay in control of your emotions. Don't let memories of past incidents overaffect your actions today. Dance to your own tune. Follow your heart.

238

Tuesday, October 31 (Moon in Aquarius to Pisces 9:11 a.m.)   It's a number 4 day. Your organizational skills are highlighted. Take care of your obligations. You're at the right place at the right time, so you can overcome obstacles with ease. Missing papers or objects are found. Happy Halloween!

NOVEMBER 2006

Wednesday, November 1 (Moon in Pisces)   Take time to retreat to a private place and spend some time in meditation. Pay attention to your dreams. Your imagination is highlighted. Your thoughts may turn to universal knowledge and eternal truths.

Thursday, November 2 (Moon in Pisces to Aries 10:47 a.m.)   It's a number 3 day. Thoughts related to spiritual values that you considered yesterday are on your mind again. Make time to listen to others. Ease up on your routines. Take time to relax and recharge your battery in preparation for a high-energy day tomorrow.

Friday, November 3 (Moon in Aries)   With the moon in your fifth house of creativity, love, and children, your energy flows smoothly today. It's a great day for initiating a new project or brainstorming new ideas. Have an adventure and take loved ones with you.

Saturday, November 4 (Moon in Aries to Taurus 11:05 a.m.)   It's a number 5 day. You're feeling versatile and changeable. It's a good day to experiment, get a change of perspective, or take a risk. Freedom of thought and action is the key phrase.

Sunday, November 5 (Moon in Taurus)   Focus on your health and diet. Get out and exercise. Take a long walk or go to the gym. You might want to be practical by combining yard work with exercise. You're opinionated and sensual today. Avoid being overstubborn if someone disagrees with you.

Monday, November 6 (Moon in Taurus to Gemini 11:47 a.m.)   It's a number 7 day. You're on a journey into the unknown. It could relate to a personal matter or a professional one. You're moving into unknown or undiscovered territory. Let go of your fears and explore this new world. Make sure you see things as they are, not how you wish them to be.

Tuesday, November 7 (Moon in Gemini)   With the moon in your seventh house of partnerships and marriage, your energy is strong today. However, be aware that you may encounter some resistance from a partner if you push too hard. Try to balance your needs *and* your partner's in order to avoid confrontations.

Wednesday, November 8 (Moon in Gemini to Cancer 2:46 p.m.)   It's a number 9 day. Take time to finish projects and reflect on how you can expand business. Look beyond the immediate. Strive for universal appeal. Don't start anything new.

Thursday, November 9 (Moon in Cancer)   With the moon in your eighth house of shared resources, you feel possessive of your things and the things you share. Your feelings may be more intense than usual, but to avoid confrontations and difficulties, don't get overpossessive. Be aware that powerful people may be watching.

Friday, November 10 (Moon in Cancer to Leo 9:35 p.m.)   It's a number 2 day. Turn around any bad feelings from yesterday by focusing on cooperation. Don't make waves. Go with the flow. Don't run or show resentment. Take time to consider where you're headed and who's going with you.

Saturday, November 11 (Moon in Leo)   Your energy flows smoothly today and you're in an expansive mood befitting Sagittarius. You might be looking to extend your base through promotion and publicity. You feel confident and vital, and you get along well with others.

Sunday, November 12 (Moon in Leo)   Philosophy, religion, and worldviews interest you today. You may discuss these subjects with others; you're passionate about your beliefs. You're impulsive and expressive, but honest. Others listen to your thoughts and opinions.

Monday, November 13 (Moon in Leo to Virgo 8:20 a.m.)   It's a number 5 day. You seek variety and change, freedom of thought and action. It's a good day to take a seminar, plan a long trip, or just find a new approach. You may want to promote new ideas through your writing skills.

Tuesday, November 14 (Moon in Virgo)   With the moon in your house of professions and careers, it's a good day for sales and dealings with the public. Pay attention to the details. Dig deep for information. You communicate your ideas well by speaking or writing.

Wednesday, November 15 (Moon in Virgo to Libra 9:15 p.m.)   It's a number 7 day. Keep any secrets or confidential information entrusted to you. Go with the flow. You may find that others are slow in making commitments or living up to their commitments. See things as they are, not as you would like them to be.

Thursday, November 16 (Moon in Libra)   You may find yourself in the role of arbiter today as disagreements break out around you. You may want to focus on your own wishes and dreams and examine your goals, but first you need to get everyone in balance around you.

Friday, November 17 (Moon in Libra)   With Venus moving into your sun sign, you exhibit a charismatic nature. Everyone's attracted to you. You get a lucky break in finances. Good fortune comes your way over the next few weeks.

Saturday, November 18 (Moon in Libra to Scorpio 9:48 a.m.)   It's a number 1 day. Don't be afraid to take the initiative to turn in a new direction. You express your opinions dynamically. A flirtation turns more serious. Make room for a new love, if that's what you want. But be aware of the consequences, especially if you're not willing to commit.

Sunday, November 19 (Moon in Scorpio)   You may be feeling intense and passionate. With Uranus going direct in Pisces, you release your pent-up energy. However, expect sudden disruptions at home. Perhaps friends stop by unannounced. You may want to retreat to a private place.

Monday, November 20 (Moon in Scorpio to Sagittarius 8:16 p.m.)   The new moon in Scorpio means you start some endeavor behind the scenes. You might begin therapy. By evening, look to the big picture. Where do you fit in it? Where are you headed? What's your goal?

Tuesday, November 21 (Moon in Sagittarius)   Matters related to publishing, law, or education come to the forefront. Your mental and emotional lives are aligned with the sun in your moon sign. You're revitalized.

Wednesday, November 22 (Moon in Sagittarius)   Your sense of humor prevails over any minor misunderstandings. You feel physically vital and passionate. Relations with the opposite sex go well. You could be planning a long trip or embarking on one soon.

Thursday, November 23 (Moon in Sagittarius to Capricorn 4:26 a.m.)   Today, Jupiter, your ruler, appears in your first house. Your personality expands. You feel more open, more magnanimous. Others are attracted to you. Others find you upbeat and fun-loving. Enjoy the day!

Friday, November 24 (Moon in Capricorn)   You could be dealing with elderly people. It might involve finances and possessions, banks and financial institutions, payments and collections. Your responsibilities increase. You may feel stressed and overworked. You need to exercise.

Saturday, November 25 (Moon in Capricorn to Aquarius 10:41 a.m.)   It's a number 8 day. Surprise money may come your way. You may feel like you've won the lottery. It's your power day, so work on your goals. Direct your energy toward success in a big way.

Sunday, November 26 (Moon in Aquarius)   You could face some resistance or unwillingness on the part of others, especially related to your dealings in the everyday world, your neighborhood, or with your relatives and siblings. Stay in control of your emotions when communicating with others, especially at a social gathering. A female relative may play a role.

Monday, November 27 (Moon in Aquarius to Pisces 3:21 p.m.)   It's a number 1 day. It's your day for a new beginning. You're at the top of your cycle. Explore and discover. Take the lead in a new project. Creative people play a role.

Tuesday, November 28 (Moon in Pisces)   With the moon in your fourth house, you may feel like withdrawing from public view and finding a quiet place for meditation. Spend time with your family and loved ones. Your intuition is highlighted. It's a good time for dream recall.

Wednesday, November 29 (Moon in Pisces to Aries 6:30 p.m.)   It's a number 3 day. You're in a fun-loving mood. You're optimistic and affectionate. Your charm and wit are recognized. Spread your good news. Ease up on your routines. It's a good day to relax and enjoy yourself in preparation for tomorrow's discipline and focus.

Thursday, November 30 (Moon in Aries)   The moon moves into your fifth house of creativity. Your strong energy flows smoothly with little resistance. It's the perfect day for brainstorming new ideas or launching a project. Your power of persuasion is magnetic, attracting the attention and interest of those around you. That's especially true when you're passionate about whatever you're doing.

DECEMBER 2006

Friday, December 1 (Moon in Aries to Taurus 8:27 p.m.)   It's a number 3 day. You're feeling vital and connected with those around you. Your optimistic and positive attitude attracts the attention and affection of others. Expect an invitation from a friend or loved one. Remember a special anniversary.

Saturday, December 2 (Moon in Taurus)   Health matters are highlighted today. Avoid any self-denial related to physical and mental health. Don't be a martyr. Take care of yourself. Find time to exercise. Pay attention to your diet. Attend to details. If you're feeling fine, attend to a friend or family member who is ill.

Sunday, December 3 (Moon in Taurus to Gemini 10:06 p.m.)   It's a number 5 day. People take note of your writing or speaking skills. Approach the day with an unconventional mind-set. Experiment; take risks. Let go of old structures so you can find a new point of view. Get ready for change, even if it causes a temporary inconvenience.

Monday, December 4 (Moon in Gemini)   With the moon in your seventh house of partnership and marriage, the focus is on relationships, both personal and business. However, the moon is also in opposition to your sun sign, which suggests you'll need to work hard to develop harmony between your business and personal lives.

Tuesday, December 5 (Moon in Gemini)   Mars goes into your sun sign and energizes your personality. Other people find you attractive, and you're not afraid to speak your mind. You also have Saturn going into your ninth house, which means that it's not a good time to take a long-distance trip. You also may be rethinking some of your viewpoints on big issues.

Wednesday, December 6 (Moon in Gemini to Cancer 1:02 a.m.)   It's a number 8 day. Your power day has arrived. Be courageous and powerful. Focus on a power play. Keep your mind open to a new approach that could lead to a financial coup.

Thursday, December 7 (Moon in Cancer)   Your interest in metaphysical matters is highlighted. Your experiences are more intense than usual. You may attract the attention of powerful people. You also may feel more possessive than usual about your belongings.

Friday, December 8 (Moon in Cancer to Leo 6:53 a.m.)   It's a number 1 day. Strike out on your own. Get a fresh start. Take the lead in a new project. Explore and discover. Stress originality.

Saturday, December 9 (Moon in Leo)   You act very energetic and spontaneous today, especially in regard to any plans for long-distance travel. You also express your interest in ideas, philosophy, and other worldviews with great enthusiasm. You're impulsive and feeling romantic.

Sunday, December 10 (Moon in Leo to Virgo 4:32 p.m.)   It's a number 3 day. Your attitude determines everything. Be happy, positive, and upbeat. Spread good news. Relax and enjoy yourself. Expect an invitation from a friend or loved one.

Monday, December 11 (Moon in Virgo)   Venus moves into your second house today; that's great for money and good fortune. You might get a raise or receive an unexpected check. You're feeling financially flush.

Tuesday, December 12 (Moon in Virgo)   With the moon in your tenth house, your professional concerns are the focus of the day. Pay attention to details. Your written communications attract attention. You're particularly responsive to the needs of a group. Warm up to a fellow worker, but avoid getting emotional in public.

Wednesday, December 13 (Moon in Virgo to Libra 5:01 a.m.)   It's a number 6 day. Service is highlighted. Be diplomatic with others. Keep everything in balance. Be willing to help. Be understanding, generous, and tolerant, but avoid scattering your energies.

Thursday, December 14 (Moon in Libra)   Romance is in the air. You make deep contact with friends. Follow your wishes and dreams. Work to achieve harmony and peace with those around you. Your skills as an arbiter are helpful.

Friday, December 15 (Moon in Libra to Scorpio 5:43 p.m.) It's a number 8 day. Your power day has rolled around again. It's a good day to hit the jackpot. A financial coup is within your grasp. Powerful people are watching you. Be courageous.

Saturday, December 16 (Moon in Scorpio) Intense emotions, possibly vengeful, come into play. You may feel like going to extremes, but it's best to forgive and forget. Control issues are at the heart of the matter. Avoid any major purchases at this time.

Sunday, December 17 (Moon in Scorpio) It's a good day to investigate something hidden or mysterious. You work behind the scenes. Take time to explore a mystical or spiritual discipline. You may want to communicate your deepest feelings to a friend.

Monday, December 18 (Moon in Scorpio to Sagittarius 4:10 a.m.) It's a number 2 day. Cooperation is the key word. Don't rush or push others to hurry. Partnership and marriage are highlighted. Be patient and go with the flow. Use your intuition to get a sense of your day.

Tuesday, December 19 (Moon in Sagittarius) It's a good day to put your face before the public. You're feeling physically vital and energized. Your mental and emotional states are aligned. Relations with the opposite sex go well. You're sensitive to the feelings of others.

Wednesday, December 20 (Moon in Sagittarius to Capricorn 11:39 a.m.) The energy from yesterday flows forward as the new moon goes into Sagittarius. The month ahead will be a new chapter in terms of your self-expression and how you present yourself. Rest up!

Thursday, December 21 (Moon in Capricorn) Your hard work is paying off. Money comes your way. You may be feeling flush, but don't speculate. Play it conservatively. Maintain your emotional equilibrium. You may need to focus more on your home.

Friday, December 22 (Moon in Capricorn to Aquarius 4:49 p.m.)   It's a number 6 day. Focus on making other people happy. Do a good deed for someone, but don't expect anything in return. Visit a sick family member or friend. A domestic adjustment works out for the best.

Saturday, December 23 (Moon in Aquarius)   In your daily life, you may face some challenge that pulls you out of the routine. If tensions arise, be sure to stay in conscious control of your emotions. Don't get lost in the details. Use your intuition and keep the big picture in mind.

Sunday, December 24 (Moon in Aquarius to Pisces 8:44 p.m.)   Family or group activities are highlighted this Christmas Eve. You may gather together with neighbors and relatives. Female relatives play an important role. You may be affected by the past and motivated to write a deep, thoughtful letter to a friend or relative who is far away.

Monday, December 25 (Moon in Pisces)   On this holiday, you might want to slip away from those around you to find time for some quiet meditation. Focus on ideals, such as compassion, deep spirituality, universal knowledge, and eternal truths. Before going to sleep tonight, tell yourself to remember your dreams. Merry Christmas!

Tuesday, December 26 (Moon in Pisces)   Pay attention to your dreams; look for synchronicities, those uncanny coincidences. Think about changing a bad habit. Your imagination is highlighted. Ideas are ripe. Your intuition is keen. However, avoid falling into the trap of self-deception.

Wednesday, December 27 (Moon in Pisces to Aries 12:05 a.m.)   With Mercury moving into your second house, you can expect checks in your mailbox. Your thoughts turn to your perspective on money. Enjoy the company of your mate and strive for cooperation.

Thursday, December 28 (Moon in Aries)   Your emotions may be volatile today. You're passionate and impatient. It's a good day for brainstorming new ideas or

247

launching a new project. You may be feeling energized and adventurous, but avoid reckless behavior.

Friday, December 29 (Moon in Aries to Taurus 3:09 a.m.)   It's a number 4 day. Your organizational skills are highlighted. Control your impulses. Persevere to get your work done. Don't get sloppy. Emphasize quality. You're building a creative base.

Saturday, December 30 (Moon in Taurus)   You may be feeling highly sensitive and sensual. Tend to health and physical activity. Cultivate new ideas. Listen to music; go to a concert or a museum. Enjoy yourself, but avoid any tendency to be stubborn. Go with the flow.

Sunday, December 31 (Moon in Taurus to Gemini 6:17 a.m.)   It's a number 6 day. Service to others is the theme on this New Year's Eve. Music plays a role. Find your rhythm. Dance to your own tune. Be understanding and diplomatic, but avoid scattering your energies.

HAPPY NEW YEAR!

JANUARY 2007

Monday, January 1 (Moon in Gemini)   You and your partner have a meeting of the minds and agree on a particular activity. Chances are it isn't anything typical! Travel is indicated, perhaps to a place near your home. This brief exploration may result in a longer trip later in the year.

Tuesday, January 2 (Moon in Gemini to Cancer 10:15 a.m.)   You may feel a pinch in terms of finances. It's probably worry about what you spent for the holidays, but just the same, finances need your attention. Your mother or another nurturing female in your life has some advice for you. Listen closely, but make your own decision.

Wednesday, January 3 (Moon in Cancer)   Venus moves into Aquarius and your third house. Romance may be as close as your backyard! Someone you previously thought of as an acquaintance seems undeniably attractive in a romantic sense. Chemistry is the hallmark of the day.

Thursday, January 4 (Moon in Cancer to Leo 4:15 p.m.)   The morning could feel iffy; your mood is hard to pin down. But by this afternoon, when the moon moves into a fellow fire sign, your mood lifts and your thoughts turn to more exotic locales.

Friday, January 5 (Moon in Leo)   Mars in Capricorn could be putting a damper on your mood. You may feel you aren't earning enough money to make ends meet. You actually are and your finances are in good shape, so get out of this mood and focus on something more productive!

Saturday, January 6 (Moon in Leo)   Resist speeding today, even if you're late. Better to get someplace late than to be stopped and ticketed for speeding. Jupiter is moving direct in your sign. Take advantage of this wonderful and expansive energy to open yourself to some new area of endeavor. You won't regret it!

Sunday, January 7 (Moon in Leo to Virgo 1:19 a.m.)   Be prepared for tomorrow's meetings by organizing your thoughts on paper. List your priorities. Be clear on what you want and what you hope to achieve. The clearer you are, the easier it will be to sell your ideas.

Monday, January 8 (Moon in Virgo)   Yes, you may feel vulnerable about your career generally, but not to worry. You're on the right track. Tend to details and do the best you can at any given time, and you'll come out way ahead of the pack. You may travel in connection with business within the next few days.

Tuesday, January 9 (Moon in Virgo to Libra 1:15 p.m.)   Friends become the focus. You may get together with people tonight for dinner, a movie, or an impromptu party at your place. You're looking for information on a particular topic, and your wide network of acquaintances is helpful.

Wednesday, January 10 (Moon in Libra)   Balance seems to elude you, even though it's what you crave most. Detachment from an outcome is necessary. Just do what you have to do, fulfilling obligations and meeting deadlines, and don't worry about the end result. Things will work out on their own.

Thursday, January 11 (Moon in Libra)   Your artistic sensibilities are greatly heightened. You may visit museums or photography exhibits or attend a musical. If none of that is possible, satisfy yourself by renting a musical on DVD.

Friday, January 12 (Moon in Libra to Scorpio 2:08 a.m.)   The moon moves into passionate Scorpio and your twelfth house. If you're involved in a clandestine relationship, it may get even more secretive. You may not be happy with keeping things hidden, and that could cause some stress in the relationship. After January 18—with a new moon in Capricorn in your house of romance—you won't go along with the agenda anymore. You want things out in the open.

Saturday, January 13 (Moon in Scorpio)   Dream recall, meditation, yoga—anything done behind the scenes, in the privacy of your own being, is beneficial for you. You can pose questions before you go to sleep on issues where you would like more insight. Keep your pen and pad handy.

Sunday, January 14 (Moon in Scorpio to Sagittarius 1:12 p.m.)   The moon finally moves into your sign. This afternoon is a high time for you. Whatever angst you feel on a daily basis is gone. Your sex appeal soars. Your mind and heart are in agreement.

Monday, January 15 (Moon in Sagittarius)   Mercury moves into Aquarius and your third house. This transit heightens your communications abilities. You may see siblings and neighbors more than you usually do and have more interaction with them. You also could be running around more.

Tuesday, January 16 (Moon in Sagittarius to Capricorn 8:50 p.m.)   Mars moves into Capricorn and your second house, energizing your finances. The moon also moves into the same sign and house, so your focus is on financial security. It's time to take a look at your retirement savings. Consult an expert.

Wednesday, January 17 (Moon in Capricorn)   Time to plan and strategize. You're in a good place to plan long-range. You may have to curb your spending for a while so that you can see your savings grow.

Thursday, January 18 (Moon in Capricorn)   The new moon in Capricorn and your second house brings in new opportunities for earning and investment. Your values come into play. It may be that you need to get into a line of work more closely aligned with what you value.

Friday, January 19 (Moon in Capricorn to Aquarius 1:16 a.m.)   As the moon moves into your third house, you may be offering support to a brother or sister who is going through a tough time. You're glad to do it and come away from the experience with a deeper appreciation for your sibling.

Saturday, January 20 (Moon in Aquarius)   The moon joins Venus in Aquarius in your third house. Romance with the person next door is certainly a possibility. Even if the relationship isn't full-fledged yet, there seems to be a lot of communications flying back and forth. Enjoy it. The romance may not be that of soul mates, but it feeds your naturally gregarious nature.

Sunday, January 21 (Moon in Aquarius to Pisces 3:49 a.m.)   You probably aren't a fan of the moon in Pisces. It makes you feel too sensitive, too moody, too everything that you don't want to feel. But take these emotions and put them to use with your family. Someone close to you needs attention.

Monday, January 22 (Moon in Pisces)   There could be some conflict between personal and professional obliga-

251

tions. You can handle it, but doing so feels uncomfortable. You hate being forced to choose.

Tuesday, January 23 (Moon in Pisces to Aries 5:33 a.m.)   This moon is more like it. You are revved for fun, pleasure, romance, and love, and your muse is whispering in your ear. Take your pick: romance, creativity, or both?

Wednesday, January 24 (Moon in Aries)   You dive into a creative project that you haven't touched since the end of last year. You discover that your passion for this project hasn't waned one iota. In fact, you're in a better place to see what needs to be done to complete it.

Thursday, January 25 (Moon in Aries to Taurus 8:29 a.m.)   Even though you usually aren't any fan of an earth moon, this one helps ground you. It also forms a nice angle to Mars in Capricorn, and helps you to see where you need to make changes in your life. You're after what's practical and efficient at work.

Friday, January 26 (Moon in Taurus)   A regular exercise routine is a must. If you don't have one, create one. There's no time like the present. Join a gym and commit to going three times a week. Or commit to walking so many miles per week or taking so many yoga classes. The point is to commit.

Saturday, January 27 (Moon in Taurus to Gemini 12:10 p.m.)   Venus moves into Pisces and your fourth house. Romance at home! Romance with someone in your personal world. It may not be a relationship where you talk each other's ears off, but a lot goes on under the surface, out of sight.

Sunday, January 28 (Moon in Gemini)   Even though the Gemini moon is opposed to your sun, the air element Gemini is more comfortable for you. You and your partner may get out of town for the day. Just the two of you.

Monday, January 29 (Moon in Gemini to Cancer 5:17 p.m.)   Your concern is on your partner's finances and how you're affected. Don't worry. Focus on your own earning capacity, and do whatever you need to do to increase what you earn. A part-time job of some kind could be in the offing.

Tuesday, January 30 (Moon in Cancer)   Your mother or another female in your life has advice you may not want to hear. Could it be too close to the truth you've suspected but haven't voiced? Everyone in your life is a teacher. What's the lesson you need to learn?

Wednesday, January 31 (Moon in Cancer)   As January winds up, get your travel plans in order for a winter getaway trip. But try not to travel between February 13 and March 7, when Mercury is retrograde. If you have to travel then, embrace the changes that surely will unfold.

FEBRUARY 2007

Thursday, February 1 (Moon in Cancer to Leo 12:15 a.m.) What a fine way to start the month, with the moon in a compatible fire sign and your ninth house. Use this energy to initiate change until February 13, when Mercury turns retrograde. Whether you're attending college classes or considering a return to college or graduate school, the universe is working in your favor.

Friday, February 2 (Moon in Leo)   Mercury moves into Pisces and your fourth house. Count on lots of activity centered in and around the home until April 10. Part of this time, Mercury will be moving retrograde, and you'll have to make adjustments in your schedule. Otherwise, this transit stimulates conversations that can be productive at home.

Saturday, February 3 (Moon in Leo to Virgo 9:34 a.m.)   The moon begins its transit of your career house and forms a harmonious angle with the current position of Mars. You should get a boost of speed and energy over the next two days, so tackle any outstanding professional matters and clear them off your desk and out of your life.

Sunday, February 4 (Moon in Virgo)   The Virgo moon is discriminating, critical, and seeks perfection. All of these qualities can be applied to your career, and the results could surprise you. A peer or boss has insights that help you in a particular project.

Monday, February 5 (Moon in Virgo to Libra 9:15 p.m.)   Breathe. The Libra moon is to your liking. Even though it's a Monday, your sociable moon carries over into this evening. Dinner with friends, time spent in a café, perhaps a movie—all are viable options.

Tuesday, February 6 (Moon in Libra)   Are you feeling ignored or unsupported by friends? You shouldn't. Today's moon brings support when you need it and friends to your doorstep. You get together with a group whose interests are like your own—probably quirky, perhaps theatrical, definitely creative.

Wednesday, February 7 (Moon in Libra)   There could be some friction with finances, or someone attacks your values, putting you in a position where you feel you must defend yourself. You can argue and debate with the best of them, but really aren't in the mood. You would just like to have peace, quiet, and happiness.

Thursday, February 8 (Moon in Libra to Scorpio 10:10 a.m.)   Here comes that intense and passionate Scorpio moon again, in your twelfth house. Basically, you're getting prepared for when the moon moves into your sign. So re-stock your reserves of energy, putter in silence, pay attention to your inner world. By Saturday, you'll be in a partying mood!

Friday, February 9 (Moon in Scorpio)   If you feel your current relationship is getting too serious too quickly, put on the brakes. You, of all the signs, love your freedom too much to compromise. On other fronts, you get information from a dream or meditation that provides insight into a current issue in your life.

Saturday, February 10 (Moon in Scorpio to Sagittarius 10:02 p.m.)   A sudden lifting in your mood happens later this evening. The moon is moving into your sign. And what great timing. Expect tomorrow to be a vast improvement over today.

Sunday, February 11 (Moon in Sagittarius)   A great book for today is by medical intuitive Caroline Myss. Even if you don't have health problems, *Sacred Contracts* will seize your attention. You're after the big picture, and that's what Myss writes about very well.

Monday, February 12 (Moon in Sagittarius)   If it's a holiday for you, get off and travel with a friend or partner. You always love the excitement of new places and people; today is no exception. Besides, you need a break from the winter doldrums. And this evening, be sure you've got your to-do list in order. Tomorrow, Mercury turns retrograde.

Tuesday, February 13 (Moon in Sagittarius to Capricorn 6:43 a.m.)   The first Mercury retrograde of the year happens in Pisces and your fourth house. During the next two weeks, there can be misunderstandings at home and tensions that result from lack of communications. Old friends may be reentering your life, and things could get mighty interesting in that regard!

Wednesday, February 14 (Moon in Capricorn)   Happy Valentine's Day! Your love life is still humming along, but your finances may be stuck. Checks you're expecting are delayed, or the paperwork hasn't gotten through. Make your calls; get things moving again.

Thursday, February 15 (Moon in Capricorn to Aquarius 11:36 a.m.)   If winter is beginning to get to you, schedule a break and get away from it all. Head south or drive to the closest shore.

Friday, February 16 (Moon in Aquarius) Looks like friends gather at your place. You can get along with just about anyone, and your wit doesn't go unnoticed by a certain someone who has tagged along. Is this one about romance or a meeting of the minds?

Saturday, February 17 (Moon in Aquarius to Pisces 1:31 p.m.) The moon joins retrograde Mercury in Pisces, in your fourth house. You may feel somewhat protective toward your family, home, and personal space. But be careful how you communicate this to others. The proclivity for being misunderstood is high.

Sunday, February 18 (Moon in Pisces) You're in the mood to repaint your home office, your bedroom or maybe your entire home. You may want to employ feng shui to enhance certain areas of your life with color and textures. If anything around your home is broken, get it fixed. If things don't work, toss them out and buy replacements.

Monday, February 19 (Moon in Pisces to Aries 2:07 p.m.) The time frame is approaching in which romance and love are the most likely to happen to you. If you already are involved, this period deepens your commitment with partner and signals very smooth sailing. First the moon in Aries and, on February 21, Venus in Aries!

Tuesday, February 20 (Moon in Aries) Your creativity is strong and powerful. If you have been ignoring the creative side of your life, indulge it. Even if you take just an hour for yourself, do it. If you have young kids, let their creative activities become yours. It can't hurt to see the world the way a young child does.

Wednesday, February 21 (Moon in Aries to Taurus 3:04 p.m.) Venus enters Aries. Strap on your seat belt. You're in for several wild and wonderful weeks, and not just in romance. Look to your creativity as a source of profound enjoyment. Who knows what may inspire you? Skydiving, hot-air ballooning, white-water rafting, maybe even rappeling.

Thursday, February 22 (Moon in Taurus) This earth moon brings you back down to the planet and urges you to be practical. Pragmatism doesn't interest you, but other qualities of the Taurus moon do—sensuality, music, and the arts.

Friday, February 23 (Moon in Taurus to Gemini 5:42 p.m.) It won't be much longer before Mercury turns retrograde. Until it does, you may want to catch up on your reading. For an innovative novel, try *The Time Traveler's Wife*. If you're more the nonfiction type, then try Michio Kaku's fascinating book *Parallel Worlds: A Journey Through Creation, Higher Dimensions, and the Future of the Cosmos*.

Saturday, February 24 (Moon in Gemini) You and your partner can't resist the call of the road. Even if it's a business trip, you're content to get out and move. Be sure to take books with you. You may find yourself with a lot of free time on your hands, and you'll want to catch up on your reading.

Sunday, February 25 (Moon in Gemini to Cancer 10:48 p.m.) Mars moves into Aquarius and your third house. This transit, lasting until April 6, triggers travel, possible charity work within your community, and more contact than usual with siblings and neighbors. Mars is symbolic of sexual and physical energy, so perhaps an affair that is pure chemistry is in the works.

Monday, February 26 (Moon in Cancer) Home, family, and hearth typify the Cancer moon. And because this moon is transiting your eighth house, you may be sorting out a family member's finances. Perhaps your mom or dad needs help with this year's taxes. Or perhaps your spouse needs help with insurance forms or a will.

Tuesday, February 27 (Moon in Cancer) The fire in you dislikes the Cancer moon. Like any water-sign moon, it urges you to feel rather than act, to intuit rather than gather facts. So try to work with this energy in a positive way by nurturing your sensitive and intuitive side.

Wednesday, February 28 (Moon in Cancer to Leo 6:30 a.m.)   Finally, a moon sign that feels great to you—more energy, more pizzazz, more flair. In fact, you're feeling so good that you dress in bold colors and get involved in all kinds of drama.

MARCH 2007

Thursday, March 1 (Moon in Leo)   Can you feel it yet? The first small breaths of spring? Even if it's cold where you are, your imagination is full and active, and you can imagine how the air will feel when it's warmer. You can imagine the sunlight on your face, the smell of spring, then summer.

Friday, March 2 (Moon in Leo to Virgo 4:32 p.m.)   With the moon moving into Virgo and your tenth house, you're sensitive about professional matters. You may be worried about your retirement or your pension, but the bottom line here is that you're worried about job security. What would make you feel secure, Sagittarius? Figure it out, and you'll have a large piece of your personal puzzle.

Saturday, March 3 (Moon in Virgo)   There's a new moon in Virgo and also a lunar eclipse. This one falls in your tenth house of career; so you may be dealing with security issues related to your career. New professional opportunities are distinctly possible.

Sunday, March 4 (Moon in Virgo)   If you're feeling besieged, just hold on a couple more days. On March 7, Mercury turns direct again. You're getting help from Mars in Aquarius and your third house. It's your booster rocket through what feels like a challenging day.

Monday, March 5 (Moon in Virgo to Libra 4:26 a.m.)   You wake this morning in a fantastic mood. The moon is in Libra and your eleventh house. You're thinking more about your wishes and dreams and may decide that you want more than you have settled for. The transiting sun is also conjunct Uranus, so your mind-set is eccentric and intuitive.

Tuesday, March 6 (Moon in Libra)   This moon forms a nice angle to Jupiter in your sign and to your sun sign. Expansive thinking is the hallmark of the day. Use this expansive, buoyant thinking to your advantage. Instead of immediately judging someone you meet, give the person the benefit of the doubt.

Wednesday, March 7 (Moon in Libra to Scorpio 5:18 p.m.)   Mercury turns direct! It's safe to pack your bags and sign contracts. Things at home—any tensions, squabbles and misunderstandings you've experienced in the last several weeks—clear up. Your emotions are a rapidly flowing river of intensity of passion.

Thursday, March 8 (Moon in Scorpio)   It's a beautiful day for romance and love. Venus forms a harmonious angle to Jupiter, so you and your partner may take your commitment to each other to a whole new level. There's a bounce in your step and a song in your heart.

Friday, March 9 (Moon in Scorpio)   As you move into the weekend, you're preparing yourself for the moon transiting into your sign. Lie low, gather your energies, and figure out what you would like to do the rest of the weekend. Give in to your urges tomorrow!

Saturday, March 10 (Moon in Scorpio to Sagittarius 5:38 a.m.)   The moon is finally in your sign again. Your optimism soars; you're ready to party or travel or both. Or you may embark on a quest this weekend that involves a puzzling spiritual or metaphysical issue. If you don't find the insight or information you need, you'll stumble over it tomorrow. Serendipity is your middle name.

Sunday, March 11—Daylight Saving Time Begins (Moon in Sagittarius)   Your energy is nothing short of remarkable. Whether you're rock climbing, hiking, or digging in ancient ruins, you can go from dawn to dusk without tiring. You and your partner are in sync.

Monday, March 12 (Moon in Sagittarius to Capricorn 4:35 p.m.)   Yes, it's true that you have a few problems with the Capricorn moon—namely, that it brings you back down to earth and forces you to deal with the practical world. That practical world is focused on your earning capacity. Set up a plan and stick to it.

Tuesday, March 13 (Moon in Capricorn)   You and a coworker have a great idea for increasing production. Be sure you have all the details lined up before you present this. Timing, as they say, is everything. For you to garner needed support, other people have to be able to grasp the merits of the idea.

Wednesday, March 14 (Moon in Capricorn to Aquarius 10:53 p.m.)   In a few days Venus will leave your fifth house. That doesn't mean your time for romance and love is over for the year. But it does point to a transition in your energy. Take advantage of the time that remains and plan a long weekend with your partner.

Thursday, March 15 (Moon in Aquarius)   There are places to go, things to do, and errands to run. It's a frantic sort of day, but keep your options open, remain alert for synchronicities, and stay upbeat. Life is much easier when you nurture optimism.

Friday, March 16 (Moon in Aquarius)   It's a very fine day. Expansive Jupiter in your sign forms a beautiful angle to Saturn in Leo. The combination gives you plenty of get up and go. Your thoughts may be turning to that overseas trip you've hoped to take. You also may be considering college or graduate school choices.

Saturday, March 17 (Moon in Aquarius to Pisces 1:31 a.m.)   Venus moves into Taurus and your sixth house. This transit, lasting until April 10, could signal an office romance. It also indicates a calmer, more productive time at work, when women are helpful. If you're in the arts, the Venus transit brings good fortune generally.

Sunday, March 18 (Moon in Pisces)   The solar eclipse in Pisces highlights family issues. During the next six months, events are triggered that allow you to see something that eluded you before. This moon also highlights your artistic and spiritual sensibilities.

Monday, March 19 (Moon in Pisces to Aries 1:42 a.m.)   As the moon enters Aries, you're revved up about a creative project. It's something completely new and different for you, and all you need to do is make time to dive into it. This could be harder than you might think. Romance is knocking on your door again!

Tuesday, March 20 (Moon in Aries)   You're a daredevil, a risk taker, and it involves a creative project or something you do for pleasure. If you aren't skydiving, perhaps you're writing the great American novel. Today it's possible to do both!

Wednesday, March 21 (Moon in Aries to Taurus 1:16 a.m.)   The moon joins Venus in Taurus in your sixth house. You and a coworker or an employee work long after everyone else has quit for the day. You're trying to meet a deadline you have imposed on yourselves. You can do it. And the project will succeed.

Thursday, March 22 (Moon in Taurus)   Your resilience is remarkable. Whether it's nipping a cold in the bud or going back to a project that stalled, you know what to do and when to do it. In health matters, you're experimenting with alternative treatments—vitamins, antioxidants, herbs, homeopathy.

Friday, March 23 (Moon in Taurus to Gemini 2:07 a.m.)   The moon lights up your seventh house of partnerships. You and your spouse or significant other are discussing going into business together. It's a good time for discussions, planning, and dreaming, but don't move on to contracts just yet.

Saturday, March 24 (Moon in Gemini)   You're in search of a certain piece of information and hit bookstores and the Internet. You find what you need in both places. Your partner is going into contract negotiations and would like your emotional support.

Sunday, March 25 (Moon in Gemini to Cancer 5:49 a.m.) If you feel uncharacteristically clingy, blame the Cancer moon. You may be feeling nostalgia for the good ol' days. But if you look back at those days and honestly think about them, you'll find your nostalgia is actually for something else—perhaps a simpler, less cluttered life?

Monday, March 26 (Moon in Cancer) An issue surfaces with one of your parents. It involves resources that you share with them—finances, land, perhaps a house or building. Or they may just need help with taxes and insurance matters.

Tuesday, March 27 (Moon in Cancer to Leo 1:05 p.m.) Just after noon, a weight is lifted. You feel it. The moon has moved from intuitive Cancer to dramatic Leo, and its fire energy is perfectly compatible with yours. Put your optimism and warmth to work for you in the areas of your life where you feel you've lost touch with yourself.

Wednesday, March 28 (Moon in Leo) You've got your tickets for that far-flung spot in the world. What to pack? What to take? You and a friend hit the mall for some spring bargains. Be sure to buy a travel book!

Thursday, March 29 (Moon in Leo to Virgo 11:28 p.m.) As the moon moves into your tenth house, you're looking for the quickest, most efficient way to do something. The answer lies in the details. Be meticulous in your research.

Friday, March 30 (Moon in Virgo) Saturn turns retrograde on April 19, in Leo and your ninth house. Try not to travel before then. You won't run into as many delays and restrictions. On the other hand, don't stress out by changing your itinerary if it means you have to pay extra fees.

Saturday, March 31 (Moon in Virgo)   Read *Life of Pi* by Yann Martel. And enjoy the nice energy that comes from Venus and unpredictable Uranus forming a great angle to each other. This pair attracts unusual experiences and people.

APRIL 2007

Sunday, April 1 (Moon in Virgo to Libra 11:45 a.m.)   A kind of magic happens for you when the moon is in Libra. Your inner world feels softer and gentler, and there's a distinctive artistic flair to your appearance and emotions. Your friends gravitate toward you, and you are glad to lead them.

Monday, April 2 (Moon in Libra)   With Mars still in Aquarius and your third house, you're seen as a powerful force in your neighborhood. You're the one others come to when they want things done. Even if you feel you don't have the time to head up some community or neighborhood project, you do it anyway.

Tuesday, April 3 (Moon in Libra)   Go to bed before midnight, and you'll be a happy camper! That way you'll miss the moon's transit into Scorpio, not your favorite moon. Otherwise, the day is great, with lots of activities and interactions with friends. You may send out a mass e-mailing to promote a product.

Wednesday, April 4 (Moon in Libra to Scorpio 12:37 a.m.)   Okay, so things seem tense at home. You're feeling the intensity of the Scorpio moon. Use this energy in a positive, focused way, and you and everyone around you will be much happier.

Thursday, April 5 (Moon in Scorpio)   Jupiter turns retrograde in your sign. This isn't like a Mercury retrograde—for one thing, it lasts longer, until early August. It's apt to make you more introspective. You'll be scrutinizing your personal beliefs, perhaps defining your personal quest.

Friday, April 6 (Moon in Scorpio to Sagittarius 12:57 p.m.)   Mars moves into Pisces and your fourth house. You aren't enamored of water signs—they're much too passive for you! This transit could bring you into deeper contact with the intuitive side of your life, particularly relating to your family. It lasts until May 15.

Saturday, April 7 (Moon in Sagittarius)   Like yesterday, today should be great, what with the moon in your sign. You're in a partying, upbeat mood, and you feel that the sky is the limit. That actually may be true.

Sunday, April 8 (Moon in Sagittarius to Capricorn 11:36 p.m.)   For most of the day, you're busy with all the things that interest you. Then, this evening, a sudden downer. The moon slides into earthy, practical Capricorn and your second house. Now finances are your new focus.

Monday, April 9 (Moon in Capricorn)   Keep tabs on your stocks, bank accounts, and daily expenditures for the next two days. How much money is going out? How much is coming in? Do they balance? Are you saving enough? Is money being put away for your kids' college educations?

Tuesday, April 10 (Moon in Capricorn)   Mercury moves into Aries and your fifth house. Your mind is on romance and fun, and not necessarily in that order. Until April 27, in fact, you have an opportunity to do strikingly original creative work. It could be part of your profession, but more than likely it's something you simply love to do.

Wednesday, April 11 (Moon in Capricorn to Aquarius 7:23 a.m.)   Venus moves into Gemini and your seventh house. This beautiful recipe for love and romance should light up your partnership. It's also excellent for business partnerships and for negotiating and signing contracts. In fact, wait until tomorrow, when the moon is forming a smooth angle to Venus, to sign those contracts.

Thursday, April 12 (Moon in Aquarius)   You and friends visit various neighborhoods to get a feel for how communities sustain and beautify themselves. Perhaps your

264

community has something special going on. Maybe it's time to put up a Web page about it.

Friday, April 13 (Moon in Aquarius to Pisces 11:39 a.m.)   If you get the midmorning blues, don't worry. You're not bipolar! It's just the moon slipping into dreamy Pisces and your fourth house. You would like to leave work early and head to an artist's colony, a beach resort, or some other laid-back place that has a dreamy atmosphere.

Saturday, April 14 (Moon in Pisces)   Are your taxes ready to be mailed? It's a bit late to think about them, but just the same, be sure everything is lined up the way it should be. Pay close attention to your dreams. Information comes to you while you sleep.

Sunday, April 15 (Moon in Pisces to Aries 12:47 p.m.)   Prepare yourself for the new moon in Taurus on April 17. This lunation is certain to bring about new opportunities in romance and creativity, and for your children. Be on the lookout for synchronicities that light up the path you should take.

Monday, April 16 (Moon in Aries)   With Venus still in Gemini and the moon in Aries, you're in rare form. You're outspoken, which may turn some people off, but others listen closely. Your partner has issues that beg for discussion, and discussion is easy and honest.

Tuesday, April 17 (Moon in Aries to Taurus 12:12 p.m.)   The new moon in Taurus is very nice for all the areas mentioned on April 15. So for the next month, keep your options open. New creative opportunities may fall in your lap. Even if you're unsure whether you want to take on these projects, definitely do so. The payoff down the line could be substantial.

Wednesday, April 18 (Moon in Taurus)   You must be stubborn and persistent about an issue at work. Don't worry about offending anyone. You have the charm to talk your way out of almost anything. But don't compromise your principles.

Thursday, April 19 (Moon in Taurus to Gemini 11:52 a.m.) Saturn turns retrograde in Leo and your ninth house. You're done with just thinking about foreign travel. You're ready to head off with just a backpack and your ATM card. Suggested reading for your trip? *Parallel Worlds: A Journey Through Creation, Higher Dimensions, and the Future of the Cosmos* by Michio Kaku.

Friday, April 20 (Moon in Gemini) You and your partner are in agreement about most things. But one small thorny issue could surface. Deal with it and move on. On other fronts, you're in search of information, and you turn to the Internet to find it.

Saturday, April 21 (Moon in Gemini to Cancer 1:51 p.m.) Early this afternoon, the moon moves into Cancer and your eighth house. Time to check on insurance policies and wills and to set up your files for this tax year, if you haven't done it already. A foray into metaphysical topics is also likely.

Sunday, April 22 (Moon in Cancer) Mothers and other nurturing females play into the day's activities. The nurturing part of this equation could be meant for you.

Monday, April 23 (Moon in Cancer to Leo 7:39 p.m.) Early this evening, the moon joins Saturn in Leo in your ninth house. If you're on the road, you could feel this is a delay or a postponement. If you're at home, your dad or a father figure drops by for a visit. Or possibly an in-law contacts you.

Tuesday, April 24 (Moon in Leo) You're in the public eye. Look your best, be courteous, and be sure you had enough sleep. Sometimes, you run yourself ragged.

Wednesday, April 25 (Moon in Leo) Children—yours or someone else's—teach you an important lesson in humility and simplicity. Perhaps it's time to prioritize and to ask yourself what is most important in your life? Look within to uncover your deepest beliefs and strive to change those

266

that are negative and may be holding you back in some way.

Thursday, April 26 (Moon in Leo to Virgo 5:25 a.m.) How far can you take an idea? You have an opportunity to find out. Share your time with someone who believes in the same things that you do, and allow your collective imaginations to roam.

Friday, April 27 (Moon in Virgo) Mercury moves into Taurus and your sixth house. Until May 11, you spend more time with coworkers and employees. You're willing to put in long hours because you believe in this project. Don't be so stubborn that you hold things up.

Saturday, April 28 (Moon in Virgo to Libra 5:46 p.m.) Your sister or brother delivers a message. Or the message comes through e-mail or a call. It changes the course of the day—for the better!

Sunday, April 29 (Moon in Libra) Museums, art galleries, photography, dance, music and the arts—the Libra moon loves all these pursuits. So indulge yourself. Get out and enjoy the spring weather; don't worry about tomorrow. Be in the moment.

Monday, April 30 (Moon in Libra) You can really feel spring in the air. The sight of new growth, the warmth, the good humor of the people around you—it all feeds your creative side. Maybe it's time to finish that novel you started!

MAY 2007

Tuesday, May 1 (Moon in Libra to Scorpio 6:42 a.m.) The moon enters Scorpio very early. You wake with a mission: to get to the bottom of an issue concerning your past, your childhood, or perhaps even unfinished business from another life. You get help from Mars, but only if you follow the intuitive signs, and also from Venus in

Gemini, whose energy manifests itself through a partner or close friend.

Wednesday, May 2 (Moon in Scorpio)   Your dreams and imagination are important. You aren't the type for therapy—you probably can't sit still long enough—so any therapy you get will have to come from within. Work with who you are—even the parts of yourself that you can't see.

Thursday, May 3 (Moon in Scorpio to Sagittarius 6:48 p.m.)   All day, you have felt an increase in your self-confidence and optimism building. The moon is moving into your sign this afternoon, and life will get very interesting.

Friday, May 4 (Moon in Sagittarius)   You have the big picture. It may concern a relationship, a career matter, or a family issue. Whatever it is, you have a better idea about how to proceed to succeed. A partner may need your support and advice.

Saturday, May 5 (Moon in Sagittarius)   You're sexy, smart, and cool. Just don't let it all go to your head. You may be tempted to put someone down, but resist the urge. Tomorrow, you'll be glad that you did.

Sunday, May 6 (Moon in Sagittarius to Capricorn 5:21 a.m.)   If you have a Capricorn moon or rising, then you'll enjoy today. You'll feel resilient and ambitious. But if you have a lot of fire in your chart, the Capricorn moon annoys you. It urges you to bring everything down to the here and now.

Monday, May 7 (Moon in Capricorn)   Money, money, money. You fret, you rage, and it's all for nothing, really. You have the abilities, the talent, and the capacity to make as much money as you want. You simply need to draw on your considerable intuition to find the right path. While you're at it, invest in companies whose products you use.

Tuesday, May 8 (Moon in Capricorn to Aquarius 1:48 p.m.)   Venus moves into Cancer and your eighth house.

This beautiful transit should get you to probe more deeply into the larger questions about life.

Wednesday, May 9 (Moon in Aquarius)   With the moon in visionary Aquarius and Venus in intuitive Cancer, you have all the answers you need at your fingertips. But your perceptions need fine-tuning. And since travel seems to do that, perhaps a trip is in order.

Thursday, May 10 (Moon in Aquarius to Pisces 7:32 p.m.)   Back to that trip. Maybe it's time to pack the family and the dog in the car and head for some spot you've never explored before.

Friday, May 11 (Moon in Pisces)   Mercury moves into Gemini and your seventh house. Partnerships are definitely on your mind until May 28. Time to pay attention to your partner. If you aren't attached, keep your options open.

Saturday, May 12 (Moon in Pisces to Aries 10:20 p.m.)   Here comes that great Aries moon again. You're really at home with fire- and air-sign moons, but the Aries moon could be your favorite—after the moon in your own sign, naturally. Romance, love, creativity—all are highlighted. You tend to be impatient and restless under this moon. Find a way to satisfy those urges.

Sunday, May 13 (Moon in Aries)   You could be short-tempered with one of your kids. Ranting and raving won't get the job done. Cooperation and patience might!

Monday, May 14 (Moon in Aries to Taurus 10:50 p.m.)   Late this evening, the moon moves into Taurus. Yes, it's an earthy moon. But one thing you love about it is its sensuality. It's not just a sexual sensuality. It extends to every part of your life. It's about appreciation for the earth and your physical being.

Tuesday, May 15 (Moon in Taurus)   Mars moves into Aries and stays there until June 24. This transit heightens your sexuality and makes you something of a daredevil when it comes to the pursuit of pleasure. The more outrageous the activity is, the more it appeals to you. Be careful that you don't gamble away your paycheck!

Wednesday, May 16 (Moon in Taurus to Gemini 10:35 p.m.) A business venture with a partner finally gets off the ground. Use your intuitive knowledge to make the right choices, and try not to let your exuberance push you too far, too quickly. Be sure you've got all your facts.

Thursday, May 17 (Moon in Gemini) Facts and information are the hallmarks of the Gemini moon. But these things feed into your emotional being, into the hidden you, so whatever facts you gather can burst through obstacles in your external life.

Friday, May 18 (Moon in Gemini to Cancer 11:39 p.m.) Work with your deepest beliefs to change your external experiences. This is really ninth-house stuff, but the eighth house, where the moon is today, is where it all begins.

Saturday, May 19 (Moon in Cancer) Mercury turns retrograde in mid-June. So if you're planning your summer vacation, keep this in mind. Do not travel from June 15 to July 9. If you have to travel then, be flexible. Don't be wedded to any particular time frame.

Sunday, May 20 (Moon in Cancer) Your mom or dad needs help and support. Or perhaps they help and support you. Whatever the dynamics, there are emotional connections with your loved ones. Wills and legacies also figure into the day's activities.

Monday, May 21 (Moon in Cancer to Leo 3:57 a.m.) You enroll in summer courses. Or perhaps it's just a workshop or seminar that grabs your attention. It's possible that the seminar is held in a foreign country, which would really satisfy your nomadic urges.

Tuesday, May 22 (Moon in Leo) You and a business partner are seeking to expand your business into foreign markets. Consult an expert, gather your facts and information, and then come up with a strategy.

Wednesday, May 23 (Moon in Leo to Virgo 12:27 p.m.) You have some exciting things going on related to your career. A partner or friend is helpful in terms of advice and support and you have plenty of energy from Mars, so you can achieve just about anything now. All you need is belief in yourself and your talents.

Thursday, May 24 (Moon in Virgo) You're heading into summer and whole new chapters in your life. Even though Saturn is still delaying and restricting certain parts of your life, Pluto and Jupiter continue to push you toward transformation and expansion. The universe really does want the best for you!

Friday, May 25 (Moon in Virgo) There are some things you do for money and other things you do for the love of it. Writing, painting, photography, dance, and even acting are your passions. How do you want to live your life? Do you want to settle for the easy path or go for what makes you ecstatic?

Saturday, May 26 (Moon in Virgo to Libra 12:17 a.m.) You and a neighbor realize you have more in common than you thought. It could begin with an invitation to a party or some sort of social gathering in your community. From there, it quickly develops into something deeper.

Sunday, May 27 (Moon in Libra) Back to what you do for passion and the love of it. Is it writing? Is it politics? The arts? You really need to look at this. You won't be satisfied just tending to the status quo. Make the change.

Monday, May 28 (Moon in Libra to Scorpio 1:12 p.m.) Mercury moves into Cancer and your eighth house. This is where it will go retrograde on June 15, so be prepared. Have your affairs lined up and your priorities written down. The retrograde will affect things like taxes, so be sure you have paid your quarterly taxes on time.

271

Tuesday, May 29 (Moon in Scorpio)   Your kids need you. One of them may not feel well; it's up to you to decide whether this requires a trip to the doctor or just a nap.

Wednesday, May 30 (Moon in Scorpio)   There could be some sort of conflict in your family. You're just one person, with a certain amount of energy and time. Decisions, decisions. Where to go first?

Thursday, May 31 (Moon in Scorpio to Sagittarius 1:07 a.m.)   The full moon in your sign illuminates an issue that has puzzled you. You could be spending time on taxes, lining everything up for your quarterly tax payment in June.

JUNE 2007

Friday, June 1 (Moon in Sagittarius)   What a terrific way to start the month, with the moon in your sign! With the moon forming nice angles to both Mars and Jupiter, you're on a roller-coaster ride and enjoying every second of it. It's the adrenaline rush that appeals to you.

Saturday, June 2 (Moon in Sagittarius to Capricorn 11:10 a.m.)   It's that time of month again, when your thoughts turn to money. If you're feeling underpaid and unappreciated, don't despair! New opportunities for increasing your income are headed your way. Tend to practicalities.

Sunday, June 3 (Moon in Capricorn)   Relax and putter around at home with your family. Or dive into a project that you had tucked away. You have the resilience and energy to complete this project.

Monday, June 4 (Moon in Capricorn to Aquarius 7:16 p.m.)   In about twelve days, Mercury turns retrograde in your eighth house. Apply for mortgages and car loans. Consider mailing off your quarterly tax payment early, and be sure you're up-to-date on insurance payments.

Tuesday, June 5 (Moon in Aquarius)   Venus moves into Leo and transits your ninth house until July 14. With Venus forming such a beautiful angle to your sun, you're in the public eye more than usual. Romance is possible with a foreigner or someone in publishing, the law, or in higher education. These areas are more prominent in your life for the next six weeks.

Wednesday, June 6 (Moon in Aquarius)   You and a brother or sister may be planning a family reunion. Best to schedule it on either side of the Mercury retrograde period from June 15 to July 9 unless you don't mind unexpected changes. You and a neighbor are cooking up an idea for neighborhood beautification. But can you get the support of other people in your neighborhood?

Thursday, June 7 (Moon in Aquarius to Pisces 1:25 a.m.)   A parent, partner, or one of your kids needs you. This could create a delicate balancing act between your home and professional obligations. Do the best you can with the situation that exists.

Friday, June 8 (Moon in Pisces)   You feel like getting off by yourself to explore, think, or dream. It's an itch you can't scratch. But you don't have to understand it to indulge yourself. Do what you need to do without guilt!

Saturday, June 9 (Moon in Pisces to Aries 5:27 a.m.)   The moon is finally in a sign that feels like a perfect fit! It makes a harmonious angle to both Venus and Jupiter. With all this fire energy, you need an outlet. What's it going to be: a party, a creative pursuit, travel?

Sunday, June 10 (Moon in Aries)   It's another glorious day with the best planets stacked in your favor. Do something special for yourself. Maybe there's a piece of property that you would like to buy for speculative purposes. Or perhaps you collect antiques and have had your eye on a particular piece. Whatever your passion, nurture it.

Monday, June 11 (Moon in Aries to Taurus 7:30 a.m.)   As the moon moves into Taurus, your focus turns to your daily work. Is there something in your office you would like to change? Whatever it is, take steps to begin the project.

Tuesday, June 12 (Moon in Taurus)   You're conscious of your appearance, perhaps more so than usual. Go to the gym, take a yoga class, take up tai chi, or go jogging or for a long walk. Whatever you decide to do for your body, commit yourself to it.

Wednesday, June 13 (Moon in Taurus to Gemini 8:24 a.m.)   You and your partner are looking for the ideal site for your joint business. You have clear ideas about location, size, all the details. But the price may be more than you had planned on. Time to regroup and gather new information.

Thursday, June 14 (Moon in Gemini)   Mercury turns retrograde tomorrow. It's wise to have your affairs in order before the retrograde period, particularly in the area of shared finances, taxes, insurance, and wills. On other fronts, the new moon in Gemini puts you and your partner in buoyant moods. Enjoy each other!

Friday, June 15 (Moon in Gemini to Cancer 9:46 a.m.) Mercury turns retrograde in Cancer. You know the drill. One of the best ways to navigate this period successfully is to think of Mercury retrograde as a time to revise, rethink, and review.

Saturday, June 16 (Moon in Cancer)   With the moon joining Mercury retrograde in Cancer, you could feel at odds with yourself and the people around you. Don't worry. This is a passing mood. Focus your energy on developing your intuition and nurturing your creative talents.

Sunday, June 17 (Moon in Cancer to Leo 1:25 p.m.)   If you have a natal Leo moon or ascendant, these Leo lunar transits are probably some of the best days you experience each month. Regardless, the Leo moon instills in you more self-confidence and sex appeal and allows you to embrace new experiences.

Monday, June 18 (Moon in Leo)   You enroll for classes in the fall—college, graduate school, perhaps even a seminar or workshop. You're hungry for knowledge and could be launching a metaphysical quest for something in particular.

Tuesday, June 19 (Moon in Leo to Virgo 8:46 p.m.)   With the moon moving into Virgo and your tenth house and Mercury retrograde in Cancer and your eighth house, it's wise to keep your own counsel. Fulfill your obligations, meet your responsibilities. The truth lies in details.

Wednesday, June 20 (Moon in Virgo)   A boss or peer acknowledges your ideas and hard work concerning a project. You can be a team player when it suits you, and you'll have to use your diplomatic skills to get around an unpleasant coworker.

Thursday, June 21 (Moon in Virgo)   Are you up to the task? You may have to run out of town, perhaps for an overnight trip that's related to business. Since Mercury is still retrograde, be flexible in your schedule. If you're driving, be sure your car is in good shape.

Friday, June 22 (Moon in Virgo to Libra 7:44 a.m.)   As the moon moves into Libra and your eleventh house, friends you haven't seen for a while seem to be coming out of the woodwork! Some contact you through e-mails, others call, and a couple could show up at your door.

Saturday, June 23 (Moon in Libra)   Uranus turns retrograde in Pisces and your fourth house and remains that way until late November. The effect of this movement is subtle because Uranus moves so slowly. But over the next several months, you look inward and toward your family for spiritual answers and insights.

Sunday, June 24 (Moon in Libra to Scorpio 8:27 p.m.)   Mars moves into Taurus and your sixth house until August 7. This transit makes you more conscious about your health and nutrition. You may be somewhat short-tempered with coworkers and employees, so exercise patience over the next few months.

Monday, June 25 (Moon in Scorpio)   Whenever the moon transits secretive Scorpio, all kinds of odd things probably happen to you. You may experience more synchronicities. Your dreams tend to be more vivid and easier to recall. And you're more prone to getting involved in secret love affairs. Be careful. The heart that gets broken could be your own.

Tuesday, June 26 (Moon in Scorpio)   You're psychic. You seem to know what people are going to say before they say it. You have a great sense of timing. And you are able to say what you have to say without revealing too much. You're gathering your energies for tomorrow, when the moon moves into your sign.

Wednesday, June 27 (Moon in Scorpio to Sagittarius 8:25 a.m.)   Early this morning, the change in your mood is palpable. Gone is the angst you sometimes feel when your heart wants to do one thing and your mind another. You may hear about a royalty check you're receiving, but don't expect it before Mercury turns direct again on July 9.

Thursday, June 28 (Moon in Sagittarius)   Is a long weekend in order? If so, stick close to home and tend to things you've put off. Consider indulging yourself in some creative play. Your muse is eager to help! You and your partner could disagree on some small issue. Make sure it doesn't get blown out of proportion.

Friday, June 29 (Moon in Sagittarius to Capricorn 6:06 p.m.)   The moon moves into Capricorn and your second house. If your holiday bills are coming due, step back, take stock, and make changes in your spending habits as needed.

Saturday, June 30 (Moon in Capricorn)   The full moon in Capricorn sheds light on financial issues. There could be some tension in your household. Just roll with the punches; don't get caught up in the drama.

Sunday, July 1 (Moon in Capricorn) You're gearing up for the Fourth of July holiday. Whether you're leaving town or hosting visitors, expect the unexpected in terms of travel plans. Your barbecue grill may not work right. The dog might grab the ribs and steaks. You get the idea, a comedy of errors.

Monday, July 2 (Moon in Capricorn to Aquarius 1:25 a.m.) If people have been too clingy toward you lately, you can change that pattern by distancing yourself without hurting anyone's feelings. Not everyone is as independent as you are; you may have to develop a little tolerance.

Tuesday, July 3 (Moon in Aquarius) A relative gets in touch with you about some family concern. Can you travel? You can't just drop all your plans. You have obligations to people at home. So you manage to use your insight to resolve the issue through e-mail and calls.

Wednesday, July 4 (Moon in Aquarius to Pisces 6:53 a.m.) The moon moves into Pisces and your fourth house—your family and home—this Fourth of July. You have insights into friends and family that may have slipped past you in earlier years. Forgive, forget, and get on with it.

Thursday, July 5 (Moon in Pisces) Venus is still in dramatic Leo, boosting your energy and love life. You could feel down in the dumps and not understand why. It's the moon in Pisces, which absorbs the energy of everyone around you. Associate with upbeat people.

Friday, July 6 (Moon in Pisces to Aries 10:57 a.m.) Look to midmorning for a positive change in your mood. The moon moves into compatible Aries. You may want to take off with the kids this weekend. Be spontaneous. Point to a spot on the map and go for it. Keep in mind that Mercury doesn't turn direct again until July 9.

277

Saturday, July 7 (Moon in Aries) You bound out of bed this morning and head to your computer, dance studio, yoga class, film festival, or writers' group. Your muse is screaming for attention, and you're listening! This evening, you and a romantic partner head out to do the town.

Sunday, July 8 (Moon in Aries to Taurus 1:54 p.m.) With Mercury turning direct tomorrow, hold off on anything you want to discuss with coworkers or employees. You'll be in a better frame of mind to discuss your emotions and thoughts on a particular subject.

Monday, July 9 (Moon in Taurus) Mercury turns direct. Those checks you've been expecting will start to arrive, probably after the new moon on July 14. Make your summer travel plans; be sure to schedule travel before the next Mercury retrograde on October 11.

Tuesday, July 10 (Moon in Taurus to Gemini 4:10 p.m.) You and your partner have friends over this evening. It's not strictly social. You have some business to discuss, ideas to brainstorm, and possibilities to imagine. You're able to win over even the most skeptical.

Wednesday, July 11 (Moon in Gemini) The faster you move, the better you like it—even with information. There's a lot of information flowing in today—through e-mails, faxes, and phone calls. Friends and acquaintances check in.

Thursday, July 12 (Moon in Gemini to Cancer 6:40 p.m.) Your attention is drawn toward the mysterious, the transformative. It could start with an internal experience that you have this evening—a voice you hear, something you glimpse from the corner of your eye, or a presence that you sense in your home.

Friday, July 13 (Moon in Cancer) Your mother has knowledge of the mysterious. Pick her brain. And while you're at it, check the Web for a vast spectrum of articles on things that go bump in the night, weather changes, and UFO sightings worldwide.

Saturday, July 14 (Moon in Cancer to Leo 10:44 p.m.)   Venus moves into Virgo and transits your tenth house of careers until October 8. This is an excellent period for you professionally. Venus is retrograde from July 27 to September 8; your major gains will occur before or after the retrograde.

Sunday, July 15 (Moon in Leo)   Venus transiting the career sector of your chart won't happen again for another two years, so take advantage of it. If you have an agenda to push or goals to achieve, now is the time to act.

Monday, July 16 (Moon in Leo)   With the moon in buoyant Leo, you're in a fine mood. You and friends may gather this evening for some kind of political or spiritual event in which all of you believe. Afterward, everyone goes to your place. You may need to sleep in tomorrow morning!

Tuesday, July 17 (Moon in Leo to Virgo 5:40 a.m.)   The moon joins Venus in Virgo in your tenth house. This duo energizes your career. Any promotions or publicity should be well received. Your intuition is right on target. Listen to it.

Wednesday, July 18 (Moon in Virgo)   Back to the intuitive equation. If you feel an urge to take a different route to work or home, do so. You could miss a traffic jam. If you feel an urge to call a particular person, make the call. Today your intuition may manifest itself through impulses. Follow them.

Thursday, July 19 (Moon in Virgo to Libra 3:54 p.m.)   Your wishes and dreams are a priority. It may be that someone or some event has shifted things around for you. You may be putting your energies toward a completely new path. Even if all the details aren't obvious yet, don't worry. You have the big picture.

Friday, July 20 (Moon in Libra)   This moon is one of your favorites. It feeds the social, affable, artistic part of you. It makes you more aware of where in your life you need balance and how you might achieve it. No small feat!

Saturday, July 21 (Moon in Libra)   You and friends get together to help another friend move, paint, clean, or do whatever is necessary. You toss a housewarming party this evening. Then you go home and realize your place could use some work. Come up with a whole new look for your home.

Sunday, July 22 (Moon in Libra to Scorpio 4:19 a.m.)   Here comes that intense Scorpio moon. Sometimes, this lunar energy gets under your skin and really irritates you. Other times, you're in the mood for its passion and resilience. Today is one of those latter days.

Monday, July 23 (Moon in Scorpio)   If you've been carrying on a relationship in secret, that will be over and done with by tomorrow, when the moon moves into your sign. You dislike secrecy, and it grates on you when you are forced to be that way. So no more!

Tuesday, July 24 (Moon in Scorpio to Sagittarius 4:31 p.m.)   Overall, the afternoon is far better than the morning, and with good reason. The moon moves into your sign in midafternoon, and suddenly, you're a powerhouse of energy, optimism, and goodwill! If you keep track of the days in a given month when the moon is in your sign, you'll recognize the inner change in yourself.

Wednesday, July 25 (Moon in Sagittarius)   You delve into the study of a spiritual system that has intrigued you for some time. Your interest is terrific and will broaden your knowledge. But be careful that you don't get sucked in so deeply that you climb onto your soapbox at every opportunity.

Thursday, July 26 (Moon in Sagittarius)   Your inner child is playful, which surprises the people around you. You may take in a stray—human or animal—and although your partner may have second thoughts, your kids won't. On other fronts, you and a relative hit the mall for gifts.

Friday, July 27 (Moon in Sagittarius to Capricorn 2:23 a.m.)   Venus turns retrograde in Virgo and your tenth house. This retrograde period could mean some physical discomforts. Or the raise you've counted on may be delayed. Don't fret. It'll come through after Venus turns direct again on September 8.

Saturday, July 28 (Moon in Capricorn)   Tomorrow night the full moon is in Aquarius. Get ready for it by visualizing what you hope to harvest this month. Does it have to do with money?

Sunday, July 29 (Moon in Capricorn to Aquarius 9:14 a.m.)   The full moon in Aquarius lights up the communication sector of your chart. There could be some tension with in-laws or other relatives. However, you have the clarity in your perceptions that you didn't have earlier this month.

Monday, July 30 (Moon in Aquarius)   With the moon in visionary Aquarius, a sign compatible with your own, you have your eye on something innovative. Whether it is a new computer or new software, you're on the cutting edge. Tomorrow, others fall in line behind you.

Tuesday, July 31 (Moon in Aquarius to Pisces 1:41 p.m.)   Mars in Taurus and Saturn in Leo form a difficult angle to each other. This creates some tension at work. Try not to take that tension home with you. Leave it at work, where it belongs.

AUGUST 2007

Wednesday, August 1 (Moon in Pisces)   You're very intuitive where your home and family are concerned. So when your psychic antenna twitches, pay heed. Call home and find out if there's anything going on that needs your attention. You should place a call to your mom or dad just to make sure things are okay.

Thursday, August 2 (Moon in Pisces to Aries 4:43 p.m.)   The moon sails into daring Aries, and once again, you're in fine form! In fact, when Jupiter turns direct again on August 6, the month looks quite positive. Try something new at work. Take a risk. The payoff could be considerable.

Friday, August 3 (Moon in Aries)   Today's risks are in romance. With someone you meet, the chemistry is immediate, mutual, and astonishing. Take it slowly. Trade e-mail addresses and phone numbers, and see where things go.

Saturday, August 4 (Moon in Aries to Taurus 7:16 p.m.)   Yes, you should be relaxing. But when the moon is in Taurus, it seems you suddenly have five million things to do. You may steal away from the house and go into work for a few hours, just to satisfy the urge and to reassure yourself that the world won't collapse if some things wait until Monday.

Sunday, August 5 (Moon in Taurus)   You learn of a new investment opportunity. Check it out before you put money into it. Consult a friend in the know, search the Internet, or call your dad. Get advice first.

Monday, August 6 (Moon in Taurus to Gemini 10:02 p.m.)   Today should feel very good for you. Jupiter turns direct in your sign, releasing pent-up energy that sends you into a soaring mood. You feel like dancing on tabletops. You're primed for travel.

Tuesday, August 7 (Moon in Gemini)   Mars and the moon move into Gemini and your seventh house. This pair brings attention and focus to your closest partnerships. The Mars transit lasts until late September; during this time, you and your partner may spend a lot of time together. You could have your share of tiffs, mostly over small things. Negotiate and sign contracts.

Wednesday, August 8 (Moon in Gemini)   You're gathering information. In fact, you're like a sponge, soaking up everything you hear and read and then connecting this piece and that piece to find the larger picture. It could concern this overseas trip you've planned.

Thursday, August 9 (Moon in Gemini to Cancer 12:37 a.m.) Even with the moon in Cancer, you'll enjoy today. Mercury—your conscious mind—and Jupiter, your ruler, form a lovely angle to each other that facilitates communications. This pair also makes you very restless about traveling. You're ready to go!

Friday, August 10 (Moon in Cancer) The moon in Cancer trines Uranus in Pisces, creating an intuitive awareness in you about your home and family. You may be more concerned than usual about your own mortality. It's not that you need to worry, but you often wonder what happens after death.

Saturday, August 11 (Moon in Cancer to Leo 6:42 a.m.) Check out books and Web sites that deal with nature's healing secrets. On other fronts, your mother or another nurturing female in your life has something to share with you.

Sunday, August 12 (Moon in Leo) Finally, a lunar transit that makes perfect sense to you. The new moon in your ninth house means international travel. It can also indicate that your business expands overseas or that your book sells to a foreign publisher.

Monday, August 13 (Moon in Leo to Virgo 2:04 p.m.) The moon joins Venus retrograde in Virgo and your tenth house. You may feel vulnerable in career matters. You may even feel paranoid. But these feelings don't necessarily reflect the reality of your situation. Get to the root of the emotion and find the core belief behind it.

Tuesday, August 14 (Moon in Virgo) Are you up for a challenge? There could be a possible communications clash between you and an in-law or you and a publisher or attorney. The best way to get through this is to postpone the discussion until after August 19. If that's not possible, hold on to your temper.

Wednesday, August 15 (Moon in Virgo) It's a beautiful day for romance. Venus in Leo and Pluto in your sign are courting each other in the heavens. You and your partner should get away and explore your relationship from the inside out. Chances are, you'll discover points in the past where your paths may have crossed.

Thursday, August 16 (Moon in Virgo to Libra 12:05 a.m.) A fun day. The greatest challenge you face is about making choices. Should you do one thing or another? Should you go out with this person or that person? The Libra moon really dislikes hurting anyone, thus the ambivalence.

Friday, August 17 (Moon in Libra) Mercury and Venus are extremely compatible, which means you and your partner should be able to communicate in an honest, meaningful way. Half the problems you have in relationships are due to lack of communications. One of you talks too much, the other not enough.

Saturday, August 18 (Moon in Libra to Scorpio 12:14 p.m.) You wake in a mellow mood, your dreams still vivid in your mind. One dream in particular seems to hold a message. What does the symbolism mean? Check out dream dictionaries. Figure out the lexicon of your internal landscape.

Sunday, August 19 (Moon in Scorpio) Mercury moves into Virgo and your tenth house. You suddenly become quite meticulous about everything you say and write. That's Virgo: discriminating and detailed. You feel compelled to go into work and tidy up your office.

Monday, August 20 (Moon in Scorpio) Yesterday's tidying up pays off. You're in a rare mood, buoyant and optimistic about the course of your life and everyone in it. Your experiences reflect this.

Tuesday, August 21 (Moon in Scorpio to Sagittarius 12:45 a.m.) The transiting sun and Saturn are together in the sky, a combination that should spur you to greater deeds and more penetrating insights. It could also focus your attention on the men in your life.

Wednesday, August 22 (Moon in Sagittarius)   If your mind is moving ahead in time, you may want to make a list of things you would like to achieve or experience before year's end.

Thursday, August 23 (Moon in Sagittarius to Capricorn 11:20 a.m.)   If the midmorning blues hit you, pour a cup of strong coffee and figure out how to use the energy of the Capricorn moon over the next two days. Your finances are in good shape. Perhaps the focus should be your values.

Friday, August 24 (Moon in Capricorn)   It's one thing to list your priorities, but quite another thing to actually put your energy into these areas. How can you go about it? How much control do you have over these areas? How can you have greater control?

Saturday, August 25 (Moon in Capricorn to Aquarius 6:35 p.m.)   You really do enjoy the energy of the Aquarian moon. It allows you to detach somewhat emotionally and to use your mind in a different way. Your perceptions are sharp, and you may see something about your community or neighborhood that needs improvement. You head up the beautification committee.

Sunday, August 26 (Moon in Aquarius)   You and a friend or sister shop till you drop. It's not traditional mall shopping. You hit the specialty stores: electronics, computers, software, gadgets.

Monday, August 27 (Moon in Aquarius to Pisces 10:35 p.m.)   Tomorrow, there's a solar eclipse in Pisces and your fourth house. Prepare by focusing on something you would like to see in terms of your home life. Something that has eluded you before.

Tuesday, August 28 (Moon in Pisces) Solar eclipses trigger external events that help us to realize something we didn't understand before. Since this one is in Pisces and your fourth house, the events could concern your home and family life and your spiritual beliefs.

Wednesday, August 29 (Moon in Pisces) You should stay up and celebrate for the moon's transit into Aries. Aries and Leo are the signs that complement your own most closely. Tonight, this one could bring you an unexpected surprise in love and romance.

Thursday, August 30 (Moon in Pisces to Aries 12:25 a.m.) Aries is a pioneer, a trailblazer, so when the moon is in this sign, you feel emotions that make you restless, eager to experience something new and drastically different. Embrace these feelings.

Friday, August 31 (Moon in Aries) It's great to end a month on such a positive lunar transit. You're ready to greet the fall, and you feel quite good about where things stand in your life. On September 2, Saturn enters Virgo and begins to transit your tenth house of careers.

SEPTEMBER 2007

Saturday, September 1 (Moon in Aries to Taurus 1:36 a.m.) The month starts with the moon in Taurus and your sixth house. You and coworkers team up for a project. It could be a charity project of some kind.

Sunday, September 2 (Moon in Taurus) Saturn moves into Virgo and transits that sign for the next two and a half years. This transit happens only once every twenty-nine years; it will have a major impact on your career. While you could experience delays and restrictions in professional matters, you may change jobs or professions, be recognized for your work, or find the proper venue for your professional talents.

Monday, September 3 (Moon in Taurus to Gemini 3:21 a.m.)   With the moon moving into your seventh house, your focus is partnerships. It's Labor Day, so perhaps you and your partner and kids should plan to do something together. You and your partner can communicate well; if there's something bothering either of you, express it.

Tuesday, September 4 (Moon in Gemini)   Venus is still moving retrograde, through your tenth house. Are you moving offices? Is your building being painted? Something about the physical space in which you work is troubling you. But don't worry. It'll all be over after September 8, when Venus turns direct again.

Wednesday, September 5 (Moon in Gemini to Cancer 7:09 a.m.)   Mercury moves into Libra for a three-week stay. This transit makes you more conscious of the need for balance in your life. You could become involved in a community or neighborhood project that requires a lot of your time. Don't commit unless you have the time.

Thursday, September 6 (Moon in Cancer)   You aren't crazy about this moon. But you've learned to use its energy wisely. Go within. Meditate. Do yoga. Hone your dream-recall skills.

Friday, September 7 (Moon in Cancer to Leo 1:00 p.m.)   Pluto turns direct in your sign. The effects of this movement are subtle, but you'll notice that things in your life that have been delayed move forward effortlessly. The moon also moves into Leo, stimulating your higher aspirations. You become an armchair traveler. And when you can't stand that anymore, you become a real traveler!

Saturday, September 8 (Moon in Leo)   Venus finally turns direct and your love life picks up again. Your career suddenly takes some positive turns, as well. You can see your way clear to taking that overseas trip you've been planning.

Sunday, September 9 (Moon in Leo to Virgo 9:11 p.m.)   The moon joins Venus in Virgo and your tenth house, making this a nice day for work. Mars in Gemini and Neptune in Aquarius hold hands, creating some beautiful energy for you and your partner.

Monday, September 10 (Moon in Virgo) Your latest challenge is to bring together members of your professional team and sell them a product or an idea. Even if there are skeptics, you can convince them and win their support. When you need to, you can sell just about anything to anyone.

Tuesday, September 11 (Moon in Virgo) The new moon in Virgo provides some wonderful career opportunities for the next thirty days. The week following this new moon is the most important. Send out your résumés, proposals, or manuscripts. This new moon happens only once a year, so take advantage of it! There's also a solar eclipse, which is sure to trigger events related to your career that allow you to see something about it more clearly.

Wednesday, September 12 (Moon in Virgo to Libra 7:32 a.m.) It's a perfect day to publicize and promote a product or idea. Get out and about; talk to people in either formal or informal settings. It won't matter. People are receptive to what you have to say.

Thursday, September 13 (Moon in Libra) Mercury in Leo and Jupiter in your sign are in agreement. That means that you're in the right place at the right time. Serendipity plays a part in the day's events. You may have some grandiose ideas that need fine-tuning.

Friday, September 14 (Moon in Libra to Scorpio 7:37 p.m.) With Pluto and Venus both moving direct, you have enormous amounts of energy at your disposal. But you should kick back and relax. Go hiking in the woods. Read a book. Do something for yourself that nurtures your abilities and talents.

Saturday, September 15 (Moon in Scorpio) Hide out, stay in, and be by yourself. If that isn't possible, keep your contact with others limited. You're gathering your strength and resources for the moon moving into your sign on Monday.

Sunday, September 16 (Moon in Scorpio)   Fiddle with divination systems. Try the *I Ching*, the tarot, runes, or even astrology. You're looking for repetitive patterns in your life, and divination systems are all about patterns.

Monday, September 17 (Moon in Scorpio to Sagittarius 8:21 a.m.)   The moon finally moves into your sign. To make the day even more perfect, Mercury and Venus are in great angles to each other, facilitating your communications with a partner. This could be the kind of day when a heart-to-heart talk changes the relationship and deepens your commitment to each other.

Tuesday, September 18 (Moon in Sagittarius)   Your idealism is running at an all-time high; it's intimately connected to your spiritual beliefs. You're able to communicate all of that. The only problem is that you may talk about it to people who aren't interested. Be sure you're talking to someone you know well and trust deeply.

Wednesday, September 19 (Moon in Sagittarius to Capricorn 7:52 p.m.)   You worry about money, and wonder how you can earn more. Maybe it's time to hook into prosperity consciousness.

Thursday, September 20 (Moon in Capricorn)   Your practicality astonishes the people around you. But you're on an organizing kick. Once you've finished with your personal and office space, you move on to everyone else's space. Be careful! You may be intruding.

Friday, September 21 (Moon in Capricorn)   There are some difficult aspects going on that pit you against the authority figures in your life. It's as if you're being encouraged to define your beliefs about authority and power. Your idealism about a relationship may not match the reality. Before you do anything hasty, give it another couple days.

Saturday, September 22 (Moon in Capricorn to Aquarius 4:18 a.m.)   With the moon moving into compatible Aquarius, you're a much happier camper. You and your family may drive around and check out neighborhoods for one that interests everyone. You're doing the groundwork for a possible move in 2008.

Sunday, September 23 (Moon in Aquarius)   You get together with relatives you haven't seen for a while. It's not exactly a family reunion, but it serves the same purpose. By this evening, you're ready to head home—no reflection on the people you were with. You're simply eager to be on the road again.

Monday, September 24 (Moon in Aquarius to Pisces 8:56 a.m.)   Associate with upbeat people. They tend to feed your innate optimism, and the more optimistic you feel, the better your day. Your kids may resist going to school or want to come home early. Or you may have some carpooling to do that conflicts with a professional obligation.

Tuesday, September 25 (Moon in Pisces)   You have a tough time making a decision about a family matter. It might be best to wait until tomorrow, when the moon is in Aries, to decide. Your mind will be clearer then.

Wednesday, September 26 (Moon in Pisces to Aries 10:23 a.m.)   Around midmorning, it's safe to revisit yesterday's quandary. If you still have to make a decision about that family matter, do so. Somehow, the fire energy of the Aries moon burns away indecision.

Thursday, September 27 (Moon in Aries)   Mercury moves into passionate Scorpio. Whatever you tackle during the next few weeks will bear a stamp of intensity and dedication. You'll be relentless in whatever you pursue—a relationship, a project, or a mission.

Friday, September 28 (Moon in Aries to Taurus 10:18 a.m.)   With Mercury in Scorpio and Mars moving into Cancer, your intuition is finely honed. And that's what you have to focus on. While you don't enjoy transits through water signs, they have their place in your life. They force you to slow down and take time to relish the moment.

Saturday, September 29 (Moon in Taurus)   It's the weekend, and you hit the gym to take a yoga class to celebrate how good you feel. It's part of your continued commitment to physical exercise. Consider getting the rest of the family involved.

Sunday, September 30 (Moon in Taurus to Gemini 10:35 a.m.)   The month ends on a positive note with the moon moving into gregarious Gemini. You're primed for the change of seasons, and you are excited about travel.

OCTOBER 2007

Monday, October 1 (Moon in Gemini)   The gift of gab is yours. Use it to negotiate a good contract for yourself. You find a constructive channel or outlet for something you've written. You and an older person, perhaps your dad, agree on a sensitive issue.

Tuesday, October 2 (Moon in Gemini to Cancer 12:58 p.m.)   Here comes that Cancer moon. You know the drill. Apply your intuition to a thorny issue concerning taxes or insurance. And heed what your intuition seems to be telling you to do.

Wednesday, October 3 (Moon in Cancer)   Contact with one of your parents could lead to the discussion of emotional issues like wills. Consult a trust attorney, but first read up on the rules concerning living wills for your state.

Thursday, October 4 (Moon in Cancer to Leo 6:28 p.m.)   On October 11, Mercury will turn retrograde in Scorpio and your twelfth house. All the usual rules and suggestions apply for this retrograde period. But because it's in your twelfth house, you have an opportunity to delve into your own unconscious and get to the root of long-standing issues. Old friends you haven't seen for a while may appear.

Friday, October 5 (Moon in Leo)   Money could arrive. Something unexpected. Or perhaps this is a long-overdue royalty check. If you have a lottery in your state, buy a ticket and play your hunch. It's a lucky day.

Saturday, October 6 (Moon in Leo)   If you're studying drama, you may want to rent last year's Oscar winners to study techniques. And whether into drama or writing, classic movies and novels will provide detailed examples of how to create compelling stories.

Sunday, October 7 (Moon in Leo to Virgo 3:04 a.m.)   The Virgo moon in your tenth house makes you more discriminating when it comes to your career and dealings with others. Reserve judgment.

Monday, October 8 (Moon in Virgo)   Your peers or a boss acknowledges you for work well done. You aren't shy about accepting the recognition, but be sure to include the other members of your team. On the health front, head over to the local health food store for some supplements.

Tuesday, October 9 (Moon in Virgo to Libra 1:58 p.m.)   If you're concerned about your appearance, blame the Libra moon. It brings out the artistic side of your personality, and those sensibilities start when you look in the mirror. Time for a haircut or a fashion change.

Wednesday, October 10 (Moon in Libra)   Beauty, like everything else, begins in the mind. But there are things that you can do to help: regular exercise, balanced nutrition, work that you love, stable relationships. Start thinking about how you will work on some of these things during the Mercury retrograde period, which starts tomorrow. You'll be able to access your unconscious during these three weeks.

Thursday, October 11 (Moon in Libra)   Mercury turns retrograde in Scorpio. The new moon today is in Libra, your eleventh house. This moon initiates new opportunities with friendships and groups and in your wishes and dreams. During the first week after the new moon, when the energy is strongest, accept all invitations!

Friday, October 12 (Moon in Libra to Scorpio 2:14 a.m.) Yes, Mercury is retrograde. However, you get something of a reprieve because the transiting sun in Libra forms a beautiful trine with Neptune. You feel loved and supported by the people around you. Your spiritual beliefs come into play.

Saturday, October 13 (Moon in Scorpio) The moon joins retrograde Mercury in Scorpio and your twelfth house. This pair should provide you with deep insights into the workings of your unconscious mind. You begin to grasp your own motivations and urges. Meditation is helpful during this time.

Sunday, October 14 (Moon in Scorpio to Sagittarius 2:58 p.m.) As the moon moves into your sign, you have an additional plus—Venus and Saturn form nice angles to each other. This combination provides a smoothness and beauty to physical reality. It's a feel-good aspect!

Monday, October 15 (Moon in Sagittarius) Your sex appeal and charisma are spectacular. Good colors to wear: violet, yellow, and bold reds and blues. You want to be noticed and appreciated.

Tuesday, October 16 (Moon in Sagittarius) One more day with the moon in your sign. Make the most of it! You and your partner should do something special together this evening, if possible. Maybe you aren't into candlelight dinners, but how about an impromptu dinner someplace neither of you has been before?

Wednesday, October 17 (Moon in Sagittarius to Capricorn 3:04 a.m.) The moon in Capricorn demands an accounting of your finances. You should be in a stable position. If you've been waiting for checks to arrive to balance things out, you'll have to wait until after November 1, when Mercury turns direct again.

Thursday, October 18 (Moon in Capricorn)   The moon and unpredictable Uranus are in agreement. This combination makes your emotional responses somewhat unusual. It also attracts idiosyncratic individuals who provide insights into your values.

Friday, October 19 (Moon in Capricorn to Aquarius 12:52 p.m.)   You do enjoy the Aquarius moon! It infuses you with vision and cutting-edge perception. How can you use this energy? Where in your life should you apply it? Where's it most needed?

Saturday, October 20 (Moon in Aquarius)   Siblings, relatives, neighbors, travel—all are part and parcel of the Aquarius moon. Power issues with someone close to you surface, but you come out just fine in the end.

Sunday, October 21 (Moon in Aquarius to Pisces 7:03 p.m.)   Whenever the moon joins Uranus in Pisces in your fourth house, there can be unexpected disruptions in your routine. It's actually not a bad thing, because Uranus's job is to shake up the status quo.

Monday, October 22 (Moon in Pisces)   Today could feel surreal. Physically you feel good, but your mood seems to fluctuate drastically. One moment you're up; the next moment you're down. It could be that you need to eat more frequently. Instead of three large meals a day, try six smaller meals. Are you drinking at least eight glasses of water a day? Get into the habit.

Tuesday, October 23 (Moon in Pisces to Aries 9:25 p.m.)   As the moon moves into daring Aries, your passions rise. You and your partner are entering a new period in your relationship. Mercury is conjunct with the transiting sun, so even when you speak, you sound as if you're on fire! Resist turning that sharp tongue on anyone.

Wednesday, October 24 (Moon in Aries)   Your muse is shouting your name. Time to get very creative and to approach a project as if it's the most pleasurable thing on the planet.

Thursday, October 25 (Moon in Aries to Taurus 9:08 p.m.)   You and a romantic partner run up against an issue in your relationship about which you both feel quite strongly. It probably won't be resolved until the moon moves into Gemini. You're maintaining your regular exercise routine and may want to add some other activity.

Friday, October 26 (Moon in Taurus)   The full moon in Taurus tonight signals the completion of a project that has consumed you for the past month. You feel elated. There could be some minor tension concerning something you're working on alone. Is it taking you away from your family or partner?

Saturday, October 27 (Moon in Taurus to Gemini 8:12 p.m.)   If you return to Thursday's issue, do so after the moon moves into Gemini this evening. Even better, do so after Mercury turns direct on November 1. Cultivate friends who share your values and beliefs.

Sunday, October 28 (Moon in Gemini)   It's a good day for an autumn barbecue with neighbors and friends. You're on the lookout for certain information you need. It comes to you from an unlikely source.

Monday, October 29 (Moon in Gemini to Cancer 8:50 p.m.)   Today could unfold like a chapter in a novel. You meet the players and glimpse the plot, but the story is propelled by something mysterious.

Tuesday, October 30 (Moon in Cancer)   You're looking for end-of-the-year tax breaks. If you have a home office, there may be a tax-deductible way to improve it: a new floor, carpet, or computer?

Wednesday, October 31 (Moon in Cancer)   As the moon moves into Leo, you're feeling affable and social, especially toward your in-laws. Maybe it's because you're going on an overseas trip next month, and you're in a gregarious mood. Saturn turns direct in Virgo. Career matters should move ahead.

NOVEMBER 2007

Thursday, November 1 (Moon in Cancer to Leo 12:48 a.m.)   The last Mercury retrograde of the year is over. And the moon is in Leo. It doesn't get much better than this. So do all the things that you've delayed doing for the last several weeks. And while you're at it, get your natal chart drawn up by an astrologer.

Friday, November 2 (Moon in Leo)   Money comes to you from unexpected sources: a loan repaid, a royalty check you hadn't anticipated, or a dividend on a stock. In about six days, Venus will move into Libra and your eleventh house. A nice romantic surprise awaits you!

Saturday, November 3 (Moon in Leo to Virgo 8:45 a.m.)   The moon joins Saturn in Virgo in your tenth house. Yes, this pair can feel like a giant pain at times. Saturn forces you to take stock, to meet responsibilities, to fulfill obligations. But it also brings rewards for a job well done. And with help from the intuitive moon, you can get inside the Saturn process and understand it more easily.

Sunday, November 4—Daylight Saving Time Ends (Moon in Virgo)   Your health is directly linked to your emotional and spiritual happiness. If you enjoy what you do, it increases your chances for optimum health. That's a place to start. How much do you like your career?

Monday, November 5 (Moon in Virgo to Libra 6:47 p.m.)   You have places to go and people to see. You're launching a new product for your company, and you are eager to get the word out. Publicize and promote.

Tuesday, November 6 (Moon in Libra)   You get together with a group of people who share your passions. It
could be a group of writers, bridge players, actors, astrologers, or photographers. These people are helpful to you.
They expand your knowledge and support you emotionally.

Wednesday, November 7 (Moon in Libra)   You have
plenty to cheer about. A new opportunity of some kind
comes to you through friends. It's the kind of thing that
lands at your doorstep and you have a choice to accept or
not accept it. Don't make a rash decision.

*Thursday, November 8 (Moon in Libra to Scorpio 7:19
a.m.)*   Venus moves into Libra and your eleventh house.
This beautiful transit stimulates activities with friends and
networks of acquaintances. Romance with someone you regard as a friend is possible. Or you may meet a romantic
partner through friends between now and December 5.

Friday, November 9 (Moon in Scorpio)   Here you are,
living in your twelfth house again. You're gathering your
resources and recharging your battery. This is a new-moon
day, so for the next month you have the opportunity to do
a lot of inner work. This inner work can take any number
of forms and paths, but the point is to clear up long-
standing issues.

*Saturday, November 10 (Moon in Scorpio to Sagittarius
7:59 p.m.)*   This evening the moon moves into your sign.
You feel the shift in energy—a sudden buoyancy in your
mood, a need to get out of the house and go for a drive,
or perhaps just a lift in your physical energy. Welcome it!

Sunday, November 11 (Moon in Sagittarius)   With
Venus in Libra forming a nice angle to the Sagittarius
moon and your natal sun sign, you're in a very nice place!
Your sex appeal and charisma are at an all-time high. Your
magnetism attracts exactly who and what you need when
you need it.

Monday, November 12 (Moon in Sagittarius)   No Monday blues for you! Your mind hums with ideas, and your

schedule is jammed. Aside from work obligations, your social calendar for the rest of the year is filling up quickly.

Tuesday, November 13 (Moon in Sagittarius to Capricorn 8:01 a.m.)   In two days, Mars in Cancer and your eighth house will turn retrograde and remain that way for the rest of the year. If you're waiting for approval on mortgages or car loans, try to speed up the process so that it happens in the next two days. Otherwise, you may be waiting into the new year.

Wednesday, November 14 (Moon in Capricorn)   Sudden, unexpected upsets that could be connected to money occur. Or someone challenges you about a belief you hold. Try not to fly off the handle. Patience really will get you much further than anger.

Thursday, November 15 (Moon in Capricorn to Aquarius 6:31 p.m.)   Mars turns retrograde. This movement will drive Mars's energy inward, perhaps forcing you to explore issues that you would rather not scrutinize. What happens after death? What were your past lives and how do those lives affect your present life?

Friday, November 16 (Moon in Aquarius)   With the moon in friendly Aquarius and Mercury and Saturn sending compatible energy to each other, you're able to communicate in a structured, convincing way. If you're in sales, this is particularly useful. Regardless of your field, you are a force to be reckoned with.

Saturday, November 17 (Moon in Aquarius)   Take stock of your neighborhood and your community, and decide what you would change if you could. Are there a lot of homeless people or stray animals where you live? Then do something about it.

Sunday, November 18 (Moon in Aquarius to Pisces 2:15 a.m.)   Here comes another one of those water-sign moons. The Pisces moon in particular seems to leave you feeling undecided, unable to make firm decisions and stick to them. Like your sign, Pisces is mutable, which means you can change your mind from moment to moment!

Monday, November 19 (Moon in Pisces) Your spirituality and intuitive abilities are highlighted. Expect events or situations that trigger the nature of the Pisces moon. Go with your hunches. They won't steer you wrong.

Tuesday, November 20 (Moon in Pisces to Aries 6:25 a.m.) This moon never fails to stimulate your life! The focus usually is on romance, creativity, and children. You may have to make some adjustments with your kids to fully seize the energy of this moon.

Wednesday, November 21 (Moon in Aries) With Mercury in Scorpio, Uranus in Pisces, and Mars retrograde in Cancer, there's pressure on you to enter the intuitive flow. Feel your way through your life. If you don't do this willingly, you miss an opportunity to divine your own future!

Thursday, November 22 (Moon in Aries to Taurus 7:19 a.m.) You and a coworker have come up against a difference in opinion or method. Neither of you is willing to back down. The wisest course of action is to set the issue aside until the moon is in Gemini.

Friday, November 23 (Moon in Taurus) You need Taurus's stubbornness. An employee is pushing you in a direction you aren't ready to go. Don't move on this issue until the moon is in a sign more compatible with your own—Gemini, Leo, Aries, or in your own sign.

Saturday, November 24 (Moon in Taurus to Gemini 6:29 a.m.) In addition to the moon moving into Gemini and your seventh house, Uranus turns direct. Since Uranus is a slow-moving planet, the effects of the direct motion will be subtle. Over time, things that have been confused at home and with your family will clear up.

Sunday, November 25 (Moon in Gemini) You and your partner get a financial tip. Even if it comes from someone you trust, don't just rush out and act on it. Gather information and facts; then decide what you want to do.

Monday, November 26 (Moon in Gemini to Cancer 6:07 a.m.) Your ideals play out in your love life. This pleasant state of things indicates that the one you love may put you on a pedestal. It also means that you and your partner may get involved in some type of charity or volunteer organization.

Tuesday, November 27 (Moon in Cancer) If you still have guests from the Thanksgiving holidays, you may feel a bit overwhelmed. Your mother or another female has a lot of questions and even more advice that you didn't ask for. Be patient.

Wednesday, November 28 (Moon in Cancer to Leo 8:23 a.m.) This morning, the moon moves into one of your favorite places—Leo. If you have a natal Leo rising or moon, this transit feels like paradise to you. But even if you don't, this transit is all about feeling optimistic, empowered, and bold. You gravitate toward bold colors, which make a statement to everyone with whom you come into contact.

Thursday, November 29 (Moon in Leo) As you near the weekend and the last month of the year, you may be looking for end-of-the-year tax breaks. What do you need for your home office? Take advantage of the loopholes while they still exist!

Friday, November 30 (Moon in Leo to Virgo 2:45 p.m.) Once more, the moon joins Saturn in Virgo in your tenth house. Saturn is moving direct in Virgo. Career matters are your focus, and you have a window of opportunity to move ahead until the end of the year.

DECEMBER 2007

Saturday, December 1 (Moon in Virgo) Mercury moves into your sign, a fabulous transit for someone whose mind is forever moving, learning, searching. December is incredibly active for you, so fasten your seat belt and enjoy the ride!

Sunday, December 2 (Moon in Virgo) You have the gumption to make professional strides. Your boss or a peer helps you out. On the health front, are you still doing your exercise routine? Don't stop!

Monday, December 3 (Moon in Virgo to Libra 1:02 a.m.) You're in a social mood, others are drawn to you, and you shouldn't hesitate to promote yourself or your product. Whatever you say is well received.

Tuesday, December 4 (Moon in Libra) On December 18, Jupiter will move into Capricorn and your second house. This transit should be very good for your finances. You can expect an expansion in your earning capacity, income coming in from unexpected sources, and new earning opportunities. Initially, you may feel that you're spending way too much. But that will even out during the course of the year that Jupiter transits Capricorn.

Wednesday, December 5 (Moon in Libra to Scorpio 1:32 p.m.) Venus moves into Scorpio and your twelfth house. This transit increases the possibility of a secretive love affair. But because your nature is generally open, the affair won't be secret for very long. Soon after Venus moves into your sign on December 30, things either will be out in the open or the affair will be over.

Thursday, December 6 (Moon in Scorpio) The moon joins Venus in Scorpio. This duo heightens emotions in a relationship. You could be concerned about what makes you feel secure as an individual and may decide this relationship isn't part of that equation. On the other hand, maybe the relationship is exactly what you need. If so, don't think about the future.

Friday, December 7 (Moon in Scorpio) Your intuitive connections to the world around you are strong. Associate with positive people.

Saturday, December 8 (Moon in Scorpio to Sagittarius 2:12 a.m.)   Very early this morning, the moon moves into your sign. You get such a boost that you and a friend head to the mall to celebrate and do holiday shopping. You're enjoying the last days of Jupiter in your sign. Just be careful that you don't overextend yourself financially.

Sunday, December 9 (Moon in Sagittarius)   While Jupiter will be moving into your money house, expanding your finances, Saturn in your tenth house of careers will be turning retrograde on December 19. This could mean a delay in any raises or promotions you expected before the end of the year. Use your enormous optimism to turn around any negative patterns in your life. The new moon is in your sign! Plant your seeds for 2008.

Monday, December 10 (Moon in Sagittarius to Capricorn 1:51 p.m.)   You may be thinking about the Jupiter transit on December 18. Finances are on your mind. Don't allow fear to rule your life and your choices. Practice moderation in your holiday purchases.

Tuesday, December 11 (Moon in Capricorn)   Make long-range goals for 2008. Decide what you would like to happen in your personal and professional life next year. Then set the wheels in motion and get to work!

Wednesday, December 12 (Moon in Capricorn)   Venus and Saturn form a harmonious angle to each other, so it's possible that an existing relationship enters a more committed phase. If you're unattached, you may meet someone older than you who sparks a romantic interest.

Thursday, December 13 (Moon in Capricorn to Aquarius 12:02 a.m.)   As the moon moves into compatible Aquarius, your idealism is soaring. How can you act on your compassion? Is there a volunteer group you can join or a group to which you can donate money?

Friday, December 14 (Moon in Aquarius)   You're in search of the perfect present for a sibling, relative, or neighbor. It doesn't have to be expensive—just exactly right. Look for the unusual, the offbeat, the personal.

Saturday, December 15 (Moon in Aquarius to Pisces 8:15 a.m.)   If your kids are young, this is their day to hit the mall for holiday shopping. They have a list of friends to whom they would like to give gifts. Set a dollar limit.

Sunday, December 16 (Moon in Pisces)   You're tidying up your house for guests due to arrive for the holidays. This may include new paint on the walls and new furniture, towels, or linens. You're stressing. Back off.

Monday, December 17 (Moon in Pisces to Aries 1:53 p.m.)   Is your list of resolutions ready? If not, get busy. You'll be fine-tuning it over the next few weeks. Keep your goals realistic, but don't be afraid to dream!

Tuesday, December 18 (Moon in Aries)   Jupiter moves into Capricorn for a transit that lasts about a year. Set some financial goals for 2008. You'll want to take advantage of this terrific transit!

Wednesday, December 19 (Moon in Aries to Taurus 4:38 p.m.)   Saturn turns retrograde in your tenth house of careers. This retrograde period lasts until May 2. Prepare by having all your projects and priorities lined up.

Thursday, December 20 (Moon in Taurus)   Mercury joins Jupiter in Capricorn in your second house. Focus your thoughts on money and on how you can integrate your values into how you earn your living. Don't worry too much. Come 2008, the answers will arrive when you need them.

Friday, December 21 (Moon in Taurus to Gemini 5:14 p.m.)   Ready to play? You're geared up for the holidays. You may even have guests arriving from out of town already. Regardless of your spiritual beliefs, these holidays are always about family ties.

Saturday, December 22 (Moon in Gemini) You're sending out holiday e-mails to people. Your in-box is filling rapidly, and you hear from people to whom you haven't sent e-greetings. Then there's that last-minute shopping. Get busy!

Sunday, December 23 (Moon in Gemini to Cancer 5:19 p.m.) Families and parents are featured. That's the moon in Cancer, always bringing you back to your roots. It could also stir up past-life memories of lives you have shared with your present families. What lessons are you supposed to learn from these people this time around?

Monday, December 24 (Moon in Cancer) How appropriate that the moon is fully in Cancer, and whatever cheer you are sharing creates memories that will last for a lifetime. Be cautious that you and one of your parents don't get into a tiff about an issue that is dear to all of you.

Tuesday, December 25 (Moon in Cancer to Leo 6:53 p.m.) If you decided to spend the holidays overseas, sightsee and remember the true spirit of these holidays: compassion, forgiveness, and giving.

Wednesday, December 26 (Moon in Leo) Some of Jupiter's largesse falls flat when Mars moves into an angry angle to the planet of luck. Patience is called for. It would be beneficial not to discuss sensitive topics with your visitors. We're all entitled to our beliefs.

Thursday, December 27 (Moon in Leo to Virgo 11:45 p.m.) The moon joins Saturn retrograde in Virgo. Seems to be happening a lot lately, right? Best to let work go for now. Enjoy some time off; worry about work and career matters after the new year.

Friday, December 28 (Moon in Virgo) Use your discriminating emotions to tackle a thorny problem that concerns authority. Is it the tax man, a cop, or a father figure? Figure it out.

Saturday, December 29 (Moon in Virgo)   You head to the gym to work off holiday excesses. Or you attend a yoga class. Ask your parents or siblings to join you. Make it a family outing.

Sunday, December 30 (Moon in Virgo to Libra 8:38 a.m.) Venus moves into your sign, a wonderful portent for romance in 2008! This transit enhances your sex appeal, charisma, and general mood. Carry these feelings into 2008.

Monday, December 31 (Moon in Libra)   The moon in Libra is about perfect for a gathering or even a full-fledged party. Maybe it's here that Venus in your sign kicks in!

HAPPY NEW YEAR!

SYDNEY OMARR

Born on August 5, 1926, in Philadelphia, Pennsylvania, Sydney Omarr was the only person ever given full-time duty in the U.S. Army as an astrologer. He is regarded as the most erudite astrologer of our time and the best known, through his syndicated column and his radio and television programs (he was Merv Griffin's "resident astrologer"). Omarr has been called the most "knowledgeable astrologer since Evangeline Adams." His forecasts of Nixon's downfall, the end of World War II in mid-August of 1945, the assassination of John F. Kennedy, Roosevelt's election to a fourth term and his death in office . . . these and many others are on the record and quoted enough to be considered "legendary."

ABOUT THE SERIES

This is one of a series of twelve Sydney Omarr®
Day-by-Day Astrological Guides for the signs of
2007. For questions and comments about the
book, e-mail tjmacgregor@booktalk.com.

SYDNEY OMARR'S®
SUN, MOON, AND YOU:
An Astrological Guide to
Your Personality

Discover the effects of the moon and sun on
LOVE, ROMANCE & SUCCESS

Nationally syndicated columnist Sydney
Omarr® shows readers how to turn the tides
in their lives! Included are all the keys to
finding the perfect balance between
day and night, featuring:

- An introduction to the sun and moon signs
- Easy-to-read tables
- How sun/moon signs contribute to personality, likes
and dislikes, finding ideal mates and the perfect jobs

Filled with colorful examples of historical
figures under each sign, and requiring no
familiarity with astrology, this is the
must-have guide for all fans of astrology!

0-451-21454-4

THE NEW AMERICAN
Dream Dictionary

The Complete Language of Dreams
in Easy-to-Understand Form

Wake up
to your
dream life.

JOAN SEAMAN AND TOM PHILBIN

NAL 0-451-21747-0

Unlock the Secrets
of the Mystical World

PROPHECY:
WHAT THE FUTURE HOLDS FOR YOU
by Sylvia Browne and Lindsay Harrison
0-451-21520-6

VISITS FROM THE AFTERLIFE
by Sylvia Browne
0-451-21327-0

MASTERING THE TAROT
by Eden Gray
0-451-16781-3

KARMABABE
by Barrie Dolnick
0-451-21413-7

Penguin Group (USA) Online

What will you be reading tomorrow?

Tom Clancy, Patricia Cornwell, W.E.B. Griffin,
Nora Roberts, William Gibson, Robin Cook,
Brian Jacques, Catherine Coulter, Stephen King,
Dean Koontz, Ken Follett, Clive Cussler,
Eric Jerome Dickey, John Sandford,
Terry McMillan, Sue Monk Kidd, Amy Tan,
John Berendt…

You'll find them all at
penguin.com

*Read excerpts and newsletters,
find tour schedules and reading group guides,
and enter contests.*

Subscribe to Penguin Group (USA) newsletters
and get an exclusive inside look
at exciting new titles and the authors you love
long before everyone else does.

PENGUIN GROUP (USA)
us.penguingroup.com